Wired Marketing

Wired Marketing
Energizing Business for e-Commerce

GLENN HARDAKER

Huddersfield University Business School

GARY GRAHAM

University of Salford Business School

JOHN WILEY & SONS, LTD

Chichester • New York • Weinheim • Brisbane • Singapore • Toronto

Other Wiley Editorial Offices

John Wiley & Sons, Inc., 605 Third Avenue,
New York, NY 10158-0012, USA

WILEY-VCH Verlag GmbH
Pappelallee 3, D-69469 Weinheim, Germany

John Wiley & Sons Australia, Ltd, 33 Park Road, Milton,
Queensland 4064, Australia

John Wiley & Sons (Canada) Ltd, 22 Worcester Road
Rexdale, Ontario, M9W 1L1, Canada

John Wiley & Sons (Asia) Pte Ltd, 2 Clementi Loop #02-01,
Jin Xing Distripark, Singapore 129809

Library of Congress Cataloging-in-Publication Data

Hardaker, Glenn.
Wired marketing ; energizing business for e-commerce. / Glenn Hardaker, Gary Graham.
    p. cm.
    Includes bibliographical references and index.
    ISBN 0-471-49645-6 (pbk.)
    1. Internet marketing. I. Graham, Gary, 1962- II. Title.
    HF5415.1265 .H366 2001
    658.8'4–dc21   00-069343

British Library Cataloguing in Publication Data

A catalogue record for this book is available from the British Library

ISBN 0-471-49645-6

Typeset in Palatino by Deerpark Publishing Services Ltd, Shannon.
Printed and bound in Great Britain by Biddles Ltd, Guildford and King's Lynn.

This book is printed on acid-free paper responsibly manufactured from sustainable forestry in which at least two trees are planted for each one used for paper production.

Dedication

Love and respect to Aishah and Ida

Contents

Preface

We believe that we are currently standing on the threshold of a new age – the age of a marketing revolution – knowing in our minds that for marketing the new wave has already arrived with an unprecedented shift to electronic commerce and the dawn of virtual consumer communities. Harnessing new forms of interactive marketing is viewed as the key in out-innovating the innovators and allowing you and your organization to realize a customer-centric focus. Such a viewpoint we feel is now a reality and should be seen as a necessary perspective in the pursuit of innovative Internet marketing in the post industrial age. The Internet is a radical catalyst for marketing transformation and in making the notion of one-to-one marketing a reality for many mass markets. The transformation process taking place has been the inspiration for this book and it is intended to be extremely useful for all marketing professionals both practitioners and educators alike. In addition we hope it also provides inspiration for realizing sustained success in the new age. The following quote by Nicolas Berdiaff we feel provides timeless inspiration.

Utopian ideas seem to be far more attainable than we once thought. Currently we are faced with a far more worrying question: How do we avoid their final realization to fruition? Utopian ideas are attainable. Life is heading in the direction of utopian ideas. Perhaps a new age is beginning, an age where intellectuals and cultivated people dream of ways of avoiding utopian ideas and of returning to a non-utopian society, one less 'perfect' and one that offers more freedom' Nicholas Berdiaff (English translation)

Use this book in a way that works for you. The book has been designed with consideration towards an object-orientated style, clustered around four main themes, that can be read in a sequential approach or in a more random style. The main themes are: marketing transformation, interactive marketing processes, e-commerce customer, and marketing Internet tools.

Glenn Hardaker
Huddersfield University Business School

Gary Graham
University of Salford Business School

January 2001

Foreword

That the world is changing in strange and unpredictable ways seems to be an accepted fact of life. Companies such as Marks & Spencers and Sainsbury whose market dominance, only a few years ago, seemed unassailable, now appear to be outmoded and face the prospect of having to reinvent themselves if they are to survive. Even the mighty Microsoft faces daunting questions: will it be broken up by the legislators? How big a threat is Linux? What is the future for the PC?

The question of the speed of change is partly a generational one: people in their 40s and upwards tend to view the world as changing more rapidly than those in their teens and 20s. Also, it is partly a sectoral issue: some sectors, such as computers and retailing, do seem to change faster than others. However, the main issue is that the advent of the Internet has propelled us into a new industrial revolution. Like any revolution, when you are in the midst of it, it is impossible to predict accurately its end result. Nevertheless, we can say with some certainty that, as with the advent of the motor car, it will have a profound impact on what we do, how we do it and indeed how we perceive the world around us.

Anyone who reads the popular press knows that the initial phase of the dot.com revolution appears to have run its course, and that investors and entrepreneurs are now beginning to take a more measured view of what the Internet has to offer. However, if we are to move successfully beyond the e-commerce hype, we need to take a well-thought-out and well-researched look at the advantages, possibilities and disadvantages of e-commerce. It is for this reason that I very much welcome this book by Glenn Hardaker and Gary Graham.

Wired Marketing links together four crucial elements in understanding and developing e-commerce. Firstly, it looks at how and why the Internet is changing the nature of marketing, and particularly the shift from direct marketing to interactive marketing. Secondly, it broadens out the marketing concept and shows how organizations are developing an e-based communication mix to target and serve their customers better. Thirdly, the book shows that the Internet is changing the nature of supply chain interactions, whether these be with suppliers, customers or partners. In so doing, these changes are generating a whole host of issues concerning security, privacy and ethics. Lastly, the book offers a marketing and Internet-based 'tool-kit' to help negotiate and keep up-to-date with the changing world of e-commerce.

Overall, this is a very useful, well-written and thought-provoking book. Unlike many books on the topic of the Internet, not only does it raise many questions, it also provides readers with the information and resources to begin answering them as well.

Though it is primarily aimed at students, I am sure that many managers and entrepreneurs wrestling with the dilemma that is e-commerce will also find help and inspiration in this book.

Dr Bernard Burnes
Manchester School of Management
UMIST

Acknowledgements

It has been a privilege for us to work with many inspiring colleagues and friends around the world to discuss and explore ideas and to learn from their own personal experiences in writing this book.

Special thanks and respect to our friends Professor S. Macoomalo, Professor D. Wilson, David Smith, Professor Richard Welford, Eamonn Sweeney, Dr Mike Waddington and Professor Pervaiz Ahmed for continued academic support and guidance. Further thanks to the UMIST team Dr Bernard Burnes, M. Sonmez, and Dr Jian-Bo Yang for critical evaluation and our lengthy discussion on the relationship of physical and virtual markets.

Appreciation to Bill Croson and Jessica Symons and all the team at the Manchester-based Graphic Palette who kindly provided the artwork for the cover of the book and were very helpful and enthusiastic at all times in supporting the project.

Our good friend Aishah Sabki at InterNexus, Ltd., provided technical assistance and knowledge of online payments possibilities and who continually supported our developments. Our thanks.

Cheers also to Russell Pearson at Cisco Systems for his wit and also astute observations.

Steve Hardman, Sarah Booth and the team at Wiley Publishing provided continued support and guidance through the complex process. Special thanks to Steve Hardman and Dr Simon Plumtree, at the Chichester office, for supporting the idea and having the confidence in us to do something different.

PART 1

Marketing transformation on the Internet

CHAPTER 1

An introduction to Internet marketing

Key topics

- The marketing concept: a brief history
- Electronic commerce and the Internet revolution
- Online selling through the Internet
- Evolution from direct into interactive online marketing
- Objectives of the book
- Structure of the book
- Distinctive features

After studying this chapter you will be able to:

- Understand the various web-based technologies.
- Describe the underlying reasons for the popularity of the Web.
- Identify the changing trends and directions of retailing.
- Appreciate the scope and purpose of the book.

The Internet is now truly a global medium and is gaining new users at a staggering rate (Network Wizards, 1999). When the World Wide Web (WWW) or web first attracted the attention of business, it was generally conceived to be an extension of direct marketing (Oldfield and Burnham, 1997). While many firms are setting up websites and making themselves more visible to customers and potential customers, other firms have gone beyond using it as an extension to their direct marketing activity and attempted to set up virtual models of business activity.

In traditional buying behaviour theory, there is a large onus put on the consumer to search for a number of suppliers, who are interested in selling or buying products or services. This is in order that they can compare prices and other attributes of the good or service – to make an optimal purchase decision. Then, some exchange of currency will take place for the product through some agreed upon, and ideally, secure channels. The rapid globalization of markets is threatening retailers' traditional customer franchise – with consumers being served by a variety of physical and remote channels. The retailer is beginning to use the Internet to move from mass marketing to mass customization, by using or developing new virtual channels to distribute their products and services. In order to fully exploit the potential market of the Internet, it is the online vendors' task to organize their 'Internet Marketing Function' (IMF) for the following: firstly, to be able to create a solid and reliable corporate image; secondly, to build compelling sites; and thirdly, to provide comfortable and supportive environments. The active involvement of the consumer in the buying process is needed to utilize the design of new products and the development of product and marketing strategies. This book is fundamentally about the intersection of marketing and technology; this includes its role for e-commerce. The marketing–technology fit predates the digital age.

The marketing concept: a brief history

The marketing concept was built upon the basic principle of the economic organization, which is 'to maximize satisfaction through the utilization of scarce resources'. The marketing concept really began to emerge in the 1950s and early 1960s. It was Peter Drucker in his seminal 'Practice of Management' (Drucker, 1954) who first observed that:

> Marketing is much broader than selling, it is not a specialized activity at all. It encompasses the entire business. It is the whole business seen from the point of view of its final result, that is, from the customer's point of view. Concern and responsibility for marketing must therefore permeate all areas of the enterprise.

And, later he commented that: 'Marketing is the distinguishing, unique function of the business.' Then, came Levitt's (1960) 'Marketing Myopia', in which he attributed the failure of firms and industries to be putting too much emphasis upon the products – which they made – rather than the needs which they served.

Although there is to some extent a consensus and shared understanding of the philosophy behind marketing – its implementation through the marketing function has tended to diverge widely from it. This was particularly the case, in the transaction paradigm of marketing, which came to dominate education and much academic research for almost, 30 years (1960–1990). The transaction paradigm was enshrined in decision making and in what is now known as the 'Marketing Management Model' with Philip Kotler's (1967) 'Marketing Management; Analysis, Planning and Control' acting as its bible. In the late 1980s, the dominant, unchallenged managerial doctrine, began to be challenged by – in Europe and particularly Scandinavia, who were looking at marketing in terms of interaction – networks and relationships. This led to the development of the 'Relationship Marketing' school.

The essential difference between the two is that the marketing management model seeks to understand consumer needs better, so that it can manipulate the elements of the marketing mix more effectively, which can then alter the demand to the available supply. The emphasis is very much on the transaction – with exchange seen largely to be a 'zero-sum' game, in which there are inevitably winners and losers. By contrast, relationship marketing more closely reflects the marketing concept. It is built upon the creation and maintenance of mutually satisfying exchange relationships. It enjoys a 'win-win' perspective and sees the role of a producer as doing things for customers.

As a result of accelerating technological change and global competition – during the 1980s, the failings of the marketing management model began to become apparent even in the US. The extent and nature of this changed perspective was encapsulated in an authoritative review of the marketing management school by Frederick Webster, in his 1992 article, which appeared in the *Journal of Marketing* entitled 'The Changing Role of Marketing in the Corporation'. In his own words:

> The purpose of this article is to outline both the intellectual and pragmatic routes of changes that are occurring in marketing, especially marketing management, as a body of knowledge, theory and practice and to suggest the need for a new paradigm of the marketing function within the firm.

It was the recession of the early 1990s that led Webster to call for a new approach to the practice of marketing. A view widely echoed in more practitioner-based publications (McKinsey, 1993). The crux of the argument was one of marketing being concerned with a set of relationships between and within organizations: then marketing must be everybody's business and not a functional activity, for a few. This view to some extent was magnified by several important developments in managerial thinking: benchmarking, total quality management, strategic alliances, globalization and strategic thinking. These might be considered the concern of marketers. These fields have been pre-empted by others.

In this new millennium marketers appear to be taking a more balanced view of their discipline. It is now generally accepted that the relationship marketing approach has effectively extended the marketing concept into areas such as services and business-to-business marketing, which were poorly served by the marketing management model based as it was upon concepts of mass production, mass distribution and mass marketing essentially of packaged consumer goods. At the same time, it has also been appreciated that many marketing exchanges are based upon low involvement and transactions and that two distinct approaches co-exist together. Simultaneously, a clearer distinction is being drawn between the philosophy of marketing which is encapsulated in a marketing orientation that can be held by everybody – both internal and external – relating to the organization. This is the market-orientated organization; it is customer oriented and market-driven. The former marketing oriented organization is committed to a philosophy of mutually satisfying exchange relationships, while the latter market-oriented company is more focused on how to achieve this through the professional practice and management of the marketing function.

From this brief review of the evolution of marketing, we next turn to the very recent development of the Web.

What is the WWW or Web?

Tim Berners-Lee is widely quoted to be the inventor or father of the Web. He designed the Web and its system of identification, as a way to present text conve-

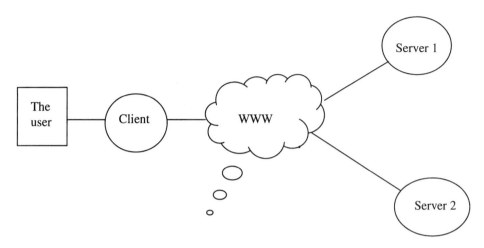

Figure 1.1   The World Wide Web

niently over the medium of the Internet. All website names, were to be known as URLs – or Universal Resource Locators – they would end in a suffix that identifies the nature of the site. The most common is .com, which indicates a commercial site, while.edu is an educational site and.org denotes a non-commercial organization. These suffixes are known as generic top-level domains, and they have remained relatively unchanged since Berners-Lee created the Web in the late 1980s. However, the expansion of e-commerce has strained this simple system to breaking point, as demand for website names has exploded and with companies having the same or similar, names. There is currently much debate about expanding the Web's identification system in accordance with recent developments.

Without a doubt the World Wide Web has confirmed that we live in the middle of an information age. Many enabling technologies have evolved and converged to make this vast amount of information so readily available. These technologies include cheaper and faster computing platforms, higher network bandwidth, more reliable data communications, improved object-oriented software technologies, protocols designed to handle the latest in information flows (data, voice, video, audio, multimedia and others), and the Internet with its paradigm as the global interoperable network of networks. Figure 1.1 illustrates that the Web utilizes all of these technologies to create a mesh of servers and clients that dispense and consume data to make information to allow users to do useful work (Harnedy, 1999, p. 4).

The information created and exchanged over the Web is most often represented in a format called hypertext. Hypertext is a representation of text that includes links associated with a word or group of words that, when selected, allows the reader to directly navigate to the new text regardless of the location. Hypertext has been extended to a new hypermedia format that allows for the addition of different types of links to audio, video, graphics, and other information that can be presented by electronic means.

Reasons for the Web's popularity

One of the prime reasons the Web has become so popular is that the web-based technologies make the Web easy to use and develop applications in. The browser interface is relatively intuitive and the graphical nature makes it 'friendly'. It also runs on different computing platforms. Web-based tools are easily accessible and considered relatively inexpensive. The notion of 'surfing' on the Web has captured the mindset of anyone – even casually acquainted with the computer – from teenagers accessing their favourite gaming websites, to university professors collaborating on the latest research to companies making information. There is a very extensive amount of information available on the Internet from latest newest products and to corporate marketers plotting their company's imminent launch into the world of e-commerce.

As a result an attractive marketspace is emerging, with consumers and businesses. In the consumer world, users seeking popular branded products subscribe today to interactive media (e.g. online services, Internet access) at rates of two or three times the national average. By 2000, there were between 30 and 40 million 'digital' consumers – most attractive in terms of demographics and shopping behaviour. In the business world it is estimated that between 10 and 20 million small businesses in the US are using interactive media to do business (Parsons et al., 1998).

Web-based marketing is likely to become integrated into part of the marketing mix for consumer marketers in the not-so-distant future. This is because of it enabling entirely new forms of interactions between consumers and marketers (two-way interactivity, seamless transactions, addressability, online demand avail-

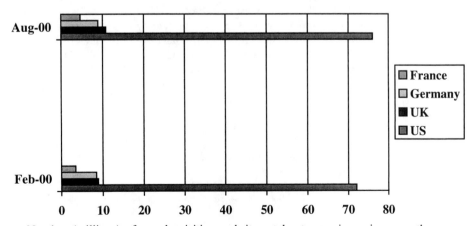

Number (millions) of people visiting websites at least once in a given month

Figure 1.2   Number of reported visitors to websites at least once in a given month. Source: Jupiter Media Metrix Company presented in the Financial Times, 11/10/00, p. 11

ability and customization), which is leading to deeper relationships and greater personalization of goods and services (ibid., p. 33). In different ways, interactive media will also substantially change business-to-business sales and marketing practices as e-commerce becomes established.

In a market where many Internet companies had little in the way of revenue to show, let alone profits, their ability to attract the attention of the growing online audience has become one way of measuring their performance. In Figure 1.2 one can see this year a significant rise in the number of reported visitors to websites from February to August 2000. The US reporting, by far the biggest number of reported visitors in February of 72.02 million, followed in descending order by the UK (8.87 million), Germany (8.44 million) and France (3.44 million). This had risen, by August in all four countries to 76.07 million in the US, 10.79 million in the UK, 8.91 million in Germany and 4.61 million in France, respectively.

CASE APPLICATION   **YAHOO!**

Yahoo! the world's largest Internet portal, announced third-quarter results in line with expectations and at record levels, but the quality of the earnings raised questions about the ability of the company to continue to expand rapidly. The group announced proforma net income of $81 million, or 13 cents a share, double the level of a year ago. Revenues jumped 89% from $155 to $295 million. Operating profits jumped from $20 to $67 million. The net results were significantly boosted by investment income, which jumped from $10 to $28 million.

At the close of market, the shares were down 3.5% at $82.69. Immediately following the results, in after hours trading, the shares recovered somewhat, down only 2.2% at $83.88.

Yahoo's traffic increased quarter on quarter from 680 to 780 million page views per day. The group said traffic was strong around the world, with Yahoo! Japan achieving 112 million views per day during September against 85 million in June. In Europe, it reached 41 million page views per day.

The proportion of revenues spent on marketing was likely to be between 33 and 37% against a previous range of 33–34%. Product development would represent about 10% of sales. The company said that one of the new services, Yahoo! by phone, would allow users to retrieve and send e-mail on their personalized Yahoo! accounts over the telephone. People would be able to call a toll free number, enter a password and get their e-mail and voicemail. E-mails would be read aloud using technology made by Speechworks also a telephony-based speech technology provider, that transfers text into speech. The voice services will be free.

Yahoo! also said it was updating its instant message system. Yahoo! Messenger, so that users could place phone calls from their personal computers to a regular telephone in the US for free.

Source: Paul Abrahams. Yahoo! meets expectations but fails to impress. Financial Times, Wednesday, 11 October, 2000, p. 11.

Electronic commerce and the Internet revolution

Electronic commerce can be defined loosely as 'doing business electronically' (European Commission, 1997; quoted in Timmers, 1998, p. 1). Electronic commerce includes electronic trading of physical goods and of intangibles such as information. This encompasses all the trading steps such as online marketing, ordering, payment, and support for delivery. Electronic commerce includes the electronic provision of services, such as after-sales support or online legal advice. Finally it also includes electronic support for collaboration between companies, such as collaborative design.

Some forms of electronic commerce exists already for over 20 years. For example, Electronic Data Interchange (EDI), in sectors such as retail and automotive, and CALS (Computer Assisted Lifecycle Support) in sectors such as defence and heavy engineering.

These forms of electronic commerce have been limited in their diffusion and take up. Recently, however, we have seen an explosive development in electronic commerce. The reasons for this are, of course the Internet and the World Wide Web, which are making electronic commerce much more accessible. They offer easily usable and low cost forms of electronic commerce. Electronic commerce on the basis of the Internet is set to become a very important way of doing business.

It was recently estimated that there were around 50 million people using the Internet world-wide, a figure that is doubling each year (Internet statistics http://adnet.com) due to the aforementioned Internet growth. Many businesses have seized the opportunity of the new and constantly expanding market; in order to establish a presence on the Internet. This is leading to the development of a market, which now accounts for $518 million of sales and $7 billion, by the year 2000 (Jupiter Communications, http://www.jup.com).

Billions of dollars have been funnelled into Internet companies by stock markets around the world, as investors demonstrated their appetite for companies linked to the dotcom suffix and agreed to back wave after wave of companies' Initial Public Offerings (IPOs). Cash came flooding into the mutual fund industry, as ordinary

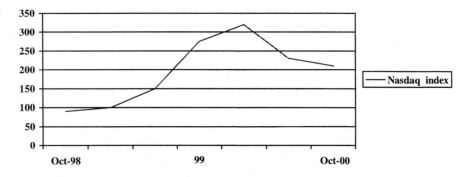

Figure 1.3   Trends in the Nasdaq Composite (rebased) index from October 1998 to October 2000. Source: Primark Datastream, Financial Times, Thursday October 12, p. 14

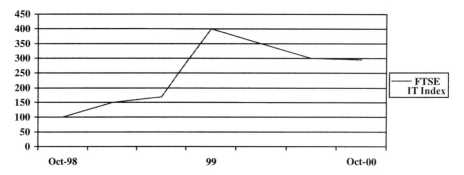

Figure 1.4 Trends in the FTSE European Information Technology Index (rebased in $ terms). Source: Primark Datastream, Financial Times, Thursday October 12, p. 14

investors were drawn in by advertising, media coverage and news of staggering outperformance of stocks.

The public hunger for Internet investment produced an imbalance between the supply of companies and the demand for dotcom stock. That was one of the reason why the Nasdaq nearly doubled between October 1999 and its peak on March 10, 2000 (see Figure 1.3). But the imbalance was even clearer outside the US. eBay's shares rose 250% on the first day of trade. Meanwhile, eToys first planned to sell its shares at $10–12 in May 1999, but eventually priced them at $20. With investors clamouring for Internet stocks, eToys shares soared reaching a peak of $86. Buoyed by new venture capital money, Mp3.com went from a small company employing six people in December 1998, to one worth a stock market value of more than $4 billion by July 1999.

In Europe, traditional venture capital funds started to wade into investing and the impact up to September, 1999 is clearly shown on the FTSE European information technology index (rebased in $ terms) presented in Figure 1.4. They were lured by the promise of extraordinary returns that their American counterparts had already began to realize.

By November, 1999 – with effectively no barriers to entry – the dynamics of supply and demand began to be shifted. The markets began to lose faith in online retailers. eToys stock has fallen to less than $5, valuing the company at $500 million. And when US Internet stocks tumbled with associated reverberations in Europe and Asia, they sucked away their funding for recent start ups like Dressmart, a Swedish e-tailer in menswear. Low on funds Dressmart hit the wall. Boo.com, the ambitious online sportswear retailer was closed down in May, 2000 less than 6 months after it started trading. QXL was forced to change its strategy away from one of acquisition and deals to profits to satisfy its investors. A month later Europatweb, an investment vehicle of Boo backer Bernard Arnault, pulled its plans for a listing. It had invested £500 million in the Internet. The key events of the Internet revolution with the major players, so far are presented in Table 1.1.

To an extent the autumn 2000 deceleration simply marks a slowdown from what has had been an unusually powerful period of demand for technology and tele-

Table 1.1   The internet revolution[a]

US events
1. September 1998: eBay's shares rise 250% on first day trade on the Nasdaq Composite index
2. May 1999: Nasdaq launch of StarMedia ignites Latin America
3. January 2000: America online pays $160 billion for Time Warner
4. March 10, 2000: Nasdaq Composite index goes to an all time high
5. March 19, 2000: growing mood of caution amongst stock market investors
6. May 2000: consolidation takes hold as Terra network agrees to pay $10 billion for Lycos

Europe events
1. April 26, 1999: Consors floats on Neuer market and sparks Internet mania in Germany
2. July 26, 1999: Freeserve floats at £1.5 billion
3. March 2, 2000: lastminute.com floats after price range increased by 67%
4. March 16, 2000: World Online floats a day before Internet stock slide in Europe
5. May 18, 2000: Boo.com comes to a spectacular end
6. June 19, 2000: Europatweb pulls its plans for a flotation

---

[a] Source: Primark Datastream, Financial Times, Thursday October 12, p. 14.

communications equipment. Intel, the world's dominant chip manufacturer, started the autumn jitters last month when it produced cautious sales forecasts. But, this is against strong sales growth of 10% in 1998, 21% in 1999 and 30% in the first half of this year (Primax datastream, quoted in the Financial Times, October 19, 2000, p. 26).

Despite such caveats, there is a grudging acceptance among analysts that the technology industry is proving far from immune to economic cycles. The broad premium that the stock markets have put on the growth of technology and Internet companies in recent years is shrinking. In March 2000, when the sector peaked, US technology companies – AOL, Cisco Systems, IBM, Lucent Technologies – were trading on the PEG ratio of a company's price/earning ratio to growth rate of 2, compared with 1.3 for companies in general. By October, the technology decline had brought the ratio down to 1.27 – identical to the market at large (ibid., p. 26). The crux of this is that the Internet company is unlikely to be immune to economic cycles, which is being exacerbated by the financial markets themselves. Even if technology takes a big share of capital spending (in the US 60% now compared to 30% in the early 1990s), it will have less room to grow.

However, it is important to emphasis that 5 years ago there was only one Internet company and that was America Online (the pioneering Internet service provider); it was worth $1 billion and that was seen as egregious. Five years later – after the bursting of the 'bubble' – there are 400 companies with a combined market capitalization of a trillion dollars, which by any measure is quite awesome value creation. Moreover, there are a myriad of entrepreneurs who managed to raise funds before the collapse of Internet stock prices who are still inspired by the potential of the Internet to fuel a second wave of Internet start ups.

CASE APPLICATION

NEW YORK TIMES DROPS TRACKER PLAN

The New York Times Co yesterday became the latest US media company to withdraw plans for an Internet trading stock, reflecting the tough market faced by online media and Internet stocks.

At the peak of the Internet boom, many large media companies viewed Internet tracking stocks as a way to keep pace with well-capitalized upstarts. The New York Times was seen as the most aggressive newspaper in pursuing this strategy, filling in January to spin off its digital properties.

The April sell-off of Internet stocks, however, forced many companies to stall or abandon IPO plans. Viacom recently announced that it would not seek to spin off its MTVi division, which had also registered to sell shares. The company said it was withdrawing its IPO registration with the Securities and Exchange Commission, but added that it still hoped for a spin-off should the market improve.

Media spin-offs that made it into the public market have suffered this year, including NBCi that were a unit of the General Electric/NBC network. NBCi has seen its shares plunge from $106 to $5 over the last year. The New York Times yesterday said its third quarter profit rose almost 3% to 37 cents a share, against 36 cents in the same period a year ago, excluding special gains from the sale of four small newspapers. The results were in line with market expectations.

Advertising revenue at The New York Times and The Boston Globe rose in the quarter, helping to offset the effects of higher paper costs.

Source: C. Grimes. 'NY Times drops tracker plan'. Financial Times, Friday, 13 October, 2000.

CASE APPLICATION

INTERNET HOTELS

The Internet bubble may have burst but investment is still flooding into infrastructure businesses. In the apparently mundane business of 'Internet hotels', buildings that house other companies' computers and telecommunications equipment, advances are being made. TeleCity, one of the leading operators in the UK invested less than £100 million setting up nine Internet hotels or colocation centres. It floated in June and is valued at more than £1 billion. TeleCity was set up by Mike Kelly, a former business development officer in Manchester University's computer department. He invested a stake of £30 000 for a stake now worth more than £250 million. TeleCity was born out the University's irritation with having to pay to route all internet traffic via London.

Businesses such as Internet service providers, web hosting companies and application service providers – which supply software over high-speed telecoms links – are prepared to pay handsomely for the savings, convenience and resilience of facilities provided by colocation companies.

The centres offer direct connection to telecoms switches that ensure faster Internet access. In addition most centres are serviced by several telecoms suppliers, which drives down prices through competition and improves resilience. The arrangement also benefits telecoms companies that use colocation centres to connect their equipment with other carriers.

Online selling through the Internet

Online sales are still in the early stage of development in Europe, even if most experts agree that they will have a spectacular development in the early part of the twenty-first century. Customers will be the first to benefit from electronic commerce because they can find on the Internet a lot of comparative information about products, competitors and prices without leaving their home or office. Consumers, and particularly youngsters well familiarized with the computer technology, will be able to focus on objective criteria such as prices, performance, quality and so on. They will become more demanding buyers. The traditional 'one-way' mass communication methods will become more and more incompatible with the net generation.

CASE APPLICATION

ONLINE SHOPPING TRENDS

In 1999 only 1.8 million Britons shopped online spending some £97 each. The difference this year is that substantially more people are online and ready to shop. Analysts at Commerzbank estimate that 44% of UK households will have personal computers by the end of 2000, up from 39% in 1999, an increase of more than 1 million homes. According to PwC, the consultancy, very few retailers are prepared for this level of demand. Of the top 100 retailers, PwC has found that only 38% are selling goods and services online at the moment. Retailers such as Body Shop, JJD sports, Ikea, Harrods and H Samuel have only information websites. They and others like them will clearly miss out, not only on potential new sales as online shopping grows, but they could also face erosion in their stores as shoppers migrate to the Web.

Retailers such as Kingfisher, which owns chains such as Woolworths, Comet, and B&Q, have spent months sorting out issues such as product availability, delivery and order capability for Internet customers over the Christmas period. Purely web-based retailers, less familiar than established bricks and mortar operators with the sheer volume of transactions running up to Christmas are particularly vulnerable. Already under financial pressure because of the downturn in sentiment that has affected Internet shares, pure e-tailers might also find it difficult to secure stock to meet the demand says one retailer. Some suppliers are reluctant to commit to deliver because of the uncertainty of Internet companies' financial position.

Source: Peggy Hollinger 'Festive Internet rush may surprise retailers'. Financial Times, Monday, 30 October, 2000, p. 6.

Electronic commerce will stimulate price competition as a result of the greater facility of price comparisons provided by the Web. For example, Music Boulevard is aggressively expanding in Europe in a joint venture with the French Company Hachette; buyers do not have to pay custom duties. The same situation prevails for books whose wholesale prices are higher in the UK than in the US. Until recently, it was more interesting to buy online with Amazon (based in Seattle) than with Internet Bookshop (IBS) based at Cambridge. Price comparisons are further facilitated since January 1999, with retail prices quoted in Euros.

TESCO EXPANDS HOME SHOPPING

Tesco is planning to roll out its home shopping service in stores across the country in the next few months, as the supermarket group attempts to cash in on the success of its free Internet service. The Tesco service allows customers to order their shopping online and have it delivered for £5. It will offer the service from 100 of its stores, enabling it to reach most of the country. The move comes after a 2-year trial of the service involving 11 stores during which Tesco experimented with allowing customers to order by phone or fax. However, it has concluded that costs will be kept down if customers only order via the Internet. Tesco expects the service to expand its customer base by tempting shoppers who cannot travel or who live too far away from a supermarket. The offer is also likely to appeal to Tesco's free Internet service, which was launched earlier this year. More than 200 000 people use Tesco as their Internet provider, with a further 10 000 joining each month.

Source: The Independent, 14 April, 1999.

In an increasingly competitive and fluctuating, but potentially lucrative e-commerce market the need for effective marketing is evident. This is a unique form of marketing, however, which is at the intersection of marketing and technology; it is to some extent an evolution of direct marketing.

The evolution from direct into interactive online marketing

Direct marketing (that is when you have a zero intermediary level channel) is current practice in industrial markets when there are few potential customers and the products are sophisticated or custom made and of high unit value. The surprising fact is the development of this selling system in the field of consumer goods, largely as a result of the development of new communication media, such as telemarketing, direct response, radio and television, electronic shopping (minitel) and so on.

Direct marketing is defined by the Direct Marketing Association as:

An interactive system which uses one or more advertising media to effect a measurable response and/or transaction at any location. Thus according to this definition, direct marketing does not necessarily imply non-store marketing, and this is a marketing system without intermediaries. To clarify the field, a distinction must be made between 'direct-order' marketing and 'direct-relationship' marketing'. (Baier, 2000, p. 65).

In direct-order marketing, purchases are made from home and delivered to the home, and the firm distributes directly without using intermediaries. This is non-store marketing, and the techniques used are mail order catalogues, direct mail, telemarketing, electronic shopping, and so on.

There are several factors which explain the development of more direct marketing and communication systems:

1. The considerable cost increase of personal communication. According to a study by Forsyth (1988), the average cost of a business sales call rose to $251.63 in 1987, that is 160% of the 1977 cost of $96.79.
2. Simultaneously, one observes a weakening of mass media advertising's effectiveness, caused by the proliferation of advertising messages and changing viewing habits in TV (zapping, VCR) combined with the rising cost of brand image advertising campaigns.
3. Shopping is no longer associated with fun and excitement, and is perceived as a bore and as time-consuming by educated consumers who tend to give their time higher value. For consumers, catalogue shopping is a convenient shopping alternative.
4. For the manufacturers, direct marketing represents several potential advantages. It allows greater selectivity in communicating with the market, personalization of messages and the maintenance of a continuous relationship. From a strategic point of view, direct marketing gives the producer a way to bypass intermediaries and to reduce the firm's dependence on the goodwill of too powerful retailers.
5. Finally, the formidable development of low-cost computers, with their immense storage and processing capabilities, has greatly facilitated the use of databases to record and keep track of commercial contacts with customers. This information is then used to reach them individually with highly personalized messages.

Associated with this evolution has been an evolution in the tools of direct marketing.
   Direct marketers can use a large variety of tools to reach potential customers, from traditional face to face to Internet online marketing. The most important tools have developed over a period of time and reflect the growing sophistication of technology:

1. Face-to-face selling. This remains the preferred tool in business-to-business markets, where firms, having a limited and well-identified number of prospects, use their sales force to locate them and develop them into customers.
2. Direct mail has grown spectacularly during recent years thanks to the development of personalized data banks which permit high target-market selectivity. One European, in average receives 46 mailings per year against 200 in the US.
3. Catalogue selling. This accounts for 5% of retail sales in the UK. In Europe several companies hold strong positions in the market – Redoute, Manufrance, Otto Versand and Schikedanz.
4. Telemarketing or telephone marketing is experiencing a spectacular development with the generalized adoption of green (freephone) numbers. The most spectacular success has been achieved by Direct Line, a telephone sales service set up in Britain by the Royal Bank of Scotland. The great advantage of telemarketing is the rate at which calls can be made. It is quite realistic for even untrained sales personnel to make more than 50 telephone calls a day, compared to 300 face-to-face calls in a year. With specialist telesales personnel the call rate can rise to hundreds per day.
5. Television marketing consists of television spots, which persuasively describe a

product and provide listeners with a green telephone number for ordering; this form of distance selling is still modest in Europe. It lends itself particularly well to products where the demonstration effect is important. The development of interactive marketing is indicative of a significant change to exchange and communication processes between producers and consumers in affluent economies.

The Internet has built a further dimension into interaction, with it the marketing monologue which prevails in most direct marketing situations is being replaced by a marketing dialogue, mass or segment marketing being substituted by customized online marketing. The most promising distance marketing method today is undoubtedly on the Internet and the reasons for this are outlined below.

Marketing communications on the Web tend to be much more consumer-driven than traditional forms of media. In addition, the recreational uses of the medium, which is manifested in the form of non-directed search behaviour, can be an important benefit to consumers, who are intrinsically motivated to use the medium. In order to adopt a 'market orientation' firms must understand their customers and engage in consumer research. Donaton (1995) perceived fairly early that the development of business on the Internet and the commercial success of a firm's website presence would be dependant, in part, on the accurate information attained on market potential and customer needs.

In turn, Gupta (1995, HERMES: http://www.umich.edu/~sgupta/hermes/) suggested that 'convenience of access is at the core of the adoption of any technological application and determines its ultimate use'. He suggested that surveys of web users tended to indicate that vendor reliability and security of financial transactions were important factors to users in buying and selling on the Web. Such limitations impact on consumer behaviour on the Web. The marketing function can be organized in entirely new ways, giving retailers the opportunity to apply new skills and resources to communicate with customers.

Objectives of the book

Given this context it is our main objective to show you to the ways in which the Internet can be used for marketing activities. It will in particular provide you with the necessary Internet skills required to be a marketing professional in the digital age.

In light of this main objective our sub-objectives to be achieved may be stated as:

1. To explore the broadening process of the marketing concept to facilitate e-commerce, by explaining and evaluating the move by more and more firms towards interactive marketing on the Web.
2. To evaluate and analyze the way that the Internet is changing how enterprises are interacting with their suppliers, partners and customers. It looks at the implications for managing the customer.
3. To look at the Web as an important channel for marketing activities. A 'roadmap' will be presented for the use by organizations of web-based marketing tools.

4. To develop awareness of the Web as an important channel for marketing activities.

This text provides a unique mix of strategic and technical knowledge designed primarily for marketing management; strategy and principles-related courses. The book focuses on the Internet as a marketing tool in the context of rapidly changing industrial and consumer markets, including the emergence of e-commerce trading on the Web.

Structure of the book

In the first part of the book we present an overall outline of the role and importance of Internet marketing for e-commerce. In particular, the technological-driven shift in the marketing paradigm – from direct marketing towards interactive marketing – on the Web. The authors provide useful web links to marketing sites of importance, offering leading edge marketing information. In particular this section will also provide a useful 'roadmap' for marketing activities on the Internet. In the second part of the book there is a consideration of the move towards new interactive forms of marketing and changing communication processes. There is proposed, for example, in the chapter on marketing communications, an e-based communications mix to illustrate the impact of new technology. This 'broadening' of the marketing concept, by the Internet is extended further in the area of distribution through a focus on supply chain management. Here, we explore the way the Internet is impacting on how enterprises interact with their suppliers, partners and customers. There is a look at the implications for managing the customer. The music industry, is one of a number of examples, which are used to demonstrate that the Internet is creating a new form of value, which is between supplier and customer. Payment systems, security issues and ethics are now viewed to be central to finding new and keeping existing customers. The final part of the book presents a Internet marketing based 'tool-kit' considering advanced web-based marketing and new forms of Internet marketing planning.

The style of the book is to encourage the application of practical knowledge, but it also attempts to offer in-depth understanding of the changing nature of marketing through trading by e-commerce. The work reflects the changing nature of marketing, by embracing the success of the Internet infrastructure and the emergence of the World Wide Web. The book's distinctive features are listed in the next section.

Distinctive features

The text offers full coverage of both strategic and operational marketing. In addition it has the following distinctive characteristics:

1. It introduces new marketing directions in this highly experimental field of e-commerce.
2. It provides an integrated treatment of consumer and business-to-business

marketing underlying practical web-based differences and conceptual similarities.

3. It integrates international and global marketing through the text rather than relegating it to a single chapter.
4. It is illustrated with numerous virtual examples and up-to-date international data and statistics.
5. It raises the issues of responsible Internet-based marketing.
6. It integrates important theoretical concepts such as buyer behaviour theory, attitude models.
7. It contains a section devoted to the distributor's strategic marketing; a topic often neglected in marketing textbooks.
8. It discusses the ideological foundations of marketing and its role in the turbulent environment of the digital age.
9. It introduces the concept of market orientation as a substitute for the traditional marketing concept.
10. It analyses the interactive needs of both the individual consumer and of the business-to-business customer.

Conclusion

In this new millennium, there is more awareness that the World Wide Web provides immediate access to a broader international customer base than ever before possible, for both business and consumers. Many businesses have been formed or expanded to target this market. Consumer protection, privacy and database legal issues will all have an impact on global electronic commerce. A reasonable balance needs to be struck between the protection of information and the innovation and creativity that has created and grown the phenomenon of the Web. In order to satisfy the need for balance and the book's objectives there is a focus on the Internet as an interactive marketing tool. This implies a detailed consideration of the necessary marketing tools that an organization needs to operate effectively in the digital economy. An evaluation and analysis that looks into the way the Internet is changing how organizations interact with their suppliers, partners and customers is presented. It looks at the associated implications for the managing of a web customer. The music industry is one of a number of examples, which is used to, demonstrate that the Internet is creating new forms of value, between the customer and supplier.

References

Anderson, P. and Rubin, L. (1986), Marketing Communications. Prentice-Hall, Inc., Englewood Cliffs, NJ.

Baier, M. (1985). *Elements of Direct Marketing*. McGraw Hill, New York.

Biocca, F. (1992), Communications within virtual reality: creating a space for research, Journal of Communications, 42.

Business Week (1998), E-shop till you drop, 9 February, pp. 14–15.

Donaton, E. (1995), Pathfinder blazes a trail to ads, Advertising Age, April 10.

Drucker, P. (1954), *The Practice of Management*. Harper and Row, New York.

Gates, B. and Hemingway, C. (1999), *Business at The Speed of Thought: Using a Digital Nervous System*. Penguin Books, London.

Gupta, S. (1995), HERMES: a research project on the commercial uses of the World Wide Web. URL: http://www.umich.edu/~sgupta/hermes/.

Harnedy, S. (1999), *Web-based Management for the Enterprise*, Prentice Hall PTR, Englewood Cliffs, NJ.

Hoffman, D.L., Novak, T.P. and Chaterjee, P. (1996), Commercial scenarios for the Web: opportunities and challenges, *Journal of Computer-Mediated Communications*, 1 (3), pp. 36–49.

IAB/Price-Waterhouse-Coopers Survey (1998), *Online Advertising in France: Year 1 at Last!* Internet Advertising Bureau.

Kotler, P. (1967), *Marketing Management, Analysis, Planning and Control,* Prentice Hall, Englewood Cliffs, NJ.

Kuttner, R. (1998), The net: a market too perfect for profits, *Business Week*, 11 May, p. 12.

Levitt, T. (1960), Marketing myopia. *Harvard Business Review,* July-August, p. 45.

McKinsey Quarterly (1993), Marketing mid-life crisis.

Network Wizards (1999), available at http://www.nw.com.

Oldfield, C. and Burnham, N. (1997), Internet brings home the bacon. *The Sunday Times*, 2 March, p. 10.

Parsons, A., Zeisser, M. and Waitman, R. (1998), Organising today for the digital marketing of tomorrow, *Journal of Interactive Marketing*, 12 (1), pp. 31–53.

Riccciuti, M. (1995), Database vendors hawk wares on Internet, *InfoWorld*, 17 (2), p. 10.

Timmers, P. (1998), *Electronic Commerce Strategies and Business Models*. John Wiley and Sons, Chichester.

Webster, F. (1992), The changing role of marketing in the corporation, *Journal of Marketing*.

CHAPTER 2

Business models for interactive marketing

Key topics

- Evolution of Internet-based business models
- Emerging role of syndication
- Model implementation and evaluation

After studying this chapter you will be able to:

- Understand the various models that can be applied to e-commerce.
- Evaluate the different models.
- Develop digital business strategies.
- Suggest future trends and developments.

The digital economy is going to change the way of defining a business model. The power of the Web lies in the creation of new business models. It has become fashionable to talk of 'new business models' when discussing the Internet. This phrase has emerged as a catch all way to highlight the impact of the dot-com operations. We do need to be more precise: new business models are those that 'offer, on a sustained basis, an order-of-magnitude increase in value propositions to the customers compared to companies with traditional business models'. In doing so, these new models disturb the status quo and create new rules of business. An important part of the strategic thinking for every company is to develop scenarios of new business models – even though they might challenge the status quo and cannibalize current revenue and margin streams (Venkatraman, 2000).

A simple definition of a business model is that it is:

> An architecture for product, service and information flows, including a description of the various business actors and their roles: and a description of the potential benefits for the various business actors, and a description of the sources of revenue (Timmers, 1998).

There is a distinct need to create new business models for the digital economy. For example, in the case of information intensive industries like music, software, publishing and education, there is a much quicker time to market.

Evolution of Internet-based business models

There is no single, comprehensive taxonomy of web business models, which one can point to. There is offered here some generic forms of business models, which we have observed on the Web. These come under the following categories:

1. Brokerage
2. Advertising
3. Infomediary
4. Merchant
5. Affiliate
6. Community
7. Subscription
8. Utility

A number of underlying themes transcend these categories and offer a rich potential for future development – commercial electronic environments, online communities, knowledge networks and social modes of interaction – on the Internet.

Brokerage model

Brokers are market-makers: they bring buyers and sellers together and facilitate transactions. These can be either business-to-business (B2B), business-to-consumer (B2C) or the consumer-to-consumer (C2C) markets. A broker usually charges a fee for each transaction it enables. Brokerage models can take a number of forms, such as:

1. Buy/sell fulfilment. This might include online financial brokerage, like eTrade, whereby customers place, buy and sell orders for transacting financial instruments. Other examples include travel agents, and those which work on volume and low overhead to deliver the best negotiated prices, e.g. CarsDirect.
2. Market exchange. This is an increasingly common model in B2B markets. Good examples, are MetalSIte or ChemConnect's 'World Chemical Exchange'. The broker typically charges the seller a transaction fee based on the value of the sale. The pricing mechanism can be a simple offer/buy, offer/negotiated buy, or an auction offer/bid approach.
3. Business trading community. This is sometimes referred to as the 'vertical web community' a concept pioneered by Vertical Net. This site acts as an essential, comprehensive source of information and dialogue for a particular vertical market. VerticalNet's communities contain product information in buyers'

guides, supplier and product directories, daily industry news and articles, job listings and classifieds. In addition, VerticalNet's sites enable B2B exchanges of information, supplementing existing trade shows and trade association activities (see also the website of Buzzsaw.com).

4. Buyer aggregator. This model was pioneered by Accompany.com, which describes buyer aggregation as the process of bringing together individual purchases from across the Internet – to transact as a group – so they can receive the same values traditionally afforded to organizations, who purchase in volume. Sellers pay a small percentage of each sale to Accompany, on a per-transaction basis. The US Patent Office has granted Mercata a business method patent on part of its 'Powerbuy' purchasing system to let customers join together online to win group discounts on merchandise.

5. Distributor. A catalogue-type operation that connects a large number of product manufacturers with volume and retail buyers. B2B models are increasingly common. The broker facilitates business transactions between franchised distributors and their trading partners. For buyers, it enables faster time to market and time to volume as well as reducing the cost of procurement. By providing the buyer with a means of retrieving quotas from recommended substitutions transactions are more efficient. For distributors, it decreases the cost of sales by performing quoting, order processing, tracking order status, and changes more quickly and with less labour.

6. Virtual mall. This is a site that hosts many online merchants. A mall typically charges set-up, monthly listing, and/or per transaction fees (see, for example Yahoo! store's terms). The virtual mall model may be most effectively realized when combined with a generalized portal. Also, more sophisticated malls will provide automated transaction services and relationship marketing opportunities. Some examples are Yahoo! stores, ChoiceMall, iMall, Women.com's shopping network.

7. Metamediary. It brings buyers and online merchants together, in order to provide transaction services such as financial settlement and quality assurance. It is a virtual mall, but one that will process the transaction, track orders, and provide billing and collection services. The metamediary protects consumers by assuring satisfaction with merchants, and they charge a set-up fee and a fee per transaction, e.g. HotDispatch, Amazon's zShops.

8. Auction broker. A site that conducts auctions for sellers (individuals and merchants). The broker charges the seller a fee, which is typically scaled with the value of the transaction. Then the seller takes highest bid(s) from buyers above a minimum. Auctions can vary in terms of the offering and bidding rules, e.g. eBay, Auctionnet and Onsale.

9. Reverse auction. There are a variety of names for this model on the Web including the following: 'name-your-price,' 'demand collection' or 'shopping by request'. This is where the prospective buyer makes a final (sometimes binding) bid for a specified good or service, and the broker seeks fulfilment. In some models, the broker's fee is spread between the bid and the fulfilment price and perhaps a processing charge. This is frequently aimed at high price items,

which could be automobiles or airline tickets, e.g. Priceline, Respond.com, eWanted, MyGeek.com.

10. Classifieds. A listing of items for sale or wanted for purchase, which is typically run by local news content providers. The price may or may not be specified and listing charges are incurred regardless of whether a transaction occurs.

The advertising-based model

The Web-advertising model is an extension of the traditional media broadcasting model. There is a broadcaster, in this case, a website provider which supplies content (usually, but not necessarily, for free) and services (like e-mail, chat, forums) mixed with advertising messages in the form of banner ads. The banner ads may be the major or sole source of revenue for the broadcaster. The broadcaster may be a content creator or distributor of content created elsewhere. The advertising model only works when the volume of viewer traffic is large or highly specialized. Some of the different variants of the advertising model are summarized below:

1. Generalized portal. This is high-volume traffic – typically tens of millions of visits per month that are driven by generic or diversified content or services; it consists of search engines and directories like Excite, AltaVista and Yahoo! or content driven sites like AOL. The high volume makes advertising profitable and permits further diversification of the site services. Competition for volume has led to the packaging of free content and services such as e-mail, stock portfolio, message boards, chat, news, and local information.

2. Personalized portal. The generic nature of a generalized portal can undermine user loyalty. This has led to the creation of more personalized portals – My Yahoo! My Netscape – that allow customization of the interface and content. This increases the degree of loyalty through the user's own time investment in personalizing the site. The profitability of this portal is based on volume and possibly the value of information being derived from user choices.

3. Specialized portal. This is usually called a 'vortal' (i.e. vertical portal). Here volume is less important than a well-defined user base (perhaps 0.5–5 million visits per month). In the case of a site that attracts only golfers, or home buyers, or new parents, it can be highly sought after as a venue for certain advertisers, who are willing to pay a premium to reach that particular audience.

4. Attention/incentive marketing. The 'pay for attention' model pays visitors for viewing content and completing forms, or sweepstakes, or a frequent flyer-type point's scheme. The attention marketing approach has the most appeal to companies with very complex product messages, which might otherwise find it hard to sustain customer interest. The concept was pioneered by CyberGold, with its 'earn and spend community' that brought together those advertisers

interested in incentives-based marketing for consumers looking to save. To facilitate transactions, the company developed and patented a micropayment system. Other loyalty-based relationship marketing approaches are Netcentives or MyPoints.

5. Free model. There is here the notion of offering users something for free – site hosting, FreeMerchant web services, Internet access, free hardware, electronic greeting cards (BlueMountain). Freebies tend to create a high volume site for advertising opportunities. The financial viability is hardest when it is based purely on advertising revenue.

It is important to stress that because much of the Web looks at first glance like a traditional publishing medium, advertising has emerged as the dominant business model to date. HotWired Ventures LLC, for example, charge companies as much as $15 000 a month to post banners about their products and services, and advertisers pay between $8 500 and $20 400 for space on Netscape Communications Corporation's site. Market research company Jupiter Communications pegs the average advertising revenue for leading websites at $1.2 million in 2000. Although high-tech sponsors are predictably numerous, web advertisers are not limited to companies targeting technical engineers. They tend to represent a range of Fortune 1000 companies. Gatorade, for example, turned up on ESPNet SportsZone, which also signed up AT&T Corp., Visa International and others for what Jupiter calls a 'groundbreaking' $100 000 per quarter. NBC, has used its advertising budget to have a presence on Infoseek Corp, HotWired and Yahoo.

What this shift enables is one-to-one advertising or 'narrowcasting' which is wonderful in theory, but often difficult in practice. This has caused advertisers and web publishers to think about how to price advertisements on the Web and monitor their effectiveness. The result is that advertisers are starting to experiment with alternatives to the traditional cost-per-thousand model – the technology is coming so that advertisers can target their audience, track click-through and monitor through intelligent software agents the behaviour of consumers searching in their website.

Infomediary model

The data which is being collected about consumers and their buying habits are extremely valuable. This is especially the case when that information is carefully analyzed and used to target marketing campaigns. Some firms are able to function as infomediaries, by collecting and selling information to other businesses. An infomediary may offer free Internet access (NetZero) or free hardware (eMachines.com) in exchange for detailed information about their surfing and purchasing habits. This is more likely to succeed than the pure advertising model.

1. Recommender System. This is a site that allows users to exchange information with each other about the quality of products or services – or the sellers with whom they have had a purchase experience (good or bad). See for example,

Deja.com, ePinions. ClickTheButton takes the concept a step further by integrating the recommender system into the web browser. Such agents monitor a user's habits, thereby increasing the relevance of its recommendations to the user needs – and the value of the data to the collector. Recommender systems can take advantage of the affiliate model (which is considered later in the chapter) offered by merchants to augment revenue from the sale of consumer information.

2. Content-based sites. These are free to view, but require users simply to register (other information may or may not be collected). With registration one is allowed the inter-session tracking of a users' site usage patterns and thereby generates data of greater potential value, in targeted advertising campaigns. This is the most basic infomediary model (NYTimes.com).

Merchant model

This includes the classic wholesalers and retailers of goods and services increasingly referred to as 'e-tailers'. Sales may be made, which are based on list prices or through auction. In some cases, the goods and services may be unique to the Web and not have the traditional 'brick-and-mortar' storefront. These includes the following:

1. Virtual merchant. A business that operates only over the Web and offers either traditional or web-specific goods or services (pure-play e-tailers). The method of selling may be list price or auction. An example of a service merchant is Facetime which calls itself an 'application service provider'. It offers live customer support for e-commerce websites with for example, Amazon, eToys, Eyewire, Onsale.
2. Catalogue merchant. The migration of mail order to a web-based order business, e.g. Chef's Catalog.
3. Surf and turf. A traditional brick-and-mortar establishment with web storefront. The model has the potential for channel conflict, but physical stores can prove to be an asset if cleverly integrated into web operations. For example, Gap, Lands End, B&N.
4. Bit vendor. A merchant that deals strictly in digital products and services, in its purest form, conducts both sales and distribution over the Web.

Affiliate model

In contrast to the more generalized portal, which seeks to drive a high volume of traffic to one site, the affiliate model, provides purchasing opportunities wherever people may be surfing. It does this, by offering financial incentives (in the form of a percentage of revenue) to affiliate partner sites. The affiliates provide purchase-point click-through to the merchant. It is a pay-for-performance model – if an affiliate does not generate sales, it represents no cost to the merchant. The affiliate model is inherently well-suited to the Web, which explains its popularity. There are variations, which include banner exchange, pay-per-click, and revenue sharing programs. However a number of potential problems loom ahead that may inhibit the diffusion of the affiliate model, which is due to the granting of a broad patent to Amazon.com (see the Website of I-revenue.net, a guide to affiliate programs on the Web, or AffiliateWorld which discusses this controversial development in detail).

Community model

Hagel (1999) believed that the dominant web-based model to be a virtual business community model. Virtual communities actually started as spontaneous social events on electronic networks, whether it was Compuserve or AOL, the early Internet, or the thousands of independent bulletin board services that sprouted up around the US. People gathered around common areas of interest, engaging in shared discussions that persisted and accumulated over time that led to a complex network of personal relationships and an increasing identification with the group as a community.

Hagel explains that any virtual community will have a distinct focus. Virtual communities are defined (Hagel) by bringing people together with a common set of needs or interests. Those needs or interests could span a variety of dimensions. Virtual communities could be organized around an area of interest (like sports or stock investments), a demographic segment (certain age groups within the population), or a geographic region (metropolitan areas). We believe this also has relevance for business-to-business markets. In these situations, virtual communities might be defined around an industry, certain types of businesses (small home office-based businesses or franchisees). In any event, the point is to create a shared focus to aggregate customers together who have similar concerns and requirements.

The viability of the community model is based on user loyalty (as opposed to high traffic volume). Users have a high investment in both time and emotion in the site. In some cases, users are regular contributors of content and/or money. Having users who visit continually offers advertising infomediary or specialized portal opportunities. The community model may also run on a subscription fee for premium services. A number of different variants of the community model have evolved in the digital age:

1. Voluntary contributor model. This is similar to the traditional broadcasting model – the listener or viewer contributor method used in not-for-profit radio and television broadcasting. The model, is predicated on the creation of a community of users who support the site through voluntary donations. Not-for-profit organizations may also seek funding from charitable foundations and corporate sponsors that support the organization's mission. The Web holds great potential as a contributor-based model because the user base is more readily apparent. A relevant example is national public radio.
2. Knowledge networks. These expert sites provide a source of information, which

is based on professional expertise or the experience of other users. Sites are typically run like a forum where persons seeking information can pose questions and receive answers from (presumably) someone knowledgeable about the subject. The experts may be employed staff, a regular cadre of volunteers, or in some cases, simply anyone on the Web who wishes to respond. Examples includes: Deia, ExpertCentral, knowPost, Xpertsite, Abuzz. Also, there is the fee-based model, e.g. Guru, Exp.

3. Subscription model. The users pay for access to the site. A high value-added content is essential (Wall Street Journal, Consumer Reports). In cases where there has been some generic news content, which is viable on the newsstand, has tended to prove less successful as a subscription model on the Web (slate). A 1999 survey by Jupiter Communications found that 46% of Internet users would not pay to view content on the Web. Some businesses have combined free content (to drive volume and ad revenue) with premium content or services for subscribers only.

4. There are a few virtual communities that are emerging to underscore some of the emerging different dimensions of interest. One of the earliest ones is a group called Motley Fool (www.fool.com). They were originally founded on AOL, but it is now available on the Internet. Despite a frivolous name, it has a serious purpose. The intent is to bring together people who are interested in stock investments. Now it has well over 800 000 active members, and has got to the point where the impact of discussions in their bulletin boards, have actually a material effect on stock prices. In some cases you can track favourable comments on these discussion forums, leading to stock prices going up, and unfavourable comments leading to stock prices going down. So there is a relatively large degree of influence emerging even at this quite early stage of development. Mediconsult (www.mediconsult.com) is another example of a virtual community organized around an area of interest – in this case health care targeted to consumers. It helps consumers to find information about various kinds of medical treatments for diseases, to compare those treatments and choose the best one for themselves. Parent soup (www.parentsoup.com) targets a specific demographic group; parents with small children. It has created an environment where parents can talk about the challenges of raising small children, and it is in the process of developing quite an attractive marketplace for a large range of consumer product vendors. Tripod (www.tripod.com) targets a different demographic group – those people leaving college, facing their first job, the challenge of renting their first apartment or house, and all the lifestyle changes that go on in that transition. An example, of a geographically-oriented virtual community would be Boston.com (www.boston.com), who are targeting people who live in the Boston area or who are interested in events there, creating a diverse set of resources for them.

5. In the business-to-business environments you can look at virtual communities like Physicians' online (www.po.com). On this site you have to be a registered physician to participate, and roughly 25% of all physicians are

members. It provides an environment where physicians can talk not only about the medical challenges of treating certain diseases, but also the business aspects of their practice, such as what to pay a receptionist and how to collect from an insurance company faster. It covers a variety of important issues for physicians.

6. Another example in the business-to-business realm is agriculture Online (www.agriculture.com). This initiative initially met with a fair amount of scepticism when it was formed because it targets farmers. The stereotype being that farmers do not know anything about computers, so why should they ever participate in a virtual community. In fact, most farmers are intensely computer literate, using them every day to manage their farms. The value of coming together in a geographically isolated job and being able to connect anytime, anywhere with other farmers is a powerful proposition. It is also an attractive marketplace for a broad range of products and service vendors who are trying to reach farmers.

CASE APPLICATION   **GEOCITIES**

GeoCities, initially derived most of its revenue from traditional banner advertising. One could click on the GeoCities website and view synchronously location filming from the streets of major cities around the world. Then in 1999 it formed an alliance with Yahoo! – the Internet's busiest portal – to generate traffic and memberships for both their sites, respectively. GeoCities provided personal webpages for Yahoo members while Yahoo supplied chat, e-mail, and web guides. GeoCities also formed partnerships with a range of Internet marketing firms; this included Amazon.com (books and music), CdNow (music), First USA (credit cards), and Surplus Direct/ Egghead (computer equipment and software). It also created GeoStore, which allowed other merchants to display their wares.

The business revenue model of GeoCities was based on:

Banner revenues and sell-through
Partnerships
Premium services

The proposed acquisition of GeoCities by Yahoo! was announced on January 28, 1999. It would combine the 35 million worldwide registered users of Yahoo! with the 3.5 million websites, grouped into 41 neighbourhoods, that made up the GeoCities community.

In mid-summer 1999 the integration between GeoCities and Yahoo! was completed. This led to a new GeoCities home page – http://www.geocities.yahoo.com). At that time Yahoo! was widely recognized as one of the most successful (and one of the few profitable) Web portals. Trade sources were said to believe that the acquisition represented an attempt by Yahoo! to develop more 'sticky' content, content that keeps users on a site longer, making possible higher advertising rates.

Source: Adapted from Roberts (2000).

ONLINE PUBLISHING

Ebrary works with publishers to bring their conventional published work to the Internet. Books can then be viewed on Ebrary's website with technology that does not allow copying or printing. If the publisher agrees, readers may print pages for sums similar to those charged to photocopy a book in a library. Links to online retailers or the publishers' websites encourage the reader to buy the book. Ebrary works on a normal library, but with substantial added value, because it integrates paper books with the Internet.

Xlibris uses print-on-demand technology to cross the bridge between the paper and electronic worlds. When you see an Xlibris book in an online bookstore, such as Amazon, clicking on the 'order' button sends a message to the printer that prints and binds one copy and sends it off. Gone are the tens of thousands that publishers needed to make a book profitable.

Xlibris offer several levels of service. On the lowest, the work is published for nothing. Works with graphics and diagrams cost the author money. But Xlibris insists it is not vanity publishing. It is, rather an enabler, using technology to lower costs. Vanity publishers charge a significant amount of money, but with Xlibris you can publish for nothing and whatever you publish is distributed.

Like Xlibris, iUniverse will publish almost anything. It also brings out-of-print books back into print. But it differs from Xlibris in that it is has entered a deal with IDG books, publishers of the 'Dummies' series and 'Frommer's' guides, to allow customers to choose a chapter from a book here and a book there, which will be sent to the print-on-demand printer.

Xlibris and iUniverse may still work with paper, but MightyWords has turned its back on anything so old economy, publishing only in electronic form. Ideally, they are looking for works from 10 to 100 pages about business, technology and computing – knowledge that people are willing to pay for.

Although anyone who writes can publish on the site, about half of the new material comes from publishers looking to boost sales of their authors, and from MightyWord's own commissions. Unlike MightyWords, Online Originals concentrates on fiction. It exercises editorial control so as to enhance the Online Original brand. As with AtRandom, the US e-book imprint of Random House, Online Original brings traditional publishing to the Internet.

Both Xlibris and iUniverse are receiving about 500 new titles a month. But who is going to read it all? One idea is that people will choose names they associate with quality, and will therefore, choose from Online Originals, Xlibris and iUniverse, on the other hand they may leave it up to authors, believing they are best at marketing their books. There is likely to be no single winner. Xlibris believes that the industry will probably have to operate on different business models. Given this and the need for authors to make themselves heard, it would be unwise to write off publishers quite yet.

Source: Paul Talacko 'Novel practices on the Internet'. Financial Times, Friday October 6, 2000, p. 14.

LASTMINUTE.COM

Lastminute has suffered from a steady drop in publicity since its much -hyped flotation in March 2000. The shares 380 p at flotation, had fallen to $137^1/_2$ p by Tuesday evening (October 10, 2000). On Wednesday (October 11), Lastminute surprised investors by appointing Allan Leighton, based at Wall Mart Europe, as chairman.

Mr. Leighton previously turned around the struggling Asda supermarket chain with Archie Norman, former chairman, before selling it to discount retailer Wal-Mart last year. He announced his intention to step down as president and chief executive of Wal-Mart Europe last month. He is expected to take an active role at Lastminute and analysts saw his appointment as giving Lastminute more operational experience to deal with its rapid growth. The founders Brent Hoberman and Martha Lane Fox are hoping to take advantage of his expertise in 'growing the business very rapidly and being very customer focused'. He will not receive a salary from Lastminute but will be granted 1 million share options exercisable at $137^1/_2$ p. He bought £100 000 of Lastminute shares yesterday. Mr. Leighton defended Lastminute's record and underlined his faith in the business model. He said: 'if you look at the business performance compared to plan it is very good… but the markets are finding it very difficult to value technology stocks. Over time they will find a way of valuing them'.

On a sour note it was evident that Mr. Leighton's appointment had failed to defend Lastminute against the slumping technology markets. The shares fell 6½ p to 131 p.

Source: Thorold Barker 'Leighton to chair Lastminute' FT Companies and Markets, Thursday, October 12, 2000, p. 1.

Subscription model

Time's and Songline Studios' decisions to pursue a subscription model – in which customers pay to access information – make sense from a normal economic perspective. However, this runs somewhat counter to much of the existing practice on the Internet, in which the consumers expect lots of free information. And, the economics of free stuff, except in the software industry, doesn't look so good. Jim Sterne, president of Target Marketing (Santa Barbara, CA) and a columnist for WebMaster (www.webmaster.com) agrees: 'The only subscription that I've seen so far that makes sense is "The Wall Street Journal", because the price is right and the brand is trusted'.

At $29 per year for readers, who subscribe to the paper version and $49 for nonsubscribers, then a personalized journal is a bargain. 'If The Wall Street Journal doesn't make it, no one will,' says Sterne.

Other high-profile publishers that have experimented with the subscription model include USA Today. But no one is showing how many customers they've signed up, so their success is tough to gauge. Paradoxically, some argue that the existence of vast quantities of free information on the Internet will actually make people more willing to pay for the best stuff. 'As the amount of free garbage on the Web goes up, more people will be willing to pay for branded information'. Stock investments and pornography sites are examples of flat-fee subscription services that are reportedly doing quite well online.

Even if mass marketing a subscription service to consumers doesn't work, business-to-business niche subscription services may have a chance. For one thing, as more and more of the Web is commercialized, the 'freebie' starts to disappear. Also, a Web start-up can survive a long time with minimal capital costs and with no expenses for printing, advertising or direct mail. 'If a company can build subscribers in a small, but rapidly growing market with [low costs] and maintain that share when the market gets bigger, it should reap good profit margins,' says Mary Meeker, an analyst of new media at Morgan Stanley and Co.'s equity research department (www.ms.com).

Another approach with revenue potential is that of micro-subscriptions, whereby hundreds of thousands of users pay pennies for snippets of information. Instead of paying $20 for an entire cookbook, for example, a consumer would shell out 5 cents for a single recipe. The software for accepting such a minuscule sum is still at the stage of 'work-in-progress', but 'any publisher with technical savvy is looking into micropayment standards for the Web browser', says Meeker.

Utility model

The utility model is a metered usage pay as you go approach. Its success may depend on the ability to charge by the byte, including micropayments (that is, those too small to pay to cover processing fees, by credit card). Some useful illustrative examples here are FatBrain, SoftLock, Authentica.

The emerging role of syndication

Syndication roles

Traditionally, companies have connected with one another in simple, linear chains, running from raw material producers to manufacturers to distributors to retailers. In syndication, the connections between companies tend to proliferate. The network replaces the chain as the organizing model for business relationships.

Within a syndication network, there are three roles that businesses can play. These are originator, syndicator, distributor and consumer, respectively. The Internet broadens the originator category in two ways. It expands the scope of original content that can be syndicated, and it makes it easier for any company or individual to disseminate that content globally. Anything that can exist as information – from products and services to business processes to corporate brands – can be syndicated.

Syndicators are a form of infomediary, collecting and packaging digital information in a way that adds value to it. In the physical world, stand-alone syndicators are rare outside the entertainment field, but this business model is increasingly becoming prominent on the Internet.

Originators create the original content. Syndicators package that content for distribution, often integrating it with content from other originators. Distributors deliver the content to customers. A company can play one role in a syndication network, or it can play two or three roles simultaneously. It can also shift from one role to another over time.

CASE APPLICATION   **LINKSHARE**

LinkShare is an online syndicator. It syndicates commerce rather than traditional content. More than 400 online retailers have contracted with LinkShare to administer their affiliate programs – programs that enable other sites to provide links to the e-tailers in return for a small cut of any sales, which they generate. LinkShare aggregates all the programs on one site, providing an easy, one-stop marketplace for affiliate sites. In this network, the e-tailers act as the originators, LinkShare is the syndicator and the content sites are the distributors. In effect, one can see that LinkShare acts to provide the technical infrastructure for monitoring transactions and tracking and paying affiliate commissions. It also offers ancillary services such as reporting, for both affiliates and retailers. The e-tailers pay LinkShare a combination of up-front fees and per-sale commissions.

Will syndication change the nature of e-commerce?

In relation to its impact on individual companies' strategies and relationships, syndication promises to change the nature of business. As organizations are being constructed out of the components syndicated from many other organizations, the result will be a mesh of relationships with no beginning, end or centre. Companies may look the same as before to their customers, but behind the scenes they will be in constant flux, melting with one another in ever changing networks. The shift won't happen overnight, and of course, there will always be functions and goods that do not lend themselves to syndication. But in those areas where syndication takes hold, companies will become less important than the Internetworks that contain them.

Indeed, individual companies will routinely originate, syndicate, or distribute information without being aware of all the others participating in the Internetwork. A particular originator may, for example, have a relationship with only one syndicator, but through that relationship it will be able to benefit from the contributions of hundreds or even thousands of other companies. While every participant will retain some measure of control –choosing which syndication partners to have direct relationships with and deciding which business rules to incorporate into its syndicated transactions – no participant will control the overall network. Like any highly complex, highly adaptive system, a well-functioning syndication network will be self-organizing, constantly optimizing its behaviour in response to an unending stream of information about the transactions taking place among its members.

Syndication may not be a new model in the physical world, but it takes on a new life thanks to the Internet. Virtually any organization can benefit from syndication, often in several different ways if it is willing to view itself as part of a larger, interconnected world rather than seeking exclusive control at every turn. The tools and intermediaries that facilitate syndication relationships will become more sophisticated over time. Already, though, there are many syndication networks in place and many examples of syndication strategies. As the Internet economy continues to grow in importance, syndication will grow along with it as the underlying structure of business.

Model implementation and evaluation

The emphasis of the virtual community model is in building relationships with customers. There are two different approaches to how you can implement this, which is essentially a type of collaborative (relationship) marketing (Hagel, 1999, p. 63). One approach is the 'funnel' model. This involves putting banner advertisements out in a variety of context sites that are emerging on the Internetwork. A context site addresses a broader experience, which is relevant to a vendor's product or service. For example, a virtual community for gardeners might be a relevant context site for vendors of gardening tools, or a virtual community for parents with small children might be a context site for financial services providers offering savings plans for college. Essentially, you are using those banner advertisements as a device to intercept and divert

An alternative approach, which is just beginning to be developed, is what Hagel calls the 'sponsorship' model. Rather than intercepting and diverting customers, it involves using some of the context sites that are developing online as the primary environment where you can help more, know more, and sell more. As a result, your own site, and the vendor's site, ultimately becomes an invisible back-office operation as opposed to the primary marketing environment. In the music industry there is such an arrangement between CDNow and its affiliated e-tailer operations.

Recently, Amazon took on a new syndication role – zShops. It now hosts hundreds of small e-commerce providers on its own site. These shops gain access to Amazon's 13 million customers as well as its sophisticated tools for smoothing the online ordering process. In return, they pay Amazon a listing fee for each item plus a 1.25–5% commission on each sale. ZShops turns Amazon into a distributor – not of books or of other products, but of online shops. In addition, to the revenue boost, Amazon gets additional traffic from customers interested, in the niche zShops. Amazon has also started signing distribution deals with larger e-tailers such as Drugstore.com and Living.com, which offer products complimentary to its own. Amazon receives substantial payments, and equity from these partners in exchange for placement on its site, and it also gives customers fewer reasons to shop elsewhere.

Amazon's experience holds a very important lesson for all companies. In a syndicated world, core capabilities is its ordering system. Instead of keeping the system to itself – as traditional strategists might have counselled – Amazon uses syndication to sell the capability, to both stores and content sites throughout the Web. Like Amazon, companies can use syndication to broaden their distribution in an efficient manner. Syndication can also bring data about customer usage patterns. And, this can generate leads and reinforce brands

Inktomi generates revenues from per-query charges and by sharing dollars its customers generate from selling banner advertisements on their search pages. The company has applied the same business model and core technologies to other services such as content catching and comparison shopping. During the last quarter it answered 3.4 billion search queries, its quarterly revenues hit $36 million, and its market capitalization surpassed $10 billion.

Scott Adams, an originator, draws the popular Dilbert cartoon strip. He licenses it to a syndicator, United Features, which packages it with other comic strips and sells them to a variety of print publications. A newspaper such as the Washington Post, acts as a distributor by printing the syndicated cartoons, together with articles, photographs, television listings, advertisements, and many other pieces of content, and delivering the entire package to the doorsteps of readers. To date this has proved a very successful business model for Inktomi.

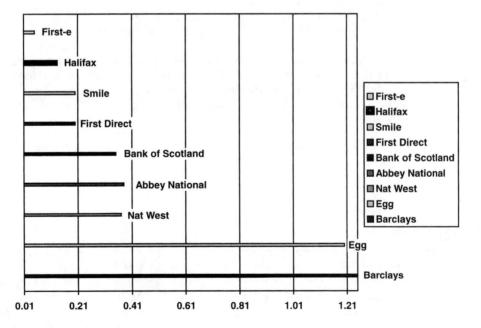

Figure 2.1   Internet banking

CASE APPLICATION   **ONLINE BANKING**

Recently, Allied Irish Banks became the biggest European bank to scale back its online ambitions, dropping plans for an Internet only bank it was due to launch in early next year. Figure 2.1 shows the biggest players in Internet banking. Analysts at ABN Amro estimate that between them the UK online banks were aiming for 3.5 million customers by the end of 2002, against a market calculated by Forrester, the research company, at just 2 million people.

Lloyds TSB is more optimistic, estimating the UK market for Internet only accounts at 2.25 million by 2003, with the European market at 8.5 million. It wants to take 10% of this European total, and have 575 000 online-only customers in the UK, through its Evolvebank subsidiary due to be launched this year.

The banks operating in the UK have only just started to come up against this mismatch between expectation and reality. First-e, which operates in the UK but is run by Dublin-based Internet incubator Enba, has embarked on a cost-cutting programme and is understood to have told staff there will be redundancies, under consultation procedure required by Irish law.

The bank has also cut back on its advertising, cancelling an expensive series of television advertisements at the last minute and incurring a large penalty as a result. Meanwhile growth has slowed at Egg, the leading Internet bank, as a move away from loss-leading savings account rates led to savers withdrawing £443 million in the 3 months to the end of September.

At the same time traditional banks like Barclays (biggest online account) are improving their interest rates to savers partly in response to the market-leading rates set by the Internet banks.

This reflects a tendency for customers to do Internet banking with banks that also had branches. In the US, this figure is 96%. However, the new online banks are not giving up. First-e says that despite scrapping its advertising plans, it is getting more new customer applications than ever. And Egg argues that customers who left it after it reduced loss-leading rates are those unlikely to be profitable customers anyway.

But there are clear signs that the banks are feeling the pain. The question each has to face is whether it – and its financial backers – grit their teeth and hang on in the market, or give up and accept the loss of face.

Source: Adapted from: James Mackintosh. 'How banking on the Internet has become a fallen icon?' Financial Times, October 20, 2000, p. 4.

Conclusion

The chapter outlines various business models that are appropriate to electronic commerce. As this is a developing field, it is vital to remain alert and be aware as new models make their appearance. It is also important to realize that as a website evolves, business models might have adapted to suit the changing needs of the business. Whatever model(s) is adopted, it is important to plan, control, monitor, adjust and manage quality.

Checklist

1. Internet environments are changing the architecture of business models from organizing mechanisms through to revenue generation.
2. Brokerage models charge a fee to bring the buyer and seller together in either the B2B or B2C contexts.
3. The advertising model characterized many new start-up Internet companies due to it offering a natural extension of pre-existing physical-based broadcasting models.
4. Some firms are able to function as infomediaries, by collecting and selling on information to other parties. who
5. In the merchant model – 'e-tailers' act as distributors for the virtual supply of goods and services.
6. The affiliates provide purchase-point click-through to the merchant. It is a pay-for- performance model – if an affiliate does not generate sales, it represents no cost to the merchant.
7. The speed and extent to which virtual communities are e-merging on the Web has led to a feeling amongst academics and practitioners alike that it is now the dominant digital model.
8. A subscription-based approach offers some potential but in a way this is the antithesis of the underlying pillars and philosophy of the Web.
9. The utility model is a metered approach, which is based on micropayments.
10. Syndication, although well established in physical-based businesses like entertainment may hold the key to the future web-based business model.

References

Deloitte Research (2000), Online B2B exchanges: the new economics of markets. http://www.dc.com/research.

Hagel, J. (1999), Net gain: expanding markets through virtual communities, *Journal of Interactive Marketing*, 13 (1), pp. 55–65.

Venkatraman, N. (2000), Five steps to a dot-com strategy: how to find your footing on the Web, *Sloan Management Review*, Spring, pp. 15–28.

Roberts, M.L. (2000), Geocities (A) and (B), *Journal of Interactive Marketing*, 14 (1), pp. 60–72.

Timmers P. (1998), Business models for electronic markets. *Electronic Markets*, 8 (2), pp. 3–8.

CHAPTER 3

Infrastructure and online information resources

Key topics

- The interactive marketing information market
- Route map to the foundations of Internet technology
- Communications infrastructure for web-based marketing
- Cyberspace information for interactive marketing
- Building your market intelligence tools

After studying this chapter you will be able to:

- Understand the development in marketing information through Internet technology
- Explain various methods of Internet connection
- Describe the communications infrastructure supporting web-based marketing
- Use cyberspace information in your web-based marketing
- Build your own market intelligence tools

The Internet is changing the way that organizations conduct business and as a consequence communicate. Internet related business activities have moved from a relatively small market to quite a large market at an unprecedented speed. What was previously viewed as a market segment is moving towards a global market at a rapid pace of growth. The Web in the context of marketing is very much a marketing communications channel, which is rapidly developing into an online trading environment for all sizes of organizations.

This chapter is intended to provide you with knowledge of the foundations of the Internet and practical tools for information searching on the Web, with a focus on relationship, one-to-one and loyalty marketing initiatives. The web is viewed as being an ideal platform for a shift towards more one-to-one marketing and we will now provide a 'route map' to the infrastructure and appropriate information sources on the Internet.

The interactive marketing information systems

Our approach to interactive marketing information systems encompasses three main participants that include: (1) organizations that create, process and distribute information in the context of time, relevance and form, (2) organizations and individuals that buy information, and (3) consumers who provide information about their specific demographics, lifestyle and transactions. The Internet can be seen as the 'glue' and as a consequence the enabler of value-added information (Kannan et al., 2000). Marketing information market can be seen through a process and content orientated viewpoint, with the former concerned about how the consumer will react to the medium and the latter concerned with the impact of the medium on the market. In considering a process oriented perspective it can be seen that many organizations, such as Neilsons have set up interactive surveys through focus groups, Web panels, and e-mail surveys. Process-based surveys are typically used for product positioning, consumer attitudes surveys with regard to branding and buyer behaviour patterns (Wylie, 1997). A content orientated perspective is more focused on information generation both on and outside the Internet. The primary source of information both in the physical and virtual world is primarily through marketing databases. Data warehouses have grown significantly through the Internet, as companies have realized the value of capturing and tracking behavioural data and selling it over the Internet (McCullough, 1998). The focus of this chapter is more concerned with a content perspective primarily based on behavioural rather than attitudinal marketing information on the Internet.

Interactive marketing information, similar to other types of information, can be manipulated in four fundamental ways: generation, processing, storage, and transmission (Davis and Davidson, 1991). News agencies such as Reuters (www.reuters.com) and Bloomberg (www.bloomberg.com) are typical examples of organizations involved in the *generation* of information. Bloomberg also *processes* data to create news headlines and also graphical representations. CCN (www.ccn.com) *store* vast amounts of market information including demographics, lifestyle and general population statistics. Many companies provide the physical access to the Internet such as telephone carriers including British Telecom (www.bt.co.uk), NTL (www.ntl.com) and MCI (www.mci.com). In manipulating information organizations may do this by focusing on one of the activities or by integrating them in a chain that adds value at various stages (see Figure 3.1). Bloomberg Financial Services is an example of a company that undertakes all activities in a information value chain (Nee, 1996).

As you use the Internet you are participating, in both experiential and goal directed surfing for valuable and useful information, which is enabling the process of exchange. The Internet is frequently viewed as a 'cybrary' (global digital library). With the Internet being a global information source we need to find effective ways of navigating through the complexed maze of routes and sources. If you compare the Internet to more traditional sources of information – such as a community library – the Internet offers all types of information: reference information (catalogues, dictionaries, textbooks and science and technology articles), news informa-

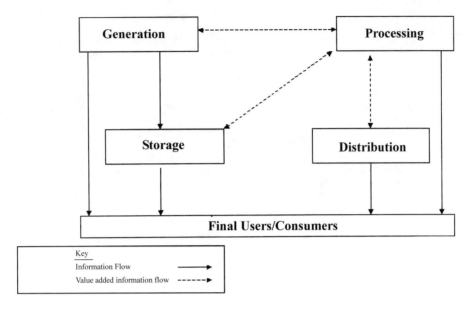

Figure 3.1

tion (places and events, technological developments), cultural information (history, philosophy, and the arts), formal and informal communications (chat rooms, newsgroups and discussion boards).

The information on the Internet is provided in various forms, which is reflecting the ever increasing use of multimedia applications. The Internet provides information through text, graphics, video and sound. For example, browsers are currently being developed through the XML 'voice for voice' driven websites that can also easily share voice content between sites.

Route map to the foundations of Internet technology

We are all aware of the Internet and what has been termed cyberspace. For many it creates a more even platform, which has its own rules and methods of working. Cyberspace is associated with anarchic online communities that to date have self-organized through rapid transformations. This new form of reality is described in many ways – the information superhighway, the electronic frontier, surfing the Net, wired world, and the information society. These metaphors are associated with ideas of exploring, surfing, searching, locating, the 'flow experience', and exchanging information. The basic structure of the Internet is based on the interconnection of computers on geographically remote locations across a complexed and ever changing telecommunications network. In comparison an Intranet is based on the same principle but gives an internal focus to a particular organization (see Figure 3.2).

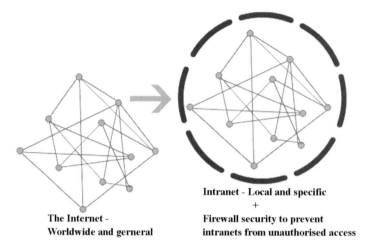

The Internet -
Worldwide and gerneral

Intranet - Local and specific
+
Firewall security to prevent
intranets from unauthorised access

Figure 3.2   Information manipulation value chain. Adapted from Lopes and Galleta (2000)

Internet technology infrastructure

The Internet in its most basic form is the interconnection of thousands of academic, research, government, business, and other organizations' computer networks. Networks are used for the sharing of hardware, software, and other information with end users. The two main types of networks that exist are Local Area Networks (LANs) and Wide Area Networks (WANs). A LAN as it infers is a network within a relatively small area, for example within the same building or on a single site/ campus. WANs are dispersed over geographical remote locations, for example across a town or even around the globe. Such networks function using various protocols (standards for exchanging messages) and as a consequence it can be difficult to communicate between WANs using different protocols. The Internet emerged through the need for open standards across global networks in the 1960s until the present day. The Advanced Research Projects Agency (ARPA) of the US Department of Defense developed techniques for interconnecting LANs and WANs that became known as Internetworks. ARPAnet soon became known as the 'Internet'. The Internet as we know it today, comprises thousands upon thousands of networks interconnected by dedicated servers with a specific purpose and these are called 'routers'. When messages are sent on the internet they are broken into packets. Each router sends a packet to another router, and so on, until the packet reaches its final destination. When the packet is delivered to the destination it is reassembled into the original message.

Users of the Internet are connected by a combination of hardware devices including cables, modems, telephone lines, satellite and other telecommunications technology. The computers on the Internet require standard communications software to allow the virtually real time interaction. The communication software must follow the same protocols, of which there are two, which are called Transmission Control Protocol and Internet Protocol (TCP/IP), respectively. All services connected to the Internet use TCP/IP and as a consequence a computer must have TCP/IP software before it can use the Internet (refer to Figure 3.3).

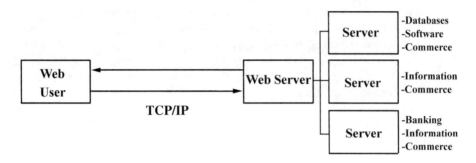

Figure 3.3   Basic structure of the Internet

The Internet community

The Internet is viewed as being a mix of objects including more than just technology. The Internet comprises technology, people and organizations located anywhere on the planet. The Internet community comprises various groups and individuals including the following:

- Individual users: people from both business-to-business, consumer-to-business and just pure information seekers that may be directed or experiential in nature.
- Internet Service Providers (ISP): internet organizations that supply connections to the Internet. Many ISPs are large organizations, such as BT, AOL and AT&T, while many smaller organizations provide a similar service such as Magic Moments. More recently the Internet has seen the arrival of free ISPs including companies such as Freeserve (http://www.freeserve.co.uk) and Supanet (http://www.supanet.net). ISPs seem to be split between business providers who charge for a premium service, while organizations such as Supanet offering a free connection are more focused on the consumer market, who are driven by fast and cheap services. Freeserve support an important market that is currently still using the Internet for 'click and play' experience.
- Content providers: individuals and various types of organizations that produce, publish or distribute information available on the Internet. Content providers include newspapers, research organizations, government bodies, museums, plus, many more. Many individual users of the Internet are also content providers through both formal and informal channels, publishing their ideas, research reports, and promotional material. As the technology gets more interactive,

through the developments of advanced multimedia tools, content provision gets faster and more dynamic in nature. Future content providers may be through people and also through intelligent software agents.

- Software and hardware companies: commercial companies that produce and distribute a wide range of Internet related products, including servers, web-based applications tools and browsers.
- Other organizations: http://www.w3.org provides a driving force across the Internet through the development and evaluation of new Internet-based tools. Many organizations exist, including voluntary groups and governments agencies, that are not directly commercial by nature but are still integral to the Internet. Governments influence the Internet by placing legalities on information content and access.

Internet addresses

On the Internet it is the case that every user requires a unique address, so that the information can be routed to the correct destination, similar to a home address so that the postal service can deliver mail to the correct residence. An Internet address is made up of two parts separated by the familiar @ sign. The part before the @ is usually a persons user name or nick name while the part after the @ represents the domain name of the computer/server.

User-name@domain-name

An example of a typical Internet address is

Joey@yahoo.com

The user name is required to validate a user account on a specific computer. The user name can be, in principle, any name but may be determined by an individual organization's conventions such as a persons initial followed by second name.

A domain name identifies a specific computer, which will be connected to a specific server on the Internet. Users are clearly assigned to a particular computer with a unique address. The address will be a sub address of the server the user connects into. The unique Internet address are abbreviated to IP address. An IP address is a string of four sets of numbers, for example 194.58.83.211. Therefore every domain name, such as ibm.com, is represented by a string of numbers. The Domain Name System (DNS) on the Internet translates the familiar domain names into an IP address automatically. Domain names are divided into several level domains. In the UK for example many organizations use the suffix.co.uk which represents an organization in the UK. The suffixes used at the end of the domain names are now becoming more varied and from a users point of view provide an easier indication of the type of organization and generally the country of origin. The main extensions or suffixes are as follows:

edu   universities and colleges in America
com   associated with international companies
org   organizations operating non-profit making websites
net   typically companies trading online
ac.uk   universities and colleges in UK
co.uk   private limited company in the UK (similar suffixes are available for
        most other countries)

Applications tools to access and communicate on the Internet

The Internet comprises many information services to share and find information. The Internet for many is being directly associated with the World Wide Web, but it is important to clarify other services along with the Web that are also widely used. Some are more obvious than others.

World Wide Web (WWW)

The Web is a collection of hypermedia documents created by organizations and individuals around the world. Various browsers such as Netscape (http://www.netscape.com), Explorer (http://www.microsoft.com), and more specialist emerging browsers including NeoPlanet (http://www.neoplanet.com) can access the Web. Web pages are developing from hypertext documents to what is now described more frequently as hypermedia documents. Hypermedia pages include far more than just text with graphics, audio and video included. Hypermedia documents have now become the norm and the level and complexity of interaction will increase. Hypermedia operates through the ability to click on objects that links one document to another. Through the development of HTML and the more recent emergence of XML, the types of links and the resulting interaction is becoming more complex. This is described in more detail in the section on communications infrastructure for web-based marketing

Electronic mail (e-mail)

E-mail has become the norm as an essential means for organizations' inter and intra communications. Mail messages, data files and software programs can be sent to other Internet users. In addition to personal communications, e-mail is also being used extensively for direct marketing initiatives. Direct marketing via e-mail for many reflects a similar type of direct mail received through the post. 'Span mail' (undirected mailings) is still very common but through the use of database driven web pages mailings are now generally more focused and this is an important tool in the move towards one-to-one marketing.

Newsgroups (Usenet)

The Internet provides a means of being able to participate in thousands of electronic discussion groups on most conceivable topics you can imagine. Newsgroups are generally text-based discussion groups that are primarily driven by e-mail, with archives that are frequently viewable via the Web. In addition newsgroups can be entered via the Web, for example through Hotbot.com which allows you enter and find newsgroups through its website. Newsgroups are a form of asynchronous digital communication.

Remote login

Remote login facilities, such as Telnet, are becoming less common but still an important tool for many users. Telnet, one of the more common software tools that enables remote login, can connect you to a computer at a geographically remote location and then enable the use of resources, such as library catalogues and data-bases

File Transfer Protocol (FTP)

FTP is an international standard for transferring files across the Internet (Figure 3.4). FTP is generally for more specialist users who require a 'no frills' tool for a fast

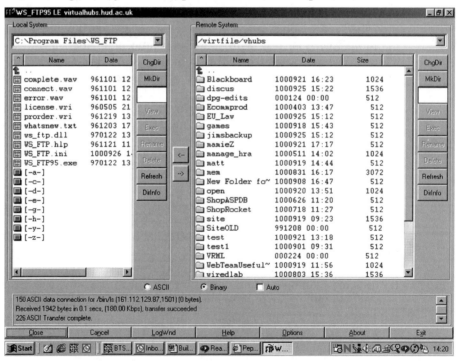

Figure 3.4   File transfer protocol (FTP)

and functionally orientated way of transferring files from and to individual servers. FTP allows individuals to access servers around the world. FTP is typically used by Internet developers with a need to transfer objects from one server to another, for example this may include: documents, software applications, graphics, audio and video.

Internet Relay Chat (IRC) and related services

Internet relay chat is often abbreviated to IRC or just chat. IRC is very popular especially among young Internet users. A very similar product to web-based IRC is instant messaging. The main difference is that to use an IRC you need to go to a special server, typically called an IRC server, while with instant messaging you need to contact the person direct using freely available software applications such as the AOL messenger. The main similarity is that they are both synchronous forms of communication.

Communications infrastructure for web-based marketing

Navigating through the marketing avenues on the Web

The World Wide Web (WWW) has become a central tool or service on the Internet and for many is seen as the commercial face of the Internet. E-commerce initiatives are currently web-driven and it facilitates online ordering. In addition, to online ordering the Web is still primarily used as a means of searching and retrieving information on an unimaginable array of subject areas (see Figure 3.5). A web document, referred to as a web page, incorporates various objects such as text, images, and other multimedia features including audio and videos clips. Web

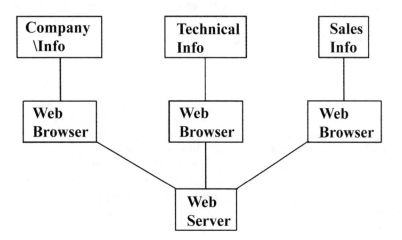

Figure 3.5   Navigating the web

pages are connected using what is called hypermedia links. These links can be created from any object on a page and as a consequence have the potential to create a web type structure. Typically a user will navigate the Web by initially entering a specific web page and then selecting links for example via text and/or images that will then jump to other related pages. Through more recent developments in web-based standards and development tools, such as XML, it is now also possible to embed links along a time line of a video sequence. For the user this allows far greater interactivity in terms of the information accessed and the level of potential feedback.

It is useful to understand how a web page is located on the Internet, as it provides a route to understanding the complexity and structure of the World Wide Web in general. Each web page has a specific address called a *Uniform Resource Locator* (URL). The URL includes the protocol for transferring data across the Internet, the domain name of the particular server containing the web page, and the path through the hierarchical structure of directories to the resource on the host. A typical URL is http://www.wired-lab.com/. This URL is for Wired Lab, a website dedicated for marketing professionals with a specific interest or desire for knowledge in the area of one-to-one Internet marketing, and to keep abreast of the latest, innovative thinking. The website comprises many web pages that include articles, reviews and online courses. The *http://* represents hypertext transfer protocol, which is the specific protocol for all web pages. www.wired-lab.com is the unique domain name related to a server connected to the Internet.

A website address may also contain numerous folders or database locations that contain further web pages or objects that are included on a web page. The most significant development on the Internet is the move away from what is termed 'flat file structure' (folders) towards a database orientation that stores objects that are called onto a web page. Database driven web pages are designed in a template format that pulls necessary information including text, images and various other multimedia objects. Such an approach has been made possible by the technology but has been primarily driven by the market in terms of speed of growth and need for greater customization.

Frequently, it is possible to guess the URL of a company, university or other type of organization. Typically an organizations will include their name or abbreviation within the standard domain name format of www.company_name.com. For example IBM's URL is www.ibm.com. UK universities are usually in the ac.uk domain, while American universities are typically in the .edu domain. A typical example of a University in the UK is www.salford.ac.uk and a comparative university in America is www.pitt.edu. It is also important to remember that in addition to web pages, most of the other resources on the Internet, including gophers, FTP, and Telnet, have URLs and are available through the Web. Specific URLs are similar to telephone numbers in that they allow you to go direct to a specific web page without going through search engines and generally allowing you to by-pass other unnecessary 'front-end' web pages.

Using a browser as a window into cyberspace

The Web has a structure designed based on the client/server model. The principles of the client/server model are based on the idea that you as the client can connect seamlessly across a computer network to various servers. On the Web you use a client program, which is called a browser that allows you to access and navigate web pages stored on web servers. Browsers are generally associated with either Netscape Communicator or Microsoft Explorer. A browser such as Netscape Communicator provides the means of requesting the desired document from a specific web server and then presents the page in the familiar hypertext format (Figure 3.6).

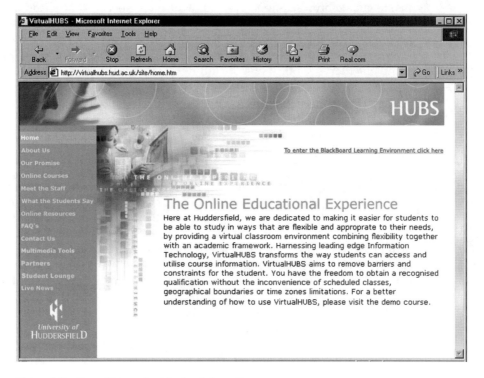

Figure 3.6   Searching and retrieving information

Even though most users associate the look and style of browsers with Netscape and Explorer there are also many more browsers available that are specifically designed for specialist applications. Browsers can be either text-based or graphical in design. Text-based browsers are clearly only designed for showing text and as a consequence particularly useful for users who require fast information rich documentation. The typical uses of a text-based browser may be on a UNIX platform designed for Linux. Graphical browsers including Netscape and Explorer can show graphics, sound, and other multimedia features such as video streaming. Such browsers have been designed primarily to operate on both Wintel and Apple computers.

New software technologies are being developed that are creating both interesting and unusual graphical presentations with quite varying degrees of success, for example, NeoPlanet (www.neoplanet.com) which is owned by Yahoo. Neoplanet attempts to offer more dynamic pages by providing extra information, through hypertext links to the Yahoo search engine. Neoplanet is able to take advantage of the Yahoo directory of web pages as a means of offering more depth of under-standing through fast and easy information access created by web agents. New software technologies are also enriching existing browsers that we have all become familiar with. You can now download and install software packages, called plug-ins, to enable browsers to support new or more specialist applications. Over time plug-ins frequently become an integral part of a browser and as a consequence are packaged with the core product. For example, if you install the current version of Netscape Communicator it also offers an option to install various plug-ins and complementary applications including Realplayer G2. Many web developers design websites that require plug-ins for web pages to be viewable in the intended format. Flash plug-in from Macromedia has been downloaded by 80% of web users browsing the Web through Netscape and Explorer.

Directories and search engines

The investigation of information indexing on the Internet needs to consider: infor-mation discovery, database technology and ranking techniques. You may be think-ing why do you need a search engine on the Web or more likely which search facility is the most appropriate for my needs. To put it simply, you need a search facility for the same reason that you need a library catalogue, but we need to consider the major search engines in more detail to identify similarities and unique features that in principle may help you in searching for valuable information. In addition, search facilities are viewed by many as fundamental drivers of the Inter-net and owners of websites need to have some understanding of the process of indexing web pages and as a consequence attempt to improve the ranking of an individual website. For example, if an organization manufactures farming equip-ment and an existing or potential customer undertakes a search on the Internet for 'tractors'; how can your organization ensure a high ranking? Clearly many complex issues need to be considered in providing a basic understanding of the fundamen-tals.

Before considering the specific services currently available on the Internet it is important to explain the differences between search engines and directories. They are often confused, but one can distinguish them by the following:

- Search engines, also called 'spiders' or 'crawlers', constantly visit web pages on the Internet as a means of creating catalogues of web pages. Search engines operate automatically and as a consequence continually update their index of web pages. The continued registration of new web pages and virtual real-time updates of existing pages ensures search engines will constantly find information not listed in directories.

■ Different to search engines, directories are created by humans and are reliant on individuals submitting website information. At the time of registration they are assigned to an appropriate category or categories. Directories are currently viewed as maintaining a valuable role on the Internet. Over time the role of directories is expected to diminish through developments in search engine technology. Currently directories frequently add more meaning to the indexing process through human involvement but are lacking in terms of being able to respond to market changes. Yahoo! is an example of a directory.

■ To further confuse matters hybrid search engines are also available. These information-based indexing facilities are primarily driven by a search engine, as the default, but also include an associated directory. Sites included in the directory have been reviewed or rated, but are not included in a basic query yet they need to be specifically requested.

The following is intended to provide an insight into the major search engines at present and useful tips in understanding their uses.

Major search engines, directories and hybrids

AltaVista

Consistently one of the largest search engines on the Internet. It provides an extensive indexing of pages with a comprehensive coverage of power search tools. AltaVista has also adopted a partnership approach with other search engines offering complimentary tools, including Ask Jeeves and LookSmart. http://www.altavista.com/

Excite

Excite is one of the most popular search tools on the Internet offering a medium sized index. In addition, Excite also integrates non-web material including company information and sports results. This was highlighted in 1996. Excite also consumed two major competitors, Magellan and Webcrawler. These both continue to operate separate services. http://www.excite.com/

Hotbot

Another search engine offering a large index of web pages and many power searching facilities. An Inktomi search engine is the power behind Hotbot. It has a partnership with LookSmart for its directory listings. Hotbot is owned by Lycos but continues to run as a separate search facility. http://www.hotbot.com/

Infoseek

Infoseek (go.com) offers one of the most popular search facilities on the Web.

Infoseek is viewed as consistently providing quality searching, but it may be limited for many broad searches due to its small to medium sized index. It also has an impressive human compiled directory of websites. Infoseek has now merged with go.com. http://www.infoseek.com/

Lycos

A relatively small index that is viewed as being less up to date than its many major competitors. Even with such limitations it remains one of the most popular search engines. An impressive feature of the search engine is the directory of search engines called Lycos Community Guides. It is interesting to note that the name Lycos comes from the Latin for 'wolf spider'! http://www.lycos.com/

Yahoo

Currently viewed as the most popular search service and has an impressive reputation for finding information required by individuals. Offering the largest human compiled guide to the Web primarily drives the reason for success. Yahoo also supplements its results through Inktomi. http://www.yahoo.com/

Alternative search engines, directories and hybrids

Ask Jeeves

This offers a human-based search service that aims to direct you to the exact page that answers your information need. If it is unable to meet your information needs it will provide matching web pages from various search engines. Results from Ask Jeeves also appear with AltaVista. http://www.askjeeves.com/

Go (Infoseek)

This was produced in collaboration between Infoseek and Disney. It offers typical portal site features including personalized and free e-mail, plus the search capabilities of Infoseek. Go was launched in December 1998 and has now merged with Infoseek. It will be interesting to monitor developments. http://beta.go.com/

Google

This search engine offers a relatively unique method of searching compared to most, placing an emphasis on link popularity as a primary method of ranking websites. This is viewed as being particularly useful in finding good sites in response to general searches such as 'finance' or 'music'. http://www.google.com/

Inktomi

Originally created in UC Berkley, before the creators went on to form their own company with the same name, but a new improved Inktomi index. The search index originally powered HotBot and then developed further collaborative arrangements with many other search index providers. The Inktomi index is only available through partners rather than direct. Inktomi offers a customized service for partners enabling them to offer a unique identity. http://www.inktomi.com/

Northern Light

A favourite for research purposes through its ability to provide clustered documents by topic. In addition it has a large indexing facility. The search engine also offers a special collection obtained from various databases, magazines and online news services. The special collection is a fee-paying service. http://www.northern-light.com or http://www.nlsearch.com/

Cyberspace information for interactive marketing

In the development of marketing applications for the Internet we need to source and evaluate information in terms of credibility and the quality of the information source. Some basic guidelines can be applied to the finding, evaluating and referencing of relevant market and product information from the complex maze of the Web.

Source and develop a marketing solution

Finding information on the Web may be necessary for various reasons, but in a marketing context primarily for enabling solutions which may be for problems or in the creation of innovative solutions from both a market and product perspective. Creativity and innovation is clearly of prime importance in the development of interactive marketing solutions. The Web is just offering one of many other sources for finding and developing information in a particular context. The primary difference with web-based information, is that it offers far more dynamic sources through the ability to add and update information virtually real time. For a marketing professional this creates an important need to establish an important list of bookmarks/favourites in your browsers plus subscribing to important discussion lists. These use the available directories and search engines to locate websites of importance.

Several helpful websites for online marketing information and e-commerce ideas are given in Table 3.1.

Also, remember to use the guides provided for particular topics within each directory or search engine. More detailed descriptions of search engines and directories are provided in the section on communications infrastructure for web-based marketing. Another important source of information on the Internet is e-mail through discussion groups, and newsgroups to exchange information with experts and potential customers. Many directories and market research agency sites are also a good source of information (Table 3.2).

Table 3.1 Helpful websites for online marketing information

Electronic Commerce	http://www.brint.com/Elecomm.htm
IBM e-Business	http://www.ibm.com/e-business
Scottish Export Virtual Community (developed by Jim Hamill)	http://www.sevc.com
e-Lab (developed by Donna Hoffman and Tom Novak)	http://ecommerce.vanderbilt.edu
Wired Lab (coordinated by Glenn Hardaker)	http://www.creation.hud.ac.uk
Marketing online (produced by Dave Chaffey)	http://www.marketing-online.co.uk
Fortune Magazine	http://www.forbes.com
Mckinsey Quarterly (full text articles available)	http://www.mckinseyquarterly.com

Table 3.2 Market research agency websites

Electronic Yellow Pages	http://www.eyp.co.uk
Thomson	http://www.thomson-directories.co.uk
Freepages	http://www.scoot.co.uk
Mintel	http://www.mintel.com
MORI	http://www.mori.co.uk
AC Nielsen	http://www.nielsen.com
Verdict	http://www.verdict.co.uk
Euromonitor	http://www.euromonitor.com
Economist Intelligence Unit	http://www.eiu.com

Evaluating information from the Web

The Internet provides a platform to access diverse information sources that are of varying quality and relevance to the end user. An important starting point for you in sourcing information on the Web, is to consider basic information systems principles of time, relevance and form. This allows you to consider your rationale for using the Web, and other Internet sources plus an evaluation of the value of the information.

As we all know information needs to be current, and global digital networks, such as the Internet, are pushing information faster and faster to meet the needs of decision makers around the world. The speed of information creates further complexities in terms of quality and its relevance to the individual or organization. You can judge the credibility of sources through various factors including the purpose of the information, objectivity of source, and the authority and expertise of individuals involved in the creation of a website. All organizations put some bias on the information published, but it is being aware of the level of bias that is important in ascertaining the overall reliability. As a starting point it is important to consider the three-letter extension that appear at the end of the URL. For example, government (.gov) agencies usually have credible websites. A major purpose of some government agencies is to provide credible information to the public. In comparison, a primary goal of many commercial websites is promote and sell products and as a consequence these can influence the information provided. You need to evaluate the information published on commercial websites accordingly. The credibility of information on educational sites is variable with many academics providing leading edge information and others providing unstructured support material. Many of the issues identified as important in evaluating published information on the Web become of greater importance due to the speed of change and growth. Fee-paying websites, primarily operating in business-to-business markets are easing this process by undertaking the evaluation process and therefore providing quality assurance. What you are specifically trying to do is to determine the quality of information published on a website and it is important to consider the following points:

- Are the sources of factual information clearly identified?
- Are the links to factual information relevant and up-to-date?
- Does the information presented substantiate other similar information sources?
- How frequently is the information on the website updated?
- What is the relative value of the information compared to other sources?

The technology is clearly an enabler in providing relevant information. Websites are evolving towards database driven applications and as a consequence they provide a means of customizing information for individual needs that can be updated virtually in real time. The issue of the relevance of information being managed effectively is primarily one in business-to-business markets. Many of the most valuable sources of information via the Internet are becoming secure sites that require payment or subscription and as a consequence provide a higher level of service for 'goal directed browsing'. The relevance issue is of less importance for many users of the Internet, especially in the consumer markets, where browsing can be far more experiential in nature.

The 'form' information that is being provided to you is currently driven by our accepted web browser. Approximately 75–80% of users are currently using Explorer from Microsoft and while the latter 20% mainly use Netscape. This is expected to change with the acceptance of other browser applications arriving in the market. The browser application will have a more important role as the form it is used in becomes more flexible. For example, the beta release version of Netscape 6 provides an insight into the browser of the future that is more customizable to individual needs. The ability to customize a browser allows the form information to be directly affected by yourself and as a consequence to directly interact in the information systems process.

Referencing electronic information sources

There are two important reasons for referencing information sources on the Web – first, intellectual honesty and secondly to give the reader a means of checking the relevance and accuracy of the information sources used in the published material.

Standards for referencing Internet-based information are well established through associations such as the Modern Language Association (MLA) and American Psychology Association.

A typical citation style for Internet information resources is as follows:

Author's last name. Authors initials. Title of the document in quotes. Title of the complete work (if applicable). Date of publication or revision. Protocol and address (date of access)

You can find more detailed information on the preparation of a webliography through various sites including:

http://www.cas.usf.edu/english/walker/mla.html
http://www.cas.usf.edu/english/walker/apa.html

Building your market intelligence tools

All information needs to be sorted in some way and this becomes an even more complex task due to the speed of growth in information availability through the Web. Before the commercial acceptance of the Web data, warehousing was already offering this possibility for larger businesses. Terms such as data warehousing, data mining, or information warehousing are frequently used terms for managing the storage and data analysis process more effectively. This was and still is a specialist area that is often outsourced. The emergence of the Web and more global networks in general has seen data warehousing merge into the more fashionable Customer Relationship Management (CRM) and business intelligence arena. This has become the prime means of collecting customer data, which is then in a form that is easily managed with the right computing tools. The volume of data available on customer behaviour via the Web is formidable. 'Click stream' analysis reveals exactly where the customer came from, at what time, duration, actual activities, when they departed and also where they surfed onto. Senior analyst with Bloor Research, Dale Vine says "data is cleaner on the Web". The new web-based systems allow more seamless integration with 'backend' systems and also improved validation compared to older legacy systems. The so-called cleaner data also brings with it its own problems, in particular when considering the customer catchment area is potentially the population of the world. This means that the level of complexity in undertaking the analysis and also the need for scalability in the Web warehouse needs to be taken into account.

What can you do with all this data?

The information derived from data analysis can be fed back into the decision making and planning process which is also shifting towards a real time feedback loop. The specific analysis includes the following:

- Use the customer behaviour analysis to feed directly back into the web design process. An iterative process between the marketplace and the web-based e-business operations can allow a very dynamic operation.

■ Use the customer behaviour analysis to drive e-commerce strategy and tactics. For example, how successful was that promotion? How many banner hits did we get? What is our customer profile of web visitors? How is this profile changing? If the customer profile is changing what do we sell them?

■ Build an integrated approach to market intelligence. Combine web data with other data from more traditional sales channels. A bottom up approach to integration of customer data allows an understanding of total operations in both the marketplace and marketspace.

CRM through business intelligence?

The basic product and functionality includes: data extraction tools to get the data from database sources, either relational or more specialized Online Analytical Processing (OLAP) or Multidimensional (MDDB) software that are customized databases allowing specialist analysis and reporting services. The more specialist tools are increasingly being offered pre-packed for various vertical sectors, such as sales or financial, which dramatically cuts down on the amount of time organizations need to spend on the business intelligence process. Competition through more products becoming available has seen both costs and time to production fall dramatically. For example the entry of Microsoft into the market of data warehousing has pushed this trend even further. Many of the established data warehousing organizations are re-aligning there focus towards CRM, e.g. Hyperion and Cognos. Scalability issues need to be considered and an organization needs to decide if it is viable to undertake in-house or is it more sensible to outsource to organizations such as WhiteCross. An organization needs both scalable hardware and networking capability and as a consequence outsourcing is a relatively seamless and efficient option, especially for small to medium businesses. Business intelligence organizations targeting the Web as a new data source to capture and analyze include:

■ NCR Teradata: www.ncr.com
■ Informatica: www.informatica.com
■ Informix: www.informix.com
■ Oracle: www.oracle.com
■ Whitecross: www.whitecross.com

Benefits of business intelligence on the Web

Data warehousing has become essential for e-commerce driven sites in order to understand both marketing and product information, but most importantly on the Web in a very fast and responsive form. The return on your investment is difficult to quantify in traditional ways but as a competitive tool is integral to success. Also expect to spend at least a quarter of your web-building costs on setting up the data warehouse. The key benefits from utilizing business intelligence applications for the Web are as follows:

- Data warehousing your e-commerce business helps dramatically in understanding your performance through customer behaviour.
- Personalizations of websites are essential to success in retaining customers who are only one click away from competition. Data warehousing is an enabler of website personalization for your customers.
- Business intelligence that enables you to capture, analyze and respond to customers behaviour virtually real time is a key competitive differentiator in the ever changing e-business world.
- Website data is similar to other forms of corporate data but it is cleaner, more coherent and generally comprehensive.
- Business intelligence is an application that can easily be outsourced but seamlessly integrated into a businesses internal computing systems.

Conclusion

The Internet is clearly established in both business-to-business (B2B) and business-to-consumer (B2C) markets. The Internet infrastructure is now driving both commercial trade, especially in B2B markets at present, and also supporting more experiential searching activities in consumer markets. Consumer confidence in both Internet technology, in particular security, is rising at an unprecedented rate and as a consequence demand for online buying and information searching is also growing rapidly. This chapter is intended to support such changing market conditions. Firstly the chapter outlines the Internet infrastructure with a particular focus on issues relevant to marketing on the Internet and secondly builds on this platform of knowledge by providing a road map to online information resources. Finally the chapter considers how to utilize online information resources through building your own market intelligence tools.

Checklist

1. Interactive marketing information involves participants involved with creation, individuals buying and information providers.
2. Consideration needs to be given to the speed of information, its relevance and if the form it is provided in is appropriate for its intended purpose.
3. The accepted Internet protocol for transmission is TCP/IP.
4. The Internet is built on various elements including: individual users, ISPs, content providers, software and hardware companies and various other bodies, for example, standards organizations.
5. Applications tools for the Internet can be categorized into: World Wide Web, e-mail, Newsgroups, remote login, FTP and Internet relay chat.

6. Web browsers provide the window to the majority of marketing information sources.
7. Information indexing on the Internet is primarily through either search engines or directories and frequently a combination of both methods.
8. Due to the diversity and volume of information sources on the Internet it is important to establish quality sources for the types of market and product information required. This can be judged through considering: the purpose of the information, objectivity of the source, the authority and expertise of the authors and organization.
9. The emergence of the Web has seen data warehousing merge into what is being termed CRM and business intelligence. Information for building market intelligence and CRM are derived from both internal and external sources.

References

Davis, S. and Davidson, B. (1991), *2020 Vision*, Simon and Schuster. New York.

Kannan, P.K., Chang, A. and Whinston, A.B. (2000), *Handbook of Electronic Commerce*. Springer, New York.

Lopes, A.B. and Galleta, D. (2000), *Handbook of Electronic Commerce*. Springer, New York.

McCullough, D. (1998), *Web-based Market Research Ushers in New Age*, *Marketing News*, Sept. 14, pp. 24–38.

Nee, E. (1996), Michael Bloomberg. *Upside*, 8 (5), pp. 36–53.

Wylie, K. (1997), NFO exec sees most research going to Internet, *Advertising Age*, 68 (20), p. 50.

Further reading

Campbell, D. and Campbell, M. (1995), *The Students Guide to Doing Research on the Internet*, Addison Wesley, Reading, MA.

Lehnert, W. (1999), *Light on the Internet*, Addison Wesley Longman, Reading, MA.

Strauss, J. and Frost, R. (1999), *Marketing on the Internet. Principles of Online Marketing*. Prentice Hall, New Saddle River, NJ.

PART 2

Interactive marketing and the marketing process

CHAPTER 4

Marketing communications on the Internet

Key topics

- Process of online marketing communications
- E-business grid for integrated marketing communication
- Interactive marketing communication tools
- Marketing communication: the future

After studying this chapter you will be able to:

- Identify the changing trends and emerging directions
- Understand the different marketing applications of digital communications
- Describe new forms of interactivity emerging through web-based hypermedia tools
- Critically evaluate the implications of new media marketing initiatives.

Process of online marketing communications

Marketing communications defined

Modern marketing demands more than just developing a good product, strongly promoted with desirable pricing, and which is made available to target customers (Kotler et al., 1999). Organizations of all types, in both consumer and industrial markets, need to be able to communicate with customers in a timely and effective way. These new technological modes of communication are becoming more complex and driven at an unprecedented speed.

The basis of information technology relates to the collection, processing and transmission of information and as a consequence has a major impact on the communication process. This chapter primarily considers the opportunities to companies in using the Web for communicating to the market, which includes both the physical marketplace and virtual marketspace (Rayport and Sviokla, 1994).

A traditional approach towards an integrated marketing communications mix consists of a specific blend of advertising, personal selling, sales promotions and public relations tools. The balance and emphasis placed on the marketing communication mix will clearly be affected by the types of industry but just as importantly the specific organizational characteristics. In recent years, direct communication initiatives have gained greater importance and this reflects the need to meet individual customer aspirations and needs. For many, technological development is an enabler of radical change both in the mode and speed of communication. It is important not to take too narrow a focus and accept the ever-changing nature of marketing communication. The information collected and processed, by a consumer provides a total image of a product, which goes far beyond the advertising message. The product offering synthesizes everything the consumer needs to know about the product including the type of usage and the type of person who buys it. Accepting organizations as open social systems (Katz and Kahn, 1978) we can view the elements of a system as both interactive and interdependent (Goldhaber, 1986). By considering the decisions associated with the development and delivery of a marketing communications strategy it is possible to see the complexity and sensi-

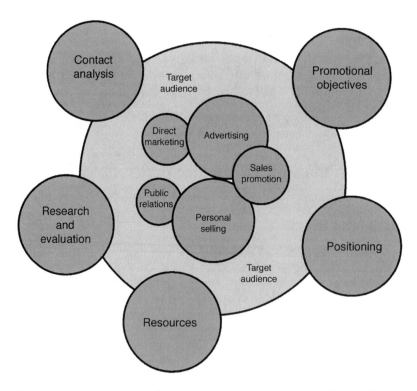

Figure 4.1   System of marketing communications (adapted from Fill, 1999).

tivity of the decision components (Figure 4.1). The traditional marketing communications mix identified below provides a basis for this chapter in further exploring issues related to the e-Business Grid (see section on e-business grid for integrated marketing communication) and interactive marketing communications tools (see section on interactive marketing communication tools). The strategically orientated e-business grid puts into context issues such as: context analysis, research and evaluation, resources, positioning, promotional objectives. The operational interactive marketing communications tools are clear extensions of the traditional marketing communications mix such as: direct marketing, advertising, public relations, personal selling and sales promotions.

The changing nature of marketing communication

The Internet offers a unique medium for communication whether it be through e-mail, newsgroups and the latest hypermedia based approach that incorporates future 3D virtual space. Figure 4.2 shows the website of www.spookyandthebandit.com, which provides diverse insight into current 3D developments using Macromedia Flash animation software.

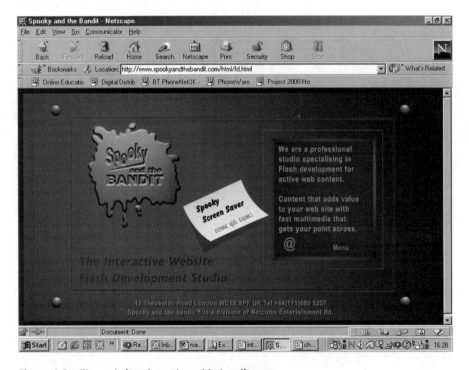

Figure 4.2   The website of spookyandthebandit.com

More significantly has been the shift away from traditional media type communications (Figure 4.3). This is typified by the shift from the one-to-one or frequently

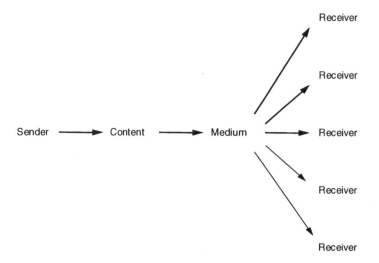

Figure 4.3   Traditional media communication (Adapted from Hoffman and Novak, 1996)

one to many approach, toward a more interactive two-way type of communication model (Figure 4.4), which is a many-to-many approach driven by the hypermedia of the World Wide Web.

The focus in Figure 4.4 is much more a two-way process that is faster and more dynamic in nature. Communication on the Internet between customer and supplier surpasses previous one-way communication, by invoices, purchase orders, online database queries, and faxes. The Internet allows one to secure trading for B2B markets via Extranets, allowing two-way access to information on delivery sche-

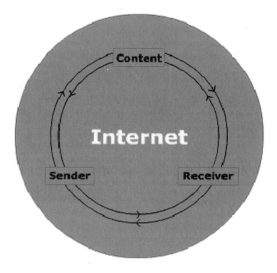

Figure 4.4   Interactive two-way communication on the Internet

dules, enterprise resource planning data and just the ability to feed into the production and development process. In B2C markets the interactive nature of the Web allows communications to be targeted at individual needs but to a mass market with virtually real time response.

The development of online communication facilitates a move towards more information rich specialist groupings (similar to user groups) or what is frequently being called communities (Selfridge, 1997). Enablers of communication development are defined as: computer infrastructure and bandwidth, international information technology standards, and shared working environments for online communities (Hardaker, 1998). Mirabilis (www.mirabilis.com) is an example of a portal driving forward global real-time communication across the Internet (Figure 4.5). Even though leisure and informal chats primarily drive usage, the website provides an invaluable insight into the potential of cost effective real-time communication on a global scale.

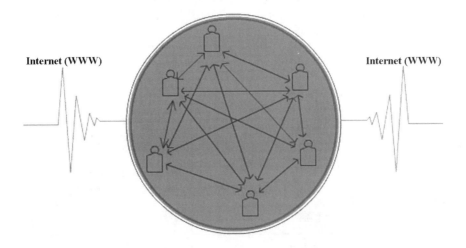

Figure 4.5   Synchronous communications process used by Mirabilis

Mirabilis.com has been a leader in facilitating online chat around the globe along with similar services. The site offers free facilities that are easy to use for both collaborating in established Internet Relay Chat (IRC) forums or setting up a new discussion group. The importance of IRCs can be seen through the level of IRC usage by AOL subscribers. AOL quote that between 30 and 40% of text-based messages in the US are via chat rooms. A natural progression for synchronous communications on the Internet is for IRCs to gradually incorporate more multimedia tools, such as 'whiteboard' tools for brainstorming activities. Over time both audio and video conferencing applications will also become the norm for interactive two-way communications processes. Such technologies (audio and video conferencing) are discussed in more detail in the final section of this chapter (see section on technological developments for marketing communication).

E-business grid for integrated marketing communication

Marketing communication through the e-business grid

It can be seen from Figure 4.6 that organizational integration encompasses a wide range of issues, as a mechanism for enabling organizations to be both responsive and adaptable through improved communication. Integration across the supply chain in B2B and B2C is identified as of prime importance in enabling creativity and innovation in the deployment of a web presence. The e-business grid is intended to provide a framework for considering businesses' web presence and development but also as a useful vehicle in identifying the relevance of the marketing communications tools described in the section on interactive marketing communication tools.

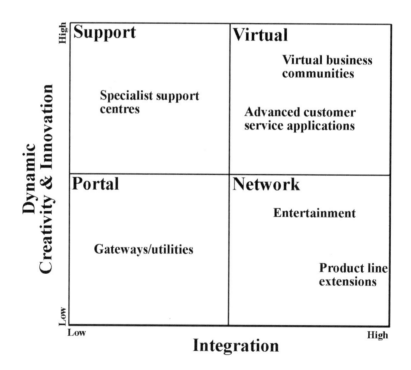

Figure 4.6   The e-business grid

CDNOW: REVOLUTIONIZING THE CHANNELS OF ENTERTAINMENT STREAMING

CDNOW is an all-encompassing online music destination offering consumers an unprecedented degree of access to music and information. The vision of CDNOW is to make every visit to the site, whether for buying or browsing, a valuable and rewarding experience.

Visitors to the site have access to over 500 000 music related products and 650 000 sound samples as well as regularly updated news, features and exclusive interviews. CDNOW is one of the most well-known and visited sites on the Internet with an average daily audience of over 800 000.

CDNOW was one of the first sites of its kind to drive digital distribution and to offer the sale of music downloads and CDs, and in addition provide free downloads – usually of new or 'up-and-coming artists'. The market of free and saleable digital downloads has seen many new entrants including MP3, however CDNOW's broad base of customers, relationships with record labels and their web technology will ensure CDNOW retain a strong market presence.

CDNOW has utilized the Internet for more than downloads and CD sales, they have also exploited new technology in streaming music live on the Internet by launching CDNOW Radio. CDNOW Radio launched eight unique programme channels focussing on different lifestyles; demographic and psychographic market segments in their audience, with each channel serving the diverse needs of the extensive monthly audience.

CDNOW Radio keeps listeners tuned into CDNOW for a longer period of time, they listen to songs, read about the artist, browse the catalogues and more.
H. Blumenthal, Senior Vice President of Media&Sales at CDNOW

CDNOW also incorporate an interactive division, CDNOW Media, which develops interactive content including allstar™ News, artist interviews and reviews and CDNOW webcasting and also incorporates a video store, CDNOW Video that includes an extensive collection of videos and DVDs and laser discs, resulting in CDNOW becoming a complete music destination on the Internet.

To support the purchasing of music through the Internet, CDNOW launched 'Cosmic Credit' the Internets largest music affiliate program and one of CDNOW's most successful customer building programs. Through the ePod™ showcase from ePod Corp, CDNOW gives affiliates a combination of advertising and merchandise revenue. CDNOW's Cosmic Credit was offered to over 250 000 affiliates giving them the opportunity to add content-rich ePod showcases to their sites. Each ePod showcase is filled with music news and reviews and offers a quick and easy way to purchase CDNOW CDs. Affiliates will add value to their sites by adding a HTML tag to their site, providing them and advertisers with the opportunity to reach a targeted and captive audience.

CDNOW Cosmic Credit creates a virtual community of music fans around the globe and bolsters the strong community of entertainment and music lovers through CDNOW's loyal customers.
H. Blumenthal, Senior Vice President of Media&Sales at CDNOW

CDNOW's affiliate program enables websites to generate revenue by linking to

CDNOW. Affiliates receive between 7 and 15% commission when visitors to their sites click on the link and make a purchase.

They continue to explore the use of 'cutting edge' technology and as a consequence lead in the distribution of music through new channels. For example, CDNOW are ensuring their leading position by selecting ViaFone, a leading provider of interactive mobile applications, to host its mobile presence. The partnership with ViaFone will allow CDNOW customers to access the site and purchase music from practically anywhere at anytime. This wireless initiative will be launched on two platforms WAP and Palm enabling customers to purchase music using an array of wireless devises including mobile phones and PDAs.

CDNOW's Internet festivals

CDNOW is an interactive initiative connecting fans to numerous American Award ceremonies including GRAMMY awards and American Music Awards providing them unique access to news, reviews and interviews. In developing this further CDNOW are implementing a festival calendar detailing tour dates of bands and are webcasting over 80 concerts including No Doubt, Britney Spears and The Who, providing visitors with coverage, interviews and photos.

CDNOW demonstrate how combining both technology and creativity can sustain a market leading company that is able to enhance the visitor experience and develop new streaming techniques to transform the distribution of today's entertainment.

The portal quadrant (Figure 4.6) represents what are becoming essential gateways and fundamental utilities for the wider world of cyberspace. Portals such as Netcentre, Lycos, Yahoo, AOL all provide essential routes to the Internet for what are viewed as growing communities. Portals attempt to demystify and smooth the complexed communications channels through the Internet by providing guides and essential sites of importance and relevance. A portal's success will clearly be reliant on being able to provide a customized service to their community and provide for the specific lifestyle, aspirations and needs. They are developing into virtual communities or specialist information sources. Portals are highly successful through the ability to offer fast, customized, up-to-date information across the Internet to the consumer.

Businesses primarily operating in the portal quadrant are viewed as having limited integration across the supply chain and also limitations in innovation and creativity. Clearly this is relative to the other quadrants and specific market conditions. The identified quadrants are particularly useful in identifying the most relevant and useful marketing communications tools for companies developing websites. Companies operating in the portal quadrant currently focus primarily on e-sponsorship, direct marketing and portal advertising described in detail in the section on interactive marketing communication tools.

Support quadrant (Figure 4.6) represents specialist support centres that offer value added information to the consumer, but with a relatively limited integration, which is reflected in a lack of customization of the service or product offering. Specialist support centres include technical support information from organizations, such as

IBM in the computer industry, on products and services. Many consultancy services and academic institutions also fall into the support quadrant, by offering a highly creative and leading edge knowledge, but with a generally limited focus on the end consumer. This results in limited integration with organizations and consumers. Specialist support services are typical of internet-based information sources, which are dynamic in nature, but are often limited in commercial concern and as a consequence meet the needs of the responsive communication channel.

Businesses primarily operating in the support quadrant are viewed as having limited integration across the supply chain but have made innovation and creativity central to business operations on the Web. Specialist support centres can be very structured or more loose in terms of development and support. For example the www.ibm.com website provides a mass of information on leading edge e-business related issues supporting quite a diverse audience. In comparison many of the more 'techi' websites supporting for example Linux or PhP developers are far more specific and functional in orientation. As previously mentioned it is relative to the other quadrants and specific market conditions. Companies operating in the support quadrant currently focus primarily on e-sponsorship, wired publicity, e-journals, e-direct marketing as described in the section on interactive marketing communication tools.

The network quadrant (see Figure 4.6) identifies limited innovation but highly integrated organizations both in terms of technology and also through organizational mechanisms, which typically include business processes along the supply chain and technical skills. Clearly companies operating in the Network quadrant will vary significantly in terms of integration and innovation but the framework provides useful guidelines. Organizations in the networked quadrant include many manufacturing businesses adopting the Internet as an essential communications channel, which is supporting supply chain management activities including the control of the flow of goods. BMW, an exemplar of the Network quadrant utilizes the Internet as an integral tool for developing superior customer relations, through providing an environment inclusive, both to existing and potential customers, through expressing views and providing feedback on product developments. Network organizations appreciate the flexibility and cost effectiveness of the Internet as a fundamental communications channel. Companies operating in this quadrant currently focus primarily on e-sponsorship, e-direct marketing, sales promotions, and web exhibitions as the main mix of marketing communications tools of direct relevance.

The Internet is viewed as replacing scarcity with abundance for both products and services and as a consequence organizations need to develop successful strategies that benefit from an over supply in many markets. Strategies need to be based on seeking out and occupying the most valuable niches in the Network quadrant or an organizations supply chain across the Internet. For many affiliate marketing strategies are an enabler in reaching the more higher value niches on the Web. In considering affiliate marketing in more detail consideration needs to be given to structure programs that have been pioneered by organizations such as CDNOW. In acquiring customers on the Web it is now widely accepted that affiliate marketing initiatives are highly effective means of driving an integrated approach towards marketing communications and typically moving organizations into the network and virtual quadrant. Affiliate marketing programs, generally agreed commission for sales through the supply chain, create an integrated approach from, for example, a music record company website (Geffen records) and a retail outlet such as CDNOW. Affiliate marketing initiatives have been driven through B2B programs in various industries but have clearly been pioneered by the CDNOW program that has created a new marketing paradigm for the Web by linking marketing communications directly to performance. Affiliate marketing is argued by many to be transforming the whole of marketing on the Web but is being driven by marketing communications. Affiliate marketing programs in B2B markets on the Web measure the amount of advertising delivered, and track the amount consumed. For example CDNOW tracks a prospect who clicks on a banner ad on a small independent music website through to the CDNOW website and onto an actual purchase. At this point the company's website from which the customer came from receives an agreed commission from the receiver of the sale (typically between 5 and 15%). Clearly this is not possible with traditional forms of advertising. The new emerging affiliate marketing programs for the Web are allowing direct performance measuring and as a consequence can measure cost per purchase in terms of advertising spend. Such programs have become highly complexed web of organizations operating across the Internet. The partnerships created offer a very dynamic and flexible structure that is responding directly to market conditions.

The emergence of the virtual business organization is for many being driven by the speed of Internet developments, in terms of bandwidth and commercial acceptance. The virtual quadrant (see Figure 4.6) represents many leading organizations that have clearly grasped the Internet as being central to commercial activities. For organizations to operate in what we have termed the virtual quadrant, high levels of creativity and innovation are required along with an integrated perspective. Advanced customer service applications are represented by organizations such as FedEx, who offer the ability to track goods via the Internet through offering the latest information on movement. CitiBank offer Internet-based banking services to increase both the level of flexibility and also integration with their consumers. CitiBank also utilize leading edge Internet based developments such as intelligent agents, and text-based tools such as 'cookies', which enable the monitoring of customers activities. 'Cookies' are now frequently used and offer organizations the opportunity to capture behavioural patterns and as a consequence act as a driver for relationship marketing initiatives. Clearly the emergence of virtual business organizations, which only exist in cyberspace, are creating new organizations and business models. Companies operating in the virtual quadrant typically focus primarily on using portal advertising, e-direct marketing, e-sponsorship and customized selling as the main mix of marketing communications tools in promoting directly virtual business operations around the Internet.

FEDEX: UTILIZING THE INTERNET TO REVOLUTIONIZE THE PARCEL DELIVERY INDUSTRY

FedEx Corporation is one of the largest integrated transportation, information and logistics solutions providers in the US. Recognizing the potential business opportunities and potential for growth, FedEx utilized the Internet for improving efficiency and customer satisfaction with a wealth of applications and Fedex tools accessible over the Web.

The customer can now benefit from the expertise of FedEx from their own desktops through FedEx InterNetShip®. This web-based shipping application streamlines the online process by allowing the home user to organize shipping to over 180 countries globally, prepare FedEx Express shipping labels, arrange for picking up and delivery, cancel shipments, track packages and so on.

The power of the Internet in particular allows users to track the shipment until delivery and receive notification of arrival by e-mail or send shipment notification to the receiver allowing them access to track the shipment. To track the shipment, users are notified of a log number. FedEx have exploited the possibilities of doing business over the Internet by implementing a digital signature for proof of delivery. Signature 'proof of delivery' is used to get a picture of the recipient's signature once the shipment has been delivered, to confirm the parcel reached the intended recipient.

FedEx Marketplace

FedEx Marketplace is FedEx online ordering facility providing direct links to a number of retailers in the 'premium store gallery' and 'main street' stores virtual shopping centres. Premium store gallery consists of retailers such as HPshopping.com, L.L Bean (clothing retailer), Williams-Sonoma (cookware retailer), Proflowers.com (florist), Greatcoffee.com (coffee retailer), Ashford.com (luxury products), Babystripes.com (baby clothing retailer). High street stores specialize in a wide range of goods and services and include store categories such as: apparel and jewellery, books and art, business and office, entertainment and leisure, flowers and gifts, foods and beverages, health and sports, home and car.

Utilizing the Internet's ability for businesses to form affiliations, FedEx is further establishing its position as a leader in e-commerce by providing direct links to websites of some of the best known brands of high quality merchandise. FedEx benefits significantly due to the incremental volume onto their site primarily through affiliates, and through the business developed due to FedEx delivery to customers who enter their websites through the FedEx portal.

Marketing affiliations over the Internet significantly increase the market for FedEx, as they are creating additional business and compliment their service by delivering products purchased over the Internet with affiliate sites. A fundamental advantage of FedEx Marketplace over other online shopping centres is that FedEx can arrange the delivery of the products purchased by their FedEx delivery services. This provides the consumer with a fully integrated service offering.

Interactive marketing communication tools

The Internet offers a new media form where new tools and techniques are required in achieving effective marketing communication initiatives. Web browsers and the hypermedia format of web pages provides a new type of 'window to the world'. The promotional mix is viewed by many as of central importance to marketing communications and includes advertising, personal selling, sales promotion, and publicity. The promotional mix needs to be extended further to form the marketing communications mix and incorporate other important communications elements, that are focused on the product itself, price, and distribution. The basic web page structure has become very powerful for marketing communications and has now become an integral part in the traditional marketing communications mix. Below we focus on marketing communication tools specific to the Web and describe in detail the unique features that have evolved as a consequence. As identified earlier in the e-business grid, e-direct marketing is a tool of central importance and is currently having the greatest impact, which is indicated through being relevant to all four quadrants (refer to Figure 4.6). The success of marketing communication on the Internet will now be considered in the context of direct marketing, e-sponsorship, customized selling, e-journals, portal advertising, sales promotions, wired relations, and web exhibitions (see Figure 4.7).

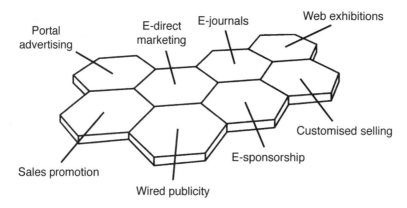

Figure 4.7   Interactive marketing communications mix

Portal advertising

The idea of portals, as already indicated, has emerged from the evolution of search engines. Portals offer virtual space, which is a gateway to the wider Internet and also an opportunity to be part of a wired community. They provide ideal space for banner style advertising for the wired world. It is also thought that the Portals of the future will offer an interactive version of traditional television advertising or what is frequently being termed interactive TV. Large portal sites such as Netscentre (www.netscapeonline.co.uk) and Yahoo (www.yahoo.com) have a major influence on traffic across the Web and as a consequence are in a pivotal position for driving current and future banner advertising initiatives. Banner advertisements are targeted at a specific audience that is driven through key word searches. When undertaking a key word search the banner appears at the top of the Web page. The motivation for placing a banner advertisement is primarily-based on: (1) anticipating a consumer will click on the banner and then receive further branding information and the opportunity to purchase; (2) and secondly visitors to a page will view the banner advertisement either consciously or sub-consciously when surfing the Web. The fundamental differences between traditional and new media advertising are:

- A performance-based advertisement model is driving the cost of advertising on the Internet. Many websites now charge advertisement banners based on actual sales of a companies product. The click stream can be monitored from the banner through to the actual purchase.
- The cost of advertising on the Internet also reduces as space becomes cheaper.
- Information, rather than image, is the primary initiator of consumer dialogue with the new medium.
- Time is becoming an ever-increasing commodity on the Internet and interaction with the user will have to be fast and a seamless process.

In addition to banner advertisements on portals, they are also frequently placed on websites that offer general news services and specialist services such as women's lifestyle magazines.

Sales promotions

Many of the traditional approaches to sales promotions, such as storecards and air miles are clearly just as applicable in the new web-based markets but need to extend the type of activities further by understanding the 'rules of the game' in the new markets. Beenz (www.beenz.com) and Zoom (www.zoom.co.uk) have adopted a traditional extension of traditional incentive schemes. Beenz is intended to be a global currency rather than a loyalty scheme specific to one country. As with other similar schemes you gain points through specific consumer behaviour. Traditional points in a store for example are gained through purchase but on the Internet this has been extended further by many websites giving points for just visiting a site. Clearly such an approach is being driven by the emergence of new business models where the medium has become the market as proposed by Hoffman and Novak (1996).

The Internet-based "Marketspace" has seen the dawn of the free product and as a consequence new business models are emerging. Sales promotion activities for many products and services will play a more central role in the supply of the process to the customer especially for the information intensive products that are transferable over the Internet. Linux provides a leading example where such an approach has been highly successful along with many other 'open source' products (refer to Chapter 11 for further details). Linux's revenue comes from support activities such as technical training and the sale of manuals. Sales promotion, in the context of commercial product such as Linux, is central to both the sale and supply process. The idealistic world of free open source software is gathering further momentum through the creation of the Gnome Foundation by Miguel de Icaza, which is hoping to bring open source to the masses with easy to use software interfaces (Syken, 2000).

Many of the new Internet promotional initiatives are viewed as still being at the high risk innovator stage in the adoption process while other promotional initiatives, such as banner advertising, are at a far later stage and more widely accepted as a valuable tool.

Wired publicity

Unlike many of the other elements of the marketing communication mix, public relations initiatives are non-personal and typically a company has little control over the actual publicity. Even though a company has little direct control over publicity, which is distributed on the Internet it can have a strong indirect influence. For example hosting your own website makes your organization a direct media owner and as a consequence you able to post publicity on the site virtually real time. Similar to traditional public relations initiatives it is knowledge of the market environment, which is of critical importance. The most significant difference on the Internet lies in the speed and complexity of developments in markets. In addition another major concern on the Internet, and in particular the Web, is the lack of controls and supporting legally enforceable rules.

A current tool on the Web, that is frequently termed "graffiti marketing", by Third Voice allows users to leave comments and opinions on any website. These can be public, for all to view, or private. Comments that can currently be found on most large websites can be favourable but are frequently quite scathing and viewed by organizations to constitute negative publicity. Graffiti marketing activities are anticipated to grow and can offer both favourable and unfavourable publicity. The main issue with graffiti marketing is the global scale and the virtually uncontrollable nature of how it operates. Third Voice requires a small software application that can be downloaded for free and it then embeds itself into your browser. The principle of how it operates is quite simple. When you visit a website it creates a three way relationship between your browser, the specific website visited and Third Voice server. You are then able to view the specific website chosen and at the same time also see on top notes both you have left and messages from the broader Third Voice community. The messages placed on top of your chosen website are being accessed from Third Voice and the three way relationship operates as illustrated in Figure 4.8.

Software tools such as Third Voice provide an insight into future business applications likely to be created in the development of far more dynamic forms of online publicity (Figure 4.9).

e-Journals

Text-based newsgroups on the Internet are still widely used forums for discussion and remain a cornerstone of Internet communications. Newsgroups are generally

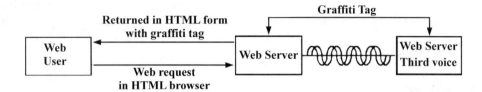

Figure 4.8   Graffiti marketing

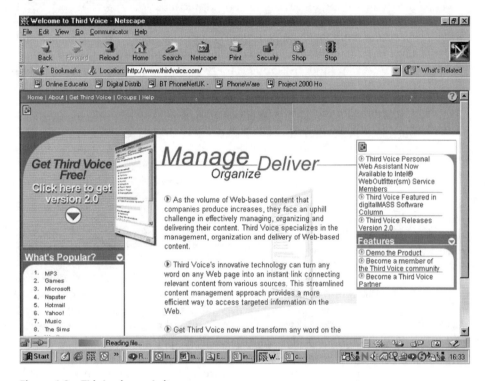

Figure 4.9   Third voice website

tightly controlled and as a consequence focus on offering value-added information. Newsgroups are still an important vehicle for marketing communication initiatives. They are similar to the traditional trade journals in offering important technical information to the specific readership. Text-based communication such as news-groups offer a valued insight and provided a foundation for the development of web-based e-journals. In establishing e-journals a similar web etiquette needs to be followed to the managing of online newsgroups whilst accepting the need for dynamic forms of communication. The e-journals of the future will harness new media-rich applications including the creation of 3D space. Many good examples are currently available that are useful benchmarks for further development. Wiley Interscience (www.interscience.com) and EBSCO represent benchmarks in the development of consumer driven information through the hypermedia format.

The web documents allow the user to read articles both in a linear and non-linear format depending on desires, preferences and needs. Both Wiley and EBSCO have adopted a process driven perspective through an object orientation towards information management.

Direct marketing online

E-mail offers an ideal mode of communication that is both a fast and responsive direct marketing tool with no geographical boundaries. The focus of direct marketing development is now via the Internet, which is providing a platform for the implementation of an integrated approach towards technology-based direct marketing initiatives. For example, various e-mail newsgroups, such as Apple computers, frequently embed there web address within value-added information-based services. The integration of communications tools on the Internet is clearly enriching the direct marketing experience and its potential for success on the Web. Multimedia developments are creating fast moving and dynamic virtual business environments (see Figures 4.10 and 4.11). Consider the e-business grid outlined earlier and the central role played by direct marketing online. In identifying the relevance and importance of the marketing communications mix to current e-business activities direct marketing initiatives on the Internet were identified as being of fundamental importance to the further development of business operations in all four quadrants.

"Word of Mouth" or what has been termed by many viral marketing is viewed as a grassroots campaign on the Internet, relying on people spreading the message and as a consequence a powerful marketing tool. You may be thinking this form of marketing has always existed but the Web opens this form of marketing up through the global communications channel of the Internet. Such an approach is clearly very informal but even so, it can be viewed as a form of associate marketing especially if you consider organizations such as Hotmail and ICQ who have used viral marketing with unprecedented success. A viral marketing campaign is successful if you learned about something, but more or less at the same time everyone in your organization or community have already just been informed through some source on the Internet. For example Hotmail, the most popular web-based e-mail system on the planet, now has over 30 million subscribers. Most of the users came by word of mouth, but the slogan at the bottom of the e-mail 'Get your free e-mail at Hotmail' has been a highly effective form of viral marketing. Every message sent and received through Hotmail carries the same simple ad for the company. Viral marketing takes advantage the Web's most potent tool, which is the ability to communicate one-on-one. People will communicate if there is a true intrinsic value, and the broader the relevance to a mass audience the greater chance there will be of global transmission through a one-to-one approach. Viral marketing is an unfortunate term but still offers a valuable informal approach that has the ability to provide an integrated approach towards marketing communications especially in B2C markets as illustrated by Hotmail.

Direct marketing using new media on the Internet needs to adopt an integrated

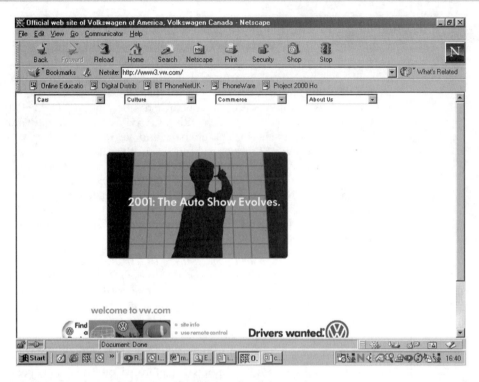

Figure 4.10   The website of the Volkswagen Beetle

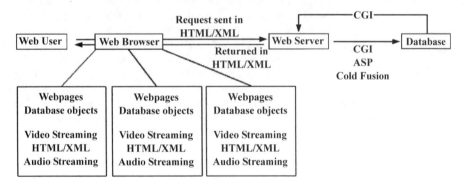

Figure 4.11   Database driven dynamic pages

approach similar to the traditional marketplace. For example Jungle.com (www.jungle.com) offers an integrated approach to direct marketing through many customers receiving a catalogue via post while more and more are now receiving a electronic catalogue via e-mail customized to there specific desires and needs. The major difference between direct marketing in the physical and virtual market is the shift in focus in the mode of delivery and how the medium has now truly become the market.

CASE APPLICATION

HOTMAIL™: HOTMAIL'S WEB-BASED E-MAIL AND VIRAL MARKETING ON THE INTERNET

Hotmail™ has undergone unprecedented growth since its launch in 1996. Its main product is a free web-based e-mail service that allows registered users free access from any PC with Internet access. Hotmail™ has become the world's largest web-based e-mail service since its launch with a subscriber base that grew more rapidly than any company in the history of the world. In its first 2 years of operation, Hotmail™ signed over 12 million subscribers to their service. In comparison with traditional print publications who typically aim to reach a 100 000 subscribers within a few years of launch, Hotmail™ demonstrates the magnitude of their success with over 66 million active users world-wide and approximately a quarter of a million new accounts opened daily. Such an unprecedented growth captured the interest of Microsoft who then acquired the free web-based e-mail company for over $400 million in 1998.

Hotmail™ has been a web-mail pioneer. It has built a strong following by offering a free, high-quality e-mail service that lets its members access a permanent e-mail address from any PC with an Internet connection. Our goal is to combine the benefits of Hotmail™ with Microsoft® services and technology to provide consumers with the best combination of free and premium e-mail services. We are committed to making it even easier for people to communicate over the Internet from anywhere in the world.

Laura Jennings, vice president, The Microsoft Network

Hotmail™ have successfully compiled an unprecedented amount of personal information on every Hotmail™ subscriber, including a detailed demographic and psychographic profile including, for example, occupation and salary. Yet, from company launch in 1996 to 12 million users, Hotmail™ spent less than $500 000 on marketing, advertising and promotion, compared to over $20 million spent on advertising and brand promotion by many close competitors.

Hotmail™ is also particularly significant through its use of viral marketing as part of their strategy, they are recognized as one of the early pioneers of viral marketing on the Internet. Hotmail™ utilize viral marketing on all their active users, whenever a subscriber sends an e-mail to friends or associates, a short marketing promotion is inserted at the bottom of every e-mail: 'Get Your Private, Free E-mail at http://www.hotmail.com'. Utilizing viral marketing in such a way enables Hotmail™ to acquire customers with no extra cost together with the repeated use of the message which allows it to grow and spread rapidly. Viral marketing and as a consequence Hotmail™ adoption follows the pattern of a virus – with spatial and network locality. People send e-mails to their friends and colleagues; many are geographically close, whilst others are scattered globally. The numbers of subscribers would proliferate considerably from a recognizable first user, hence the term virus. The major benefit of successful viral marketing, as recognized by Hotmail™, is that none of this requires a substantial marketing budget, the subscribers undertake all the work. Hotmail™ were imperative in the development of viral marketing over the Internet and due to their success other online companies have followed a similar approach.

e-Sponsorship

Many development websites, from universities to information resource centres, are primarily funded through online sponsorship deals. The primary incentive for companies to offer sponsorship on the web is driven by an ability to reach a large potential market in a cost-effective way. For example, standards bodies or information resource centres, such as www.w3.org or www.educause.edu, offer an ideal opportunity to increase a firm's profile but is also seen to be contributing to important developments. Sponsorship can be from a simple membership of an organization to significant direct funding-based initiatives. An extension of sponsorship initiatives is co-branding or what is frequently termed promotion partnering. Basically co-branding is where two or more companies agree to jointly display content and to undertake joint promotions such as banner advertisements. A co-branding approach towards banner advertisements can have the added benefit of being far more cost effective over time, especially for companies that have established websites within specific market sectors. Many examples of co-branding now exist along specific supply chains or between companies targeting a similar customer group.

Novak and Hoffman (1996) identified sponsored content sites and sponsored search engines. Sponsored content sites include newspapers and magazines, while sponsored search engines are typical of websites such as Excite (www.excite.com).

Customized selling

Businesses are striving towards the notion of offering a unique product or service to an individual customer and the Internet has become an enabler of such an environment. For products that are able to fit with such an approach, in particular information-intensive products, the Internet is potentially able to offer an infrastructure that supports highly customizable solutions. The Internet is a facilitator in taking relationship marketing principles forward in achieving a more collaborative one-to-one approach to mass markets. Customized selling is particularly dependent on the type of product or service. Dell computers offers for sale physical computing equipment from its Website with some customization. In contrast the music store MP3.com (www.mp3.com) offers far greater customization to a consumer by providing the option to download samples, full music tracks from new artists and also the facility to buy online. Customized selling will have a particular impact on information intensive products that can be supplied over the Internet such as music, software, publishing and education. The Internet is currently just beginning to show its full potential in understanding our individual desires and aspirations, and building tools to support tailored marketing communications. Many websites now incorporate intelligent applications and more basic data capture applications (cookies) into the design process. For example, retail banks such as CitiBank incorporate what are termed cookie applications into an individual computer, via the web browser, to capture basic behavioural data in an attempt to personalize and ease the Web experience. When the user of the computer re-visits the site that placed the cookie, such as CitiBank, the Website is able to identify the customer and tailor the individual web session accordingly. As a consequence Cookies, even though the technology is quite simple, is a powerful marketing tool for customized selling by being able to identify a particular customer.

Web exhibitions

The automobile industry provides various examples of using the Web as a platform for digital exhibition halls. Exhibitions on the Web are now becoming both rich and dynamic 3D environments. The use of products such as Canoma and VRML is extending the interactivity of the Web in being able to offer more immersive applications. For instance the ability to view products from all angles with functionality to zoom in and out provides an indication of the future. Volkswagen with the launch of the new Beetle (http://www.new-beetle.com/) has harnessed the power of the Web (Figure 4.10), by the development of an interactive exhibition space where users for example, are able to view the car from various perspectives. This has been developed using Macromedia Flash which is a vector-based design software.

VRML (Virtual Reality Markup Language) on the Web has seen a mixed response and has been inhibited primarily through the limited bandwidth presently available. Even though graphically limited in the level of detail it is still viewed as a powerful tool for displaying many products on the Web and for many provides a useful insight into product features. A typical useful VRML application can be found on the Palm website (www.palm.com) where you are able to chose one of the exhibited PDAs and interact directly with the device, from turning it around to testing out its functionality.

Technological developments for marketing communication

This section is intended to help you consider some of the new and emerging technology for the Internet and how it can be used effectively for marketing communications initiatives. In developing a good understanding of new Internet-based technology, and its role for marketing communications, we need also to consider the changing nature of interactivity. Eva Pascoe co-founder of the highly successful Internet cafe in London called Cyberia stated that success can only be achieved on the Internet by serving the community. In particular, web users are demanding fast and up to date information and as a consequence information is now being provided through a technology platform that can provide information on demand. Database driven websites are now becoming the norm. Figure 4.11 provides an insight into how this is delivered to Internet users. The fundamental approach is in constructing pages through the creation of web objects that can be presented in a customized form for individual consumers or market sectors. The primary technology enabler is by extending web pages from HTML format into extendable mark up language (XML) with a back end database facilitating the whole web experience.

Marketing communications on the Internet are being extended further by developments in leading edge software applications including: real time audio, real time video, internet videoconferencing, interactive chat on your website, and virtual interactive environments. RealPlayer and NetMeetings described below are intended to provide an insight into the vast array of new software products currently available or about to be released that will enrich both the communications and the process of interaction across the Internet.

RealPlayer G2 from RealNetworks (http://www.real.com)

RealPlayer for many has now become a leader on the Internet for both audio and video streaming. RealPlayer G2 is a formal partner with Netscape and is bundled with Netscape Communicator. RealPlayer enables the streaming of audio and video over the Internet and the real jukebox enables the consumer to play audio from files on an individuals personal computer (see Figure 4.12). A particularly interesting feature of the G2 edition is the use of XML applications. For the user this enables for example the linking of web pages to the timeline of a video clip. For direct marketing applications the linking of web pages to video clips allows the production of more rich interactive forms of communication that are similar in principle than the emergence of interactive TV channels.

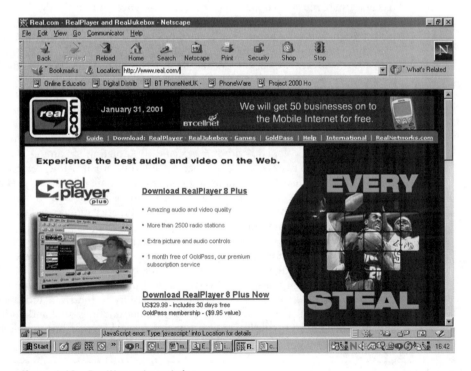

Figure 4.12   RealNetworks website

REALNETWORKS (WWW.REAL.COM):
COMPLETE STREAMERS OF MEDIA SOLUTIONS AND SERVICES

RealNetworks is viewed as the pioneer and market leader in the delivery (streaming) of media over the Internet. They continue to excel in developing software products and services designed to enable users to send and receive audio, video and other multimedia services over the web. The market for real time streaming of both visual and audio media over the Internet is growing, according to RealNetworks. Over 350 000 hours per day of live sports; music, news and entertainment are broadcast over the Internet using RealNetworks solutions. The RealNetworks product portfolio is among the top audio/video destinations on the Internet. The solutions and services they offer have ranked the site consistently in the top 25 most popular sites on the Internet.

Real.com is the main website of RealNetworks providing an online entertainment guide with information on news, movies, sports, and music resulting in an all encompassing entertainment provider. In order to fully utilize the features on the website and other similar sites across the Web, Real.com offers free downloads of past versions of RealPlayer. Through offering free the player (RealPlayer), Real.com has registered over 130 million unique users, representing the main broadest audience for streaming media delivery on the web. RealPlayer enables users to download audio and visual media and tune into to global radio stations from both Real.com and other web sources either for free or for the latest editions at a reduced price. As a means of receiving maximum revenue from their entertainment guide 'Realguide', Real.com have limited access to certain audio and visual formats by only allowing the download to occur with the latest RealPlayer which the user must pay for as a means of providing a revenue stream for the company.

In 1999 RealNetworks also launched RealJukebox which has become the latest in technological advancement for RealNetworks. RealJukebox allows users to record, organize and play MP3 and digital music on their PCs or take it on the go. RealJukebox is the market leader in digital media software with over 35 million unique registered users.

In addition to creating media streaming solutions for individual consumers, RealNetworks have developed a division specifically targeting streaming solutions for businesses. RealNetworks has developed an Internet broadcasting service targeted at providing broadcasting solutions to broadcasters, retailers and corporations. The Real Broadcast Network team provide hosting solutions that deliver streamed presentations to any size online audience whether it is for broadcasting a single live event or round the clock programming.

RealNetworks have capitalized on their expertise of streaming media by now leading in both consumer and broadcast markets by creating a complete solutions corporation. Their extensive consumer base for both RealPlayer and RealJukebox attract broadcasters to select RealNetworks to fulfil their media streaming needs. The future for RealNetworks depends on their ability to innovate and improve on the services they currently provide and bring higher quality visual and audio media to every consumer in both business-to-consumer markets and business-to-business markets.

Videoconferencing

NetMeeting and Intel Video Phone are free videoconferencing products available for download from the companies' Websites. With a sound card, microphone, and speakers, Intel Video Phone and similar products allow you to place audio calls over the Internet or a corporate intranet. By adding a video camera you are also able to have face-to-face communication over the Internet. Internet conferencing give users the ability to share data through relay text messaging, whiteboard, audio, and video with friends and colleagues in real time. Through the use of applications such as Intel Video Phone (see Figure 4.13) various marketing communications applications are being moved beyond traditional boundaries in enabling individual hyper-media-based interactivity. A typical application of videoconferencing is for personal selling where a consumer can visit a website and both sales and technical support can be provided online through telemarketing on the Internet. Currently most websites use 'callback' facilities creating quite good synergy between the Web and telephone. For videoconferencing to operate over the Internet 'callback' facilities need to integrate directly into a call management system, which uses computer-integrated telephony. The benefit of the Web is currently the ability to deal with more of the routine queries and it is relatively easy to automate while the emergence of integrated videoconferencing provides the opportunity to offer more individual one-to-one specialist advice.

Figure 4.13   Intel Video Phone

Conclusions

Marketing communication is viewed by many as the management of the customer buying process over time from pre-selling, selling, consuming, and also post-consumption stages. This involves the following: identifying the target audience, determining communications objectives, message design, choosing appropriate media to send message, and collecting feedback. Marketing programmes are focused on building closer relationships with customers in more narrowly defined markets. New Internet-based technology is speeding the development of such initiatives at an unprecedented pace. The Internet has also driven marketing communication into new avenues of opportunities with two-way interaction becoming common place. The e-business grid (see Figure 4.6) provides a valuable framework for considering the types of e-business and the direct implications to marketing communications in the near future. The Internet is also creating significant changes in the marketing communication mix with new forms of activity from new electronic journals to online exhibitions and conferences. The future for marketing communication is clearly going to be driven by a faster telecommunications infrastructure through broadband services and as a consequence the merging of multimedia technology including audio, animation and web TV.

Checklist

1. Many forms of communications are at the early stages of shifting away from mass broadcast media towards more interactive approaches.
2. Interactive communications via the Internet is reshaping the traditional communications process in terms of the relationship between sender, message and receiver.
3. It is proposed true interactivity, via two-way information flow, that needs to provide the opportunity to influence and be influenced by the exchange of ideas.
4. e-Business has emerged with organizations providing product and service offerings to specific market demands.
5. The e-business grid in Figure 4.6 identifies four primary quadrants to classify businesses and as a consequence the types of marketing communications activities that are appropriate.
6. Interactive marketing communications on the Internet can be seen as a natural extension of the traditional communications mix presented in Figure 4.1.
7. Two major developments in the creation of an interactive marketing communications mix is the emergence of portals and performance driven pricing structures for banner advertising.
8. Hypermedia is a broad term representing multimedia objects that provide links, local or remotely, to further information sources.
9. The Internet is moving towards the use of multimedia rich technology such as audio and video streaming.

References

Fill, C. (1999), *Marketing Communications, Contexts, Contents, Strategies*, 2nd ed. Prentice Hall, New Saddle River, NJ.

Goldhaber, G.M. (1986), *Organizational Communication*. W.C. Brown, Dubuque.

Hardaker, G. (1998), Benchmarking for quality management and technology: an international perspective, 5 (2).

Hoffman, D.L. and Novak, T.P. (1996), Marketing in hypermedia computer-mediated environments: conceptual foundations, *Journal of Marketing*, July.

Katz, D and Kahn, R.L. (1978), *The Social Psychology of Organizations*, 2nd ed. John Wiley & Sons, New York.

Kotler, P., Armstrong, G., Saunders, J. and Wong, V. (1999), *Principles of Marketing*, 2nd European ed. Prentice Hall, Europe.

Rayport, J.F. and Sviokla, J.J. (1994), Managing in the marketspace, *Harvard Business Review*, Nov–Dec, pp. 141–150.

Selfridge, P. (1997), Online communities and the next-generation Internet, *IEEE Expert*, Nov–Dec, pp. 4–5.

Syken, B. (2000), An evangelist for free software, *Time*, 18 September.

Further reading

Venkatrannan, N. and Henderson, J.C. (1998), Real strategies for virtual organizing. *Sloan Management Review*, Fall, pp. 33–48.

CHAPTER 5

The Internet customer and relationship marketing

- Theoretical basis of relationship marketing
- Buyer–supplier relationships on the Internet
- Developing web relations
- Strategic benefits of virtual relationships

- Identify those industries where the Internet is being used most effectively to implement relationship marketing strategies and how?
- Understand how the Internet can be used to build trust and safety in relationships or create higher customer switching costs.
- Describe new forms of relationship marketing emerging in virtual communities.
- Critically evaluate the strategic benefits of virtual relationships.

Marketing has undergone a significant transformation in the past decade. Specifically the established concept of the marketing mix, which has been challenged by the emergence of what may loosely be termed 'relationship marketing', which must be seen as a product of radical changes – in the service sector and industrial marketing. In the relationship view, marketing is the management of a complex network of interconnected relationships, and not the management of isolated transactions in consumer and organizational markets (Coviello et al., 1997).

This shifting focus is clearly evident in the emergent definitions of relationship marketing.

> Relationship marketing strategies are concerned with the development and enhancement with a number of key markets. It is concerned with the 'internal' market within the organization as well as external relationships with customers, suppliers, referral sources, influence markets and recruitment markets. (Payne et al., 1995, p. 4).

Inevitably such a fundamental shift in the underlying focus of marketing activities has had significant implications for the organization of the marketing function within the organization of the marketing function within the organization. Piercy and Cravens (1995, p. 21) argue that:

> ...as the focus of marketing moves from transactions to relationships, then the blurring of the traditional boundaries between the firm and its market will be mirrored by less distinct functional boundaries within the firm.

The centralized marketing department as the tangible expression of the marketing function is thus seen as being of increasingly less relevance to modern organizations. Rather marketing becomes a largely decentralized activity, being primarily the responsibility of staff from a rang of discrete functional areas, the activities of which impact directly or indirectly on the organization's network of external relationships.

Under such a perspective, marketing rather than being the preserve of a dedicated group of relatively isolated specialists, is of necessity part of the responsibilities of what may conventionally be seen as non-marketing staff:

> ...marketing cannot be the sole responsibility of a few specialists and everyone in the firm must be charged with developing and contributing value to the customer. Implicit here is the need to develop and nurture mechanisms for bridging the gaps between firms and for managing effectively the nexus between firms. (Spekman, 1996, p. 12).

Staff, particularly 'front of house staff' (Grove et al., 1992) have argued to have responsibility for undertaking a variety of marketing activities, particularly in respect of the ongoing management of relationships with external network members, alongside their core technical responsibilities (Gronroos, 1997). This process of empowering front-line staff is widely viewed not only as critical to the effective management of the complex network of market relationships facing modern organizations but is also a means of developing an all embracing corporate marketing culture throughout the organization.

However, reviewing the rapidly evolving marketing literature on relationships and networks, Spekman (1996, p. 120) argues that in fact:

> ...there has been a noticeable gap in attempts to understand how to manage these marketing relationships... the full effects of relationship management tools and techniques has not been fully demonstrated.

Specifically while their may be a conceptual logic and coherence in the decentralization of organizational responsibility for marketing, implementing such a concept poses significant managerial challenges in terms of the control, co-ordination and implementation of marketing, of the management of external relationships.

> One clear problem is that something which is everyone's job stands an excellent chance of actually being implemented by no-one. (Piercy and Cravens, 1995, p. 24).

In this regard it is important to recognize that such decentralization of marketing and hence empowerment of front-line staff is ultimately underpinned by two critical assumptions. Firstly that such non-marketing staff will accept responsibility for marketing activities alongside their core technical responsibilities, and secondly the primacy of organizational loyalty over external affiliations amongst staff.

Focusing on the latter of these twin assumptions, while this assumption of the primacy of organizational loyalty may be valid in the majority of organizational settings, particularly in industrial organizations, such pre-eminence of organizational loyalty cannot automatically be assumed to exist in many professional service settings. Professional activities such as medicine, law and accountancy amongst others, are frequently characterized by the primary identification of the service professional being with their profession, that is their professional peers and with their clients raters than the organization itself (Dawson, 1994). Moreover, professional services are also typically characterized by a relatively high degree of professional autonomy from direct corporate managerial control. Rather than being based on a simple linear hierarchy, management in such organizations is frequently based on negotiation and consensus.

Taken together, these twin linked characteristics arguably pose fundamental challenges to the management of inter-organizational relationships in professional service organizations and hence the effective marketing of such organizations as unified corporate identities. There is an involvement and integration of customers, suppliers and other infrastructural partners into a firm's developmental and marketing activities. Such involvement results in close interactive relationships with suppliers, customers or other value chain partners of the firm. Interactive relationships between marketing actors are inherent as compared to the arm's length relationships implied under the transactional orientation (Webster, 1992).

A significant amount of the pioneering and seminal work on relationship marketing was undertaken mainly in Europe, by Christian Gronroos at the Swedish School of Economics in Stockholm. Gronroos (1997) proposed the following definition:

> Marketing is to establish, maintain and enhance relationships with customers and other partners, at a profit, so that the objectives of the parties involved are met. This is achieved by a mutual exchange and fulfilment of promises (p. 183).

Numerous extensions and adaptations to this definition have been made, but one of the most radical in terms of its conceptual impact to marketing was made by Gummesson (1994). He suggested that a relationship needed to be put in an appropriate context of networks and interactions; this opened up a whole new field of academic study between relationship marketing and network theory. Finally, the market is viewed as a set of interconnected exchange relationships between actors, who are controlling the resources for production. The Internet-relationship fit lies with its potential role for services marketing and process orientation.

Theoretical basis of relationship marketing

Long-term relationships between companies and their stakeholders have aroused considerable interest in academic research (see, e.g. Ford et al., 1998). In addition to its commitment towards its customers, the company also become concerned with the development and enhancement of more enduring relationships with other internal or external stakeholder groups (see, e.g. Christopher et al. 1993, pp. 8–9; Gummesson, 1994; Payne et al., 1995, pp. 29–31).

The theoretical base for defining and understanding Internet relationships has roots in three various disciplinary areas of marketing. These areas include firstly, the Nordic School approach to services marketing (see, e.g. Gummesson, 1994; Gronroos, 1997, pp. 1–3); secondly, the interaction and network approach to industrial and international marketing (see e.g., Ford et al., 1998); and thirdly, relationship marketing (Gummesson, 1994).

All of these schools of thought emphasized the importance of identifying, establishing, maintaining, and enhancing long-term relationships between sellers and buyers and other internal or external stakeholders in the marketplace to a considerable extent. In fact, building and managing relationships have become one of the philosophical cornerstones of all these schools since the late 1970s (Gummesson, 1994).

The Nordic School approach emphasized that the management of marketing must ordinarily be built upon relationships rather than transactions. In particular, long-term relationships with customers and other stakeholders are important (for the findings of the Nordic School approach, see, e.g. Berry and Parasurman, 1993; Fisk et al., 1993; Brown et al., 1994; Gummesson, 1994). According to the interaction and network approach all companies are involved in a complex network of relationships with their suppliers, customers and other business partners (Ford et al., 1998).

Relationship marketing is a relatively new term, but it represents an old phenomenon. There is, however, no common agreement on the definition of relationship marketing. Several definitions of relationship marketing include explicit or implicit references to other stakeholders rather than only to customers (for a comprehensive discussion of the implicit and explicit definitions of relationship marketing, see Berry and Parasuraman, 1991; Berry, 1983; Gummesson, 1994).

Based on our prior understanding from the Nordic School approach to services marketing, the interaction and network approach to industrial and international marketing and relationship marketing, this chapter focuses on the rapidly evolving and highly inter-disciplinary research area of buyer–supplier relationships on the Internet.

The virtual triangle of relationships

In Figure 5.1 the virtual triangle puts marketing for e-commerce in a relational context. The virtual context of Figure 5.1 represents marketing, as it is developing in a rapidly growing number of online businesses. The Web firm may still have a centralized marketing and sales staff, called here the full-time marketers, but the Internet is facilitating that they do not represent all the marketers and salespeople of the firm. Markets, as masses of more or less anonymous individuals are considered less suitable in the virtual world. The online buyer is also treated on a much more personalized basis.

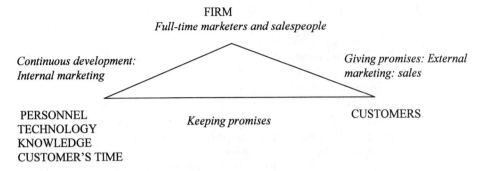

FIRM
Full-time marketers and salespeople

Continuous development:
Internal marketing

Giving promises: External
marketing: sales

PERSONNEL
TECHNOLOGY
KNOWLEDGE
CUSTOMER'S TIME

Keeping promises

CUSTOMERS

Figure 5.1   The virtual triangle (adapted from Gronroos, 1997)

In principle, no online customer should remain anonymous to the firm, unless this can be justified from an economic or practical standpoint or if the customer does not want it. On the Web it is not the product that is most transparent; rather it is the resources that are used to create value for the customer, which are in the forefront. Of course, the product is still there, but it has been conceptually divided into its basic elements, i.e. the various resources, technology, knowledge, etc. that form the product. Depending on type of offering, products as prefabricated packages of information resources do exist (computer games, music and DVD). However, often there are so many other resources required in the relationship that cannot be pre-packaged so that the notion of a product as a prefabricated package of resources becomes more meaningful. And in the case of services (travel and financial services) that are processes and not actual things it becomes quite unclear if a product can exist in the first place.

Relationship 'breadth' and 'depth'

The assumption is that the Internet will set new standards for total relationship management – both in 'breadth' and 'depth'. 'Breadth' means that a relationship will increasingly last for the entire ownership experience, including the time before and after the purchase of the product or service. For example, Coors used consumer feedback via the Web both during the development and promotion of its beverage, Zima, and thus involved consumers at all stages in the product life cycle. 'Depth' has to do with the degree of interaction with consumers at any given point in their experience of a product. An example of this is the book retailer, Amazon.com, which uses the information it obtains from consumers to create value-added services such as suggestions about books that a particular reader might enjoy.

The Internet's role in consumer relationship management has important consequences for marketers. For instance, if most car purchasers start to do their own research into different models on the Internet instead of talking to salespeople, then the dealers will have to rethink the way they manage the whole consumer relationship. Eventually, customers may approach them only to place an order. This implies that the dealers will have to find new ways to offer buyers value if they are not to disappear. Furthermore, if consumers buyer behaviour changes, so will the type of skills the salespeople will need to deal effectively with relationship management.

These salespeople need to be compensated when consumers make their purchases through channels other than in a dealership.

A great deal of the Internet's potential relies on the development of a dialogue between the consumer and the marketer, in which information is exchanged for value. Marketers need to implement new skills of rewarding consumers for giving them access to personal information, e.g. who they are, what they like and what they want to buy. This process of value exchange will become critical as new standards are created to protect consumer privacy. For instance, the proposal announced by Netscape in May 1997, for it to capture information on the consumer hard drives rather than on marketers' computers marked a step in a new direction with the implicit acknowledgement that consumers will not only 'own' the information about themselves, but also control the release of that information to marketers.

A number of marketers are beginning to manage the process of value exchange quite effectively. An example of this is Vogue, who in exchange for basic information such as name, address, age and income, the fashion magazine, provides readers with discounts, special offers and previews of forthcoming articles.

The Web brings together marketing with other business processes such as customer service, it will put more pressure on the organization of most marketers. The emergence of interactive networks will encourage the move towards new organizational models, in which marketers will structure their various functional capabilities around consumers. For example, the USAA's (a US-based insurance company) customer centre receives and manages all communications with consumers, whether direct via the telephone, mail and the Internet, or via intermediaries. The rest of the organization revolves around the consumer centre.

Sophisticated information systems help the company to process interactions in order to maximize their value. The advantage of this is that customers feel that USAA knows them better. Moreover, the company is quick to respond to a complaint or learn about important market changes such as a cut in a competitor's price in certain areas. As more and more companies reorganize themselves around their customers, intranets linked to the Internet will become crucial. They will make it economically feasible for managers within an organization to have more information about consumers, and more interactions with them.

Buyer–supplier relationships on the Internet

In the Internet-based approach to supplier sourcing, a buyer has access to a far greater supplier base than is available using conventional sourcing techniques and suppliers could be located anywhere in the world.

Cox's (1996) empirical study likened business relationships to the human situation (successful), observing successful relationships emerging after five distinct stages:

1. Courtship – where organizations are attracted to each other and discover if they are compatible.
2. Engagement – where a commitment to a lasting relationship is made.
3. Housekeeping – where it is discovered that the partners have different ideas about the way business should operate.
4. Devising mechanisms and techniques to overcome the differences.
5. Discovering that each partner has changed internally as a result of accommodating the other partner's position.

As the relationship progresses mutual trust becomes stronger. In much of the literature, the partnership approach is seen as superior to the adversarial approach (Lamming, 1993). Whilst there are benefits to the partnership approach, such as the opportunity to lower costs and improve quality, there are situations where the partnership approach may not be appropriate (refer to Chapter 7 for further details). There is no single best way to source suppliers and therefore buyers need to adopt a portfolio approach.

Some buyer–supplier relationships that start as adversarial may mature into partnerships. An explanation of this process is provided by Ellram who has applied the well established life-cycle model to the development of the buyer–supplier relationship (Ellram and Carr, 1995). The development stage is characterized by frequent face-to-face communications and low levels of trust. As the relationship matures into the commitment stage, trust grows and there is less need for face-to-face contact. In the integration stage, mutual expectations are established and the relationship stabilizes. Finally the relationship may or may not dissolve depending on specific circumstances.

In the partnership approach there is a prolonged period of bilateral adjustment during which time mutual trust becomes established. One example of this is Marks and Spencer which has established partnerships with its fresh sandwich suppliers based on mutual trust (Christopher, 1997). This approach is appropriate because of the perishable nature of the ingredients and the wide fluctuation in demand for the end product requires the type of co-operation inherent in the partnership approach. In the adversarial approach it may be assumed that trust plays no part in the relationship. However, this appears not to be the case. Sako (1992) proposes that there are three distinct types of trust. The first is contractual trust in which both parties fulfil their contractual obligations; the second is competence trust where both parties perform their roles competently; and the third is goodwill trust which is characterized by a willingness to share information and a predisposition to do more than is actually required by the formal contract. Applying this concept to buyer–supplier relationships, the adversarial approach can be seen to consist of mainly contractual and competence trust, but little goodwill trust, whilst in the partnership approach goodwill trust becomes highly significant.

A further insight is provided by consideration of loyalty in buyer–supplier relationships. It is possible to differentiate between subjective and objective loyalty, the former being based on emotional attachment and the latter on reasoned self-interest. Objective loyalty is based on things like quantitative selection criteria such as quality, price and delivery. Subjective loyalty consists of qualitative factors such as the state of personal relationships between buyers and suppliers. Buyers may remain loyal to a supplier who may not be the most appropriate to fulfil a particular requirement perhaps because of a strong and long-lasting interpersonal relationship. Next, we consider the facilitating role played by the Web in relation to buyer–supplier relationship evolution.

Facilitating role played by the Web

Corporate bonding on the Web is likely to extend beyond a previous single level – of relationship – to multiple levels. For instance, instead of a salesperson being the only person responsible for creating and maintaining relationships with customers, it is quite likely that other professionals in the company will be able to directly interact and develop psychological bonds with consumers. Similarly marketers would extend their relationships with other members of the family and friends. MCI's 'Friends and Family Program' is a good example, of how a marketer has broadened its relationship to a larger social group. Technology is the prime facilitator for such bonding. A developing feature of the bonding process is the application of electronic front-line 'intelligent agent' systems that can interface with and build virtual communities of users.

Building virtual communities

A buyer–supplier relationship can develop through the identification or internalization of similar values. e-Bay, has been very adept in developing and managing communities of users, which have a common interest. e-Bay's success is attributed to the notion of a commerce site, which has been built around a community where users are exchanging information, goods, services and merchandise. This is a peculiar community of hobbyists and serious collectors, who are together with people of established 'bricks-and-mortar' businesses, which are moving activity over to e-Bay. Also, there are members, who have left their profession or careers to start a new business on e-Bay. The traffic comes from virtually everywhere. It comes from people of all economic backgrounds and from virtually every demographic group. Table 5.1 presents appropriate financial and market information on e-Bay. The coverage is all age groups and it is globally based. e-Bay is only open to members aged 18 years. The site was opened in September 1998 and its market capitalization hit $3 billion by Halloween. At the time of writing e-Bay, is now the world's largest online trading community. The website really offers the user the opportunity to come together, and buy and trade in a wide range of items, including fine collectibles.

Small businesses are likely to benefit from the Web's ability to develop networks or communities of users for its retail products and services to or within a group. By developing networks or communities that offer within group (member) benefits, synergies for participants can be created. Co-ordinating certain functions between firms, creates a strategic advantage for the entire group of participants as well as facilitating the creation of exit barriers, for members.

Table 5.1   e-Bay financial and market information[a]

Initial stock price	$18
7 week high (11/10/98)	$140
Shares outstanding	39.7 million
Market capitalization at IPO	$714.6 million
Market capitalization (11/11/98)	$4.6 billion (Onsale $443 million; Excite, $2.5 billion; Netscape, $2.8 billion; Amazon.com, $6.3 billion; Yahoo, $15.5 billion)
Product categories	1086
Items currently for sale	863898
Items for sale inception (9/95)	28 million
Bids since inception (9/95)	105 million
Competitors	Yahoo! Auctions (items currently for sale: 51135); Onsale (bids since 5/95 launch: 8.4 million); Auction Universe (items: 21264); First Auction
Highest sale price	$17101 for a Chicago Bulls jersey signed by Michael Jordan
Lowest opening price	1 cent (several listed)
Pez dispensers for sale	1011. Highest asking price: $2100 for an unopened 'bride' model
Celebrity-related items for sale	Mark McGwire, 2314; Madonna, 614; Princess Diana, 581; Hitler, 219; Mariah Carey, 89; Bill Gates, 13; Clinton–Lewinsky, 12; Nelson Mandela, 7; Mother Theresa, 7

[a] Source: Wired, January 1999, p. 156.

Developing web relations

There is some fundamental change in relationship development as a consequence of developments in web technology. This technology is not only assisting in relationship development it is also helping in its enhancement, and even in the termination, of relationships. Through the use of web technology, consumers can enhance their relationship development with the marketing organization. For example, when a bank (Barclays) or credit card company (Marbles) goes online, the e-consumer will experience a one-stop service with multiple offerings, potentially customized, by the marketer. The consumer, who is conducting transactions over these interactive networks must also provide and obtain additional information to the marketer. The interactive nature of the system, also offers the opportunity – for the consumer – to terminate a relationship with the marketer. Consumers are able to sign off from the membership program, by simply sending an e-mail message.

The range of web-based technologies – from bulletin boards to integrated data interchange – is facilitating group and institutional influence on consumers, who are both engaging in and terminating some relationships. This is apparent with the development of interest groups, who share their views about products and marketers on electronic bulletin boards. There are also institutions – such as churches, pressure groups, and charities – who are using bulletin boards in order to shape consumer choices and expectations. There are US government institutions, such as the IRS to the Department of Commerce, who are effectively using web-based applications for business to fill in their tax returns and import–export forms, respectively. In addition, there is a range of digital technologies from fax–web, mobile phone–mail, and online television broadcasting to develop and sustain relationships with existing and potential customers.

Customers will want to develop an exchange relationship after they are satisfied with past performance and trust in future performance. Such a notion is not new to the relationship marketing approach. Within a balanced approach to relationship marketing and customer retention, however, relationship development will become and in the case of Dell is an important source of competitive advantage, for web-based suppliers.

CASE APPLICATION

DELL COMPUTING

Dell's customer-centric information became the most powerful tool ever seen in the computer industry. The Internet and e-commerce have revolutionized Dell's customer information and customer relationship management. As Michael Dell[1] puts it: 'The only medium that would be more effective that the Internet is mental telepathy'. For Dell it is one thing to create an Internet culture that works, but it is another thing to use that Internet culture in order to create a measurable advantage. The greatest threat to Dell is keeping its people and the web-based entrepreneurial spirit alive in a company that has capitalized at £18 billion and whose stock has risen 36 000% in a decade.

For Michael Dell, it can be seen that direct contact means direct feedback. From the thousands of daily e-mails, website visits, faxes, and phone calls Dell have had the most powerful advantage of all – a minute by minute feedback of the customer needs and experience to its offerings. Michael Dell points out: 'Technology, high quality and good value are just the price of entry; total customer experience is the most competitive franchise. The key is dialogue – talk with your customers, not just to them' (p. 84).

Relationship development at Dell places at the customers' disposal the right amount of information about the value offerings, the exchange relations and its conditions in a clear and reliable way which is easy to grasp, on an actual basis via a medium easy to access. In a developing exchange relationship, at Dell, the customers should obtain any relevant information as easy as possible. All information including the price should be consistent and well structured. Dell's relationship development is increased by unbundling prices for instance.

Every-Day-Low-Prices (EDLP) and product guarantees also contribute to relationship development. Changes in prices and other exchange conditions are communicated to interested customers. Dell list their recent changes in prices (price reductions and increases) in their virtual stores. Using modern information technology they are seeking to develop a broad range of creative and cost-efficient ways to enhance relationship development and contribute to a relationship of trust.

In the short-term, relationship development may conflict with corporate objectives to maximize turnover and profit. For Dell's 'hit-and-run' marketing strategy, intransparency would certainly be more appropriate. Under a long-term perspective, however, relationship development contributes to turnover and profit through the construct of customer satisfaction, both in terms of attribute satisfaction and information satisfaction.

[1] *Source: Michael Dell, Direct from Dell. Published by Harper Collins Business, 1999. Quoted in eBusiness, November 1999, p.83.*

Strategic benefits of virtual relationships

The strategic role of the Web is viewed typically to be one of how it can be used to make money, but its real benefit to supplier and consumer alike is in saving money. These savings, accrued at the expense of more traditional media, including phones, faxes, printed material, letters, etc. can be used to enhance customer service by offering the potential transfer of a much more substantive amount of information, such as technical data. In providing data bases and search capabilities at their websites, it is companies like Dell and FedEx who are allowing their customers to retrieve information on products or services. Both contain Frequently Asked Question (FAQ) pages, which are designed to save the company and customer time and/or money. These are designed to be a more expedient alternative to that of calling on help for technical assistance from a technician. Therefore, businesses are finding the Internet a cheap, efficient, and more productive way of extending customer services. The value of the Web may well vary from industry to industry or from firm to firm, as does the value of relationship marketing itself between industries.

The Web is a valuable research tool for customers, for those who are seeking out information about products/services and for vendors, who will need to provide information to inquiring consumers and also need to seek out information about consumers. Its value to customers is so significant that vendors or suppliers, which do not use it as a mechanism to reach out to prospective customers will stand the risk of simply not being 'found' in customer product searches. Consider universities, students can search for financial aid assistance (e.g. fastweb.com or finaid.org) as well as retrieve information on admissions policies or other facts regarding a university. Most universities supply this information on their sites, suggesting that universities that do not provide a site will be at a definite disadvantage.

Individuals with a particular obscure interest have found the Web a lucrative source of information, creating a marketing opportunity for the creative supplier. Medical specialist can 'be found' by prospective clients through postings in related newsgroups or by hosting chat rooms and this provides information about obscure maladies they treat. A search on the Net can give detailed information about how to care for a Venus Flytrap. And, a supplier can share problems, post FAQs or get tips from individuals with similar interests via newsgroups or chat rooms.

Not only has the Internet evolved into a network for customers/users to seek out information about topics, products, and businesses, but it has also matured as a tool with which vendors and marketers can seek out information about consumers, particularly single source data. The Web is a lucrative source of information on demographic trends, competitors, technological forces, natural resources, social and cultural trends, world and local economies, and legal and political environments. Businesses lending themselves for use on the Internet can be particularly effective at gathering customer information and are much more likely to succeed in a knowledge-based business environment.

In collecting data on the paths that visitors travel while in a site, the time spent on pages, and purchasing information (web visitor tracking) marketers can test advertising copy response, get instant feedback on new product concepts, and quickly obtain data regarding varying price structures. One creative start-up incubator, Idealab, has found an interesting way to gather and sell customer information. The company has fronted two spin-offs, Free-PC and NetZero, each of which gives you free hardware in exchange for detailed customer information. The information is then resold to other companies. Its founder, William Gross, estimates that the demographic data every Free-PC customer provides are worth $2 000 each in advertising copy[2].

Finally, the lightning speed with which news travels on the Web can be used to track the effectiveness of a firm's PR program, by monitoring comments posted on their websites or discussions in related chat rooms. Perhaps the greatest attribute of the Internet to relationship marketing is its value as a communications tool. Online surveyors, such as CyberAtlas, identify e-mail as the most important Net application. It is certainly becoming the preferred means of communication by 'Netizens' (Internet users). E-mail is revolutionizing how people and business communicate. More reliable than a fax, far less costly than a long distance phone call, and less tedious than writing and mailing a letter, an e-mail note or document can be posted anywhere in the world as quickly as it takes to click 'send'. E-mail is simply one of the most cost-effective tools a business can utilize in communicating with its customers, other businesses, and between employees. The ability to send attachments as part of an e-mail greatly enhances the obvious 'note sending' value of e-mail.

Company information, including letters/memos, resumes, promotional material, and/or technical data can be passed on in bulk, reviewed, edited, and responded to. The development of internal networks (Intranets) to facilitate communication and transactions among employees, suppliers, independent contractors, and distributors may be the Internet's principal value for multinational corporations. Transcending time zones, documents can be reviewed and edited from one international office with comments posted on the originators PC the following day. In total, the likely net result is greater, more efficient exchange of information yielding greater, all-around productivity.

---

[2] M. Duncan. *The Internet and Relationship Marketing: A Framework for Application.* AMA Winter Educators' Conference, 2000, San Antonio, Adam Mark's Hotel, pp. 72–80.

Conclusion

The Internet is a strategically vital component in the successful implementation of a relationship marketing strategy in this digital era. However, utilizing the Internet to develop a relationship marketing strategy with clients, customers, or business associates requires both a conceptual understanding of relationship marketing including the various applications, that are provided by the Internet and which can be managed through appropriate business channels to effect the desired strategy. It is likely that the Internet will begin to redefine relationship marketing's applicability and economic viability for a number of products and/or industries, from large book retailers to wine retailers being but, two examples of consumer goods. This paucity of historical data is restricting analysis to the realms of conjecture and anecdotal information.

Checklist

1. The Internet is changing the nature and form of relationship development and management.
2. Its tools are playing a growing facilitating role for relationship marketing.
3. Web-based information and communication is leading to cost savings and improving the quality and timeliness of information between buyer and supplier.
4. There is an evolution in the field of relationship marketing through the Web from the notion of a buyer–supplier network to that of virtual-based communities.
5. The Web is setting new standards for the management of relationship 'depth' and 'breadth'.
6. New virtual organizational forms are emerging that are centred on consumers.
7. Relationship value creation is largely based on an exchange information.
8. New virtual patterns of consumer behaviour are emerging with much more emphasis on the relationship to transactional approach.

References

Barnes, J. (1997), Closeness, strength and satisfaction: examining the nature of relationships between providers of financial services and their retail customers, *Psychology and Marketing*, 14 (8), pp. 765–790.

Berry, L. (1983), Relationship Marketing, In: Berry, L., Shostach, G., and Upau, G., (Eds.), *Emersing Perspetives in Services Marketing*. AMA, Chicago, IL, pp. 25–28.

Berry, L. and Parasurman, A. (1991), *Marketing Services. Competing Through Quality*. New York, Free Press.

Berry, L. and Parasurman, A. (1993), Building a new academic field - the case of services marketing, *Journal of Retailing*, 1, pp. 13–60.

Brodie, R.J., Coviello, N.E., Brooks, R.W. and Little, V. (1997), Towards a paradigm shift in marketing? An examination of current marketing practices, *Journal of Marketing Management*, 13, pp. 383–406.

Brown, S. Fisk, R. and Bitner, M. (1994), The development and emergence of services marketing thought, *International Journal of Service Industry Management*, 1, pp. 21–48.

Christopher, M., Payne, A. and Ballantyre, D. (1993), *Relationship Marketing. Bringing Quality, Customer Service and Marketing Together.* Butterworth-Heinemann, Oxford.

Christopher, M. (1997), *Marketing Logistics*, Butterworth-Heinemann, Oxford.

Cox, A. (1996), Relational competence and strategic procurement management, *European Journal of Purchasing and Supply Management*, 2 (1), pp. 57–70.

Coviello, N.E., Brodie, R.J. and Munro, H. (1997), Understanding contemporary marketing: development of a classification system, *Journal of Marketing Management*, 13, pp. 501–522.

Dawson, S (1994. :Changes in the Distance: Professionals Reappraise the Meaning of Management, *Journal of General Management*, 20 (1), pp. 1–21.

Dell, M. (1999), Direct from Dell, Harper Collins Business, extracts quoted in e-business, November, p. 83.

Duncan, M. (2000), *The Internet and Relationship Marketing: a Framework for Application.* AMA Winter Educators' Conference, 2000, San Antonio, CA, pp. 72–80.

Ellram, L.A. and Carr, A. (1994), Strategic purchasing: A history and review of the literature. *International Journal of Purchasing and Materials Management.* Spring; pp. 10–18.

Fisk, R. Brown, S. and Bitner, M. (1993), Tracking the evolution of the services marketing literature, *Journal of Retailing*, 1, pp. 61–103.

Ford, D., Gadde, L.-E., Hakansson, H., Lundgren, A., Snehota, I., Turnbull, P. and Wilson, D. (1998), *Managing Business Relationships*, John Wiley & Sons, Chichester.

Gronroos, C. (1997), Value-driven relational marketing: from products to resources and competencies, *Journal of Marketing Management*, 13, pp. 407–419.

Gummesson, E. (1994), Broadening and specifying relationship marketing. *Asia–Australia Marketing Journal*, 1, pp. 31–43.

Lamming, R. (1993), *Beyond Partnership: Strategies for Innovation and Lean Supply. The Manufacturing Practitioner Series.* Prentice Hall. Hemel Hempstead.

Payne, A., Christopher, M., Clark, M. and Pack, H. (1995), *Relationship Marketing for Competitive Advantage*, Butterworth-Heinemann, Oxford.

Piercy, N.F. and Cravens, D.W. (1995), The network paradigm and the marketing organization, *European Journal of Marketing*, 29 (3), pp. 7–34.

Sako, M. (1992), *Prices, Quality and Trust.* Cambridge University Press, Cambridge.

Spekman, R.E. (1996), A reflection on two decades of business-to-business marketing research: implications for understanding marketing relationships and networks, in: Iacobucci, D. (Ed.), *Networks in Marketing*, Sage, California.

Webster, F. (1992), The changing role of marketing in the corporation, *Journal of Marketing*, 56, pp. 1–17.

CHAPTER 6

New buyer behaviour directions through virtual communities

Key topics

- Interactive marketing directions for e-commerce
- Marketing transformation through virtual environments
- Evolution of buyer behaviour concepts on the World Wide Web
- Hypermedia support for new media-based buyer behaviour.

After studying this chapter you will be able to:

- Identify the changing trends in marketing activities on the Internet.
- Develop and implement new emerging marketing concepts for buyer behaviour.
- Identify and establish the role of virtual communities.
- Understand the role of new media for marketing.

Interactive marketing directions for e-commerce

Buyer behaviour directions for e-commerce

It is predicted, even though growth rates are very high across most of the West, the US will continue to dominate e-commerce across the globe with an estimated 80% market share. Such trends are estimated to remain the same for at least the next 5 years. Many factors can be identified for the current market share and growth rates of e-commerce across western nations. Much can be attributed to past developments in infrastructure investment and also the pricing policies of telecommunications organizations. Clearly, one finds that the speed and price of connections are an integral part of the buying process and as a consequence they determine overall market size and growth. For example, consider the US consumer market, which has widespread access to cable modem technology and also fibre-optic lines. Meanwhile in the European telecommunications sector it frequently gets blamed for inadequate technology when compared to the US. What does this mean to the consumer? This means a lot longer time on line and as a consequence much higher costs incurred in the buying process – plus less interactive communications in many instances. It is for such reasons that forecasts are indicating similar trends in market size for the next 5 years in e-commerce.

According to Cahners Business Information, buyers and specifiers are twice as likely as they were a year ago to use the Internet as their first source in locating products and technologies. Many research reports are identifying the emergence of a new model for the buying process which is common with many professionals. Cahners Business Information found that trade magazines are now used much more pervasively in the early and middle stages of the buying process, with the Web being integral to the process at the back end. Such findings indicate for example the importance of the Internet closer to the actual sale and as a consequence can be viewed as being integral to pricing decisions due to the ever increasing amount of comparable information available. The buyer behaviour model shown in Figure 6.1 is a well recognized standard model (Engel et al., 1990) and provides a platform for further consideration of the impact of e-commerce. The model presented is still applicable but the importance of the elements are radically altered in virtual markets as will be revealed through this chapter.

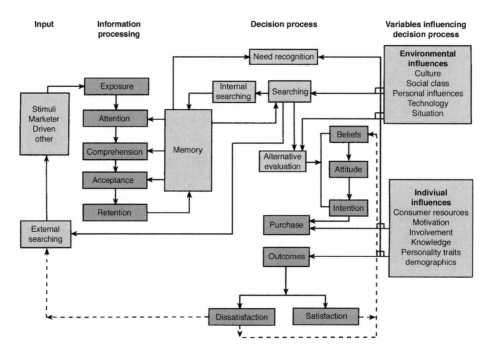

Figure 6.1   Buyer behaviour model

Accepting new forms of buying mainly through information availability on the Internet indicates that changes in pricing strategies are also emerging. For example, it would be in the realms of science fiction to suggest 5 years ago that free goods would be offered across a wired nation in 1999! Now regular users of the Internet accept certain products and services, especially with an information intensive focus such as software, which will be available for free. In addition, consider the changing views towards ownership. Organizations need to move with a growing market that will frequently require ownership of products and services for a limited period of time.

An interactive marketing approach on the World Wide Web

Due to exchange transactions increasingly being carried out electronically and online, the network will in many instances serve as the market. For traditional media it is frequently said that 'the medium is the message' but for the Web it is true that 'the medium is the market' (Hoffman and Novak, 1996). Web-based buyer behaviour patterns, as a consequence, are directly affecting organizational relationships and traditional approaches to supply chain management. You need to consider the implications of such changes for both business and consumer markets. As we have identified it is evident that significant cost savings are to be gained with the freeing up of new markets. Such developments are also viewed as having detrimental effects – for many intermediaries – in the supply chain. Changes in supply change management through buyer behaviour patterns have driven high street retailers to reconsider current distribution channels. The buyer decision making process is seen to be shifting in many business sectors towards virtual environments, which is being enabled through advanced computing technology. This in turn will have direct implications on buyer behaviour factors such as socio-economic, cultural, psychological and social factors. This fragmentation in desires and customer demands marketing needs to become ever more personalized with a shift from target marketing to one-to-one marketing (see Figure 6.2).

B^2B buyer behaviour in business markets is an integral to supply chain management, including the philosophy of Just in Time (JIT) manufacturing. Buyer behaviour recognizes the need for lean service and manufacturing delivery, which is flexible and responsive to markets. Organizations of all sizes across the globe are recognizing the central role played by information technology in current and future developments. Communication over long distances, until recently, was viewed by many as being primarily for medium to large organizations, due to the high costs incurred. The Internet offers cost-effective communications, for all industrialized nations and is consequently radically changing current buyer behaviour patterns – through facilitating access to global markets. The Internet and similar technology driven environments are central to buying behaviour in business markets for the twenty-first century. Over time computers will continue to play an integral role – with the gradual introduction of intelligent software business tools – to the desktop environment.

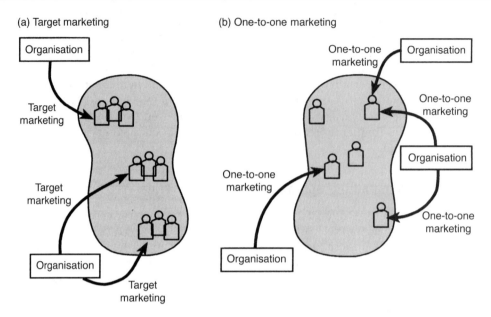

(a) Target marketing

(b) One-to-one marketing

Figure 6.2   Move to one-to-one marketing

Marketing outcomes of e-commerce in virtual markets

Bookacourse (www.bookacourse.com) along with many other websites provides an environment with variable pricing based purely on supply and demand in global markets. In many ways, there are currently only isolated examples available, but over time cyberspace will offer the potential to radically change current pricing strategies. For example, consider American Airlines, who in the mid 1980s introduced a complex pricing matrix (for the consumer) for variable flight prices – based on changing demands and customer type. Now we take for granted this variability of price fluctuations, which is found in the airline industry plus numerous other industries. Currently, there is a new wave of change which seems to be taking place, and again it is driven primarily by technology and secondly through consumer aspirations and desires. Information, especially on the Internet, is creating significantly different markets and as a consequence consumer behavioural patterns. Pricing strategies, for many industries are clearly becoming far more complex primarily through information and consumer awareness. Take for example, the publishing industry where in the traditional marketplace consumers browse may be one, two or possible three book shops comparing availability, service and for many cost. Price variations will clearly be limited to a specific area or town. Now consider the option to buy similar products via the Internet, for example, Amazon.com or similar Net-based options. International purchasing power and the ability to offer lean operations (lean needs more explanation) driven by interactive technology offers global consumer reach and as a consequence stronger purchasing power. For many purchased products, such as books the Internet offers a far more cost effective means plus very efficient distribution networks even when purchasing from overseas. Many Internet-based bookstores for example offer 2-day delivery at significantly reduced prices. Prices strategies in the marketspace are frequently based on virtually real time supply and demand fluctuations (Figure 6.3).

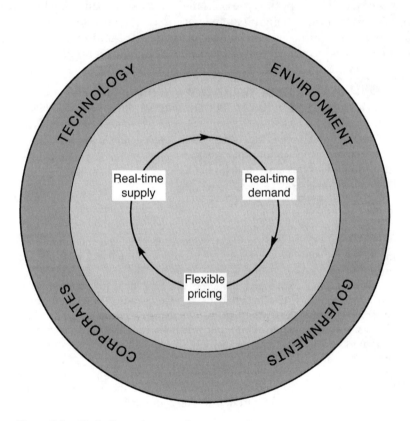

Figure 6.3   Marketing outcomes of e-commerce

Pricing considerations in the future for many organizations currently operating in the traditional marketplace will need to embrace new methods and styles of operating to survive in highly differentiated markets. The Internet is creating dynamic and chaotic markets far more in tune with consumers. This view is becoming even more exciting through the use, especially in America of shopbots – software driven shopping utilities that aid a user find products of interest at the best price. The shopbots develop their skills and efficiency through monitoring consumer behavioural patterns based on purchases but also through visits to websites.

For many these software utilities are not viewed as appropriate for some markets. e-Bay provides an environment which objects to automated software and is deemed as unfair competitive tools based on the nature of what an auction is about.

The emerging digital age will demand pricing which meets rapidly changing aspirations and needs in new emerging markets. The speed of product innovation creates consumers who desire pricing strategies that reflect the ownership of products and services for variable periods, which may be for a lifetime, or a year, or a week, or 1 h, or possibly less. In many industries, this may be viewed as rental but as products are changing at an ever increasing speed this will be viewed more and more over time as new forms of ownership and as a consequence pricing strategies need to reflect new attitudes and behavioural patterns.

CASE APPLICATION

VOLKSWAGEN (WWW.VOLKSWAGEN.COM): NO LONGER JUST A CAR SHOWROOM, NOW AN EXPERIENCE!

Volkswagen of America, Inc. is the wholly owned subsidiary of Volkswagen AG, the fourth largest producer of passenger cars in the world. Volkswagen have sold more than 10.6 million cars and markets both Volkswagen and Audi vehicles with a network of over 600 Volkswagen and 260 Audi authorized dealers.

Competition within the passenger car market is fierce, and many car manufacturers such as Volkswagen are launching their companies onto the Internet in order to seek out new customers and sustain success. As technology is developing and the potential of the Internet is being recognized, Volkswagen realized the need to make their site interactive by allowing customers to purchase the goods and form a community of users.

Volkswagen has exploited the Internet in many ways, for example, by only making it possible to purchase the first ever-special colour edition Beetle online. Volkswagen of America recognized early the growing desire of consumers to purchase online. To meet this desire Volkswagen's online buying process through their website allows interested customers to learn more about the new special edition Beetle, configure a desire car, check its availability within the Volkswagen distribution system, select their local dealer, consider financing and purchasing terms and arrange a delivery date, all online. With the exception of physically collecting the car, the customer could complete the purchase of the car directly from from the computer screen.

We know that nearly 60% of Volkswagen customers use the Internet to gather information and purchase products and services…Volkswagen plan to be a leader and an innovator in this area. This is the first step in that direction.

Liz Vanuza, Volkswagen of America Marketing Director

Through the VW website, a virtual community of customers has evolved; within this community, members can interact through the chat room, check for local events in the VW calendar, purchase merchandise and accessories in the VW store, read the online magazine 'Driver' and receive VW club benefits. The site has also been utilized to debut VW's new other media campaigns, inculding television, in an unprecedented move to create a fun and exciting brand even before it reaches the American airwaves. Customers to the website are alerted to the advertising campaigns through an e-mail directing them to log onto the website.

> *The advert lends itself well to the Web because it is completely visual with no dialogue... We know from our electronic dialogue with customers that there is a significant website audience who really connect with our advertising... This is an easy way to give this group a special preview.*
>
> Liz Vanuza, Volkswagen of America Marketing Director

Volkswagen of America have recognized the potential of the Internet in reaching new audiences and doing business; the future for VW on the Internet will clearly be leading the way for many others in the industry and it is anticipated that the future for the industry online will be a complete, all encompassing showroom, where consumers can purchase any car without leaving their computer screens, and as to collecting the vehicle – it can be organized online to be delivered.

Marketing transformation through virtual environments

Emergence of online communities

Consideration needs to be given to the fundamental principles of marketing and society within the digital age, in particular those issues related to social value, ethics and consumerism. Online communications, via the Internet, is driving the evolution of cyber-based communities – in both domestic and commercial environments. These changes in international communications are clearly at a relatively early stage of development and this raises issues, which are of a fundamental interest but also concern. Security and control are issues of prime importance to all existing and future participants in cyberspace because they have direct implications for both freedom and order. The Internet has evolved from a small specialist controlled to an online environment – both anarchic in nature and requiring new forms of marketing activities. The more recent rise of the World Wide Web (WWW), which is being driven by corporate acceptance and adoption, appears to be pushing towards the formalization of the Internet infrastructure in marketing applications.

The possibility of online marketing (http://e-commerce.vanderbilt.edu/), such as the one presented by the Internet, heralds a fundamental shifts in the experience of knowledge and behaviours. This Internet-led 'connectivity' enables new forms of interaction, in speed, scope and scale, and hence shifts the balance of the economics equation – by altering the nature of information asymmetries. The emergence of Internet technology has been utilized in a variety of ways from sole individuals to large businesses and from the associated relationships have emerged online communities. One profound impact emanating from these new relationships is in the formation of online communities (Hagel and Armstrong, 1997). Hagel and Armstrong (1997) highlight four categories of community (Figure 6.4):

- *Communities of transaction*: communities in which the core activity that brings together active participants is engagement in specific transactions.
- *Communities of interest*: communities in which participants share common inter-

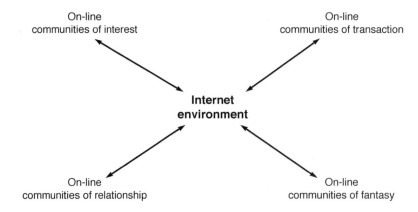

Figure 6.4 Online communities

est in some specific topic or concern. Typically these involve a higher degree of inter-personal communication.

- *Communities of fantasy:*comprise of individuals who indulge in an extensive level of make-believe and fantasy.
- *Communities of relationship* are created by the coming together of individuals who share similar experiences, world views and who wish to share these with like-minded people. Typically these communities are based on strong personal connection since the identities of individuals are often transparent.

Communities of interest

One way the Internet can facilitate sustainable development is through communities of interest. Communities of interest can bring together individuals who have expertise to closely monitor and scrutinize corporate activities. Such pools of experts often are in much stronger positions to investigate the veracity of corporate claims than the individual. This opens up the possibility of convening world-wide forums almost instantaneously thus enabling the formation of specialist colloquies able to question and challenge organizational expertise. Such online forums potentially can lead to pooling of expertise to the extent that they can out-reach even the biggest of corporations. In their discussion of the Intel-bug episode Badaracco and Useem state:

> ...Technical experts, therefore, will lend stakeholders legitimacy and power, for they know what they are talking about and they deserve to be listened to. The virtual team of mathematician and scientists who discovered the Pentium bug, documented its effects and later challenged Intel's assertions of probabilities and magnitudes believing their expertise and credibility matched or exceeded that of the Intel team that came up with the "one in nine billion" number and played down the bug's significance. Highly capable experts around the world were willing to spend time scrutinizing Intel's assumptions, rerunning its experiments,

challenging its conclusions and finally testing Intel at its own highly technical game, all with clear and detailed explanations (pp. 21–22).

In this new environment a shift in information promotes power to the stakeholders and allows them to weigh in on decisions to the benefit of society as a whole. Whilst the full ramifications were not predictable when the information revolution began, it has become increasingly clear that shifts in information handling and management holds profound implications over the governance of companies, at the individual, industry, nation and even global level. The revolution in governance and values sparked by incumbent communities can help to provoke corporations to fundamentally shift not only their business practices but their corporate cultures as well. Such shifts in the paradigms of handling information hold implications for the taxonomies, modes of discussion and analysis, as well as the search for solutions which are acceptable and aligned with the values of society (Chepaitis, 1997).

Communities of transaction

Another source force propelling online community based sustainability is that based around transactions. The Internet by facilitating direct interaction between the customer and corporation not only creates a virtual transaction market but also can be a vehicle of powerful consumerist activism. The Internet can be used to lend voice to the consumer by electronic means, especially in cases of discontentment or dis-satisfaction with the product/service of exchange. Consumers can now easily air their views by creating website consumer communities and then posting their views. This enables consumers not only to share their grievances, but also once posted the website can be the mechanism to accumulate the mass of evidence against the corporation. Without the emergence of such consumer websites it would be difficult if not impossible to build up sufficient momentum so as to induce corporate action, since contact between dis-satisfied consumers would be extremely difficult. The Internet however makes it possible to establish and collect concerns about the organizations product/service offering. The Internet thus endows and amplifies consumer voice.

The Internet by virtue of being an open and accessible platform of contact between the organization and individuals (customers, employees, shareholders, and all others with an interest in the company) becomes a forum for driving stakeholder accountability. The Internet in particular makes the organization more visible to outsiders. This transparency is the impetus towards ensuring that the organization monitors its activities much more carefully. The Internet however is not just a source of discordant expression from the consumer, it can in fact facilitate the corporation to listen into and respond sooner and more effectively to consumer concerns. Positively, the Internet can be used in several ways to build closer contact with customers. First by simply reading postings about the company and its product/service offering the company can gauge consumer opinion and sentiment. The Internet thus can act as a focus group barometer for marketing research. In fact such posting can provide richer and more contextually embedded information allowing companies to capture subtle shifts in trends.

The Internet offers the possibility to contact the consumer either as a community/group or as subgroups or even as an individual. This opens up the possibility for the organization to deal with issues as they arise both personally as well as on a global community level. The Internet thus helps to remove traditional layers and filters which often dampen and introduce 'noise' in the communications between the organization and its consumer. By peeling away the layers, better and more effective dialogue between the customer and organization can be stimulated and sustained.

Communities of relationship

Quite apart from specialist interest groups, the Internet enables establishment of communities who constantly monitor actions and activities of the organization world-wide. For example the corporate watch site (http://www.corpwatch.org) provides an impressive array of links to sites that acts as a transnational communication mechanism promoting decentralization of information and enhancing citizen democracy. The corporate watch site provides hot-links to sites all around the world. For example the emergence of an electronic watchdog is steadily but increasingly taking hold. Websites such as the corporate watch site focus and encourage specifically the monitoring of sustainability and ethical issues by online communities.

Communities of fantasy

Much of the community within this grouping deals with make-believe and virtual realities. However, not withstanding that as more and more individuals begin to experiment with virtual reality then the experiences stemming from these interactions will begin to shape attitudes, values, and moral perspectives. The effects could be both positive and negative. Positively fantasy based communities could be based on heightened sensitivity to an idealized state for mankind through a process of simulation. Negatively fantasy communities may easily degrade into a total absence of values leading to new levels of moral latitude and realism in all spheres.

CASE APPLICATION   **E-BAY: THE ONLINE TRADING COMMUNITY**

e-Bay was founded from an idea conceived from a passion at a time when the opportunities and possibilities of the Internet were only just beginning. Founders Pierre Omidyar and his wife recognized the need for a central location on the Internet to buy and sell unique items and to meet other consumers with similar interests and needs. e-Bay was launched on the Internet in September 1995 and quickly became the leading personal online trading community, pioneering a new market of person-to-person trading in an auction format over the Web.

e-Bay has successfully created an online community comprising of nearly 10 million registered users, interacting through mediums such as e-Bay café, bulletin boards. With more than 4000 categories and over 500 000 new items available every day, the story of e-Bay is one of major success. The vision of e-Bay, and a significant factor in their success is trust, between the buyers and sellers who constitute the community of e-Bay.

In addition to e-Bay users trading online, they are also provided with bulletin boards that enable them to interact, discuss topics of mutual interest and seek out information from others. The bulletin board encourages further communication between users. The sense of e-Bay community is strong in that a self policing policy operates, and users frequently form 'neighbourhood watch' groups to ensure against improper use of the site.

As reluctance to trading over the Internet is frequent and a barrier for many, e-Bay revolutionized e-commerce by developing and implementing the first electronic information exchange exclusive to one-to-one trading – The Feedback Forum. Through the innovative Feedback Forum, e-Bay users can submit comments regarding their dealings with other users. To safeguard users against fraud, e-Bay established SafeHarbor™, an in-house customer support team dedicated to providing a safe environment for users to trade with protection against fraud. Users of e-Bay are also supported by 24-h customer service representatives, 7 days a week via e-mail together with live real time support through e-Bay café.

e-Bay affiliations

In order to overcome e-Bay's primary limitation of shipping and mailing of goods purchased over the site, e-Bay formed a strategic relationship with E-Stamp in which e-Bay will promote E-Stamp exclusively on the website. The agreement provides E-Stamp with access to 10 million community members, in return members will be able to take advantage of a convenient way to purchase and ship merchandise.

We are committed to offering the e-Bay community a range of services that will make trading more convenient, efficient and add value to the core auction process.

President and CEO of e-Bay

The strategic relationship between e-Bay and E-Stamp illustrates the advantages of partnerships online and the benefits of the relationship to the communities of users. The future for companies such as e-Bay and E-Stamp will depend heavily upon further strategic partnerships.

Creation of virtual markets

The transition for some traditional marketplaces is now being realized through the growth of Internet-based environments. Marketspace is now a frequently used term to describe the new Internet environments. Rayport and Sviokla (1998) described virtual markets on the Internet as being where information is handled, processed and utilized, and where virtual chains are created through data networks. The viewpoint of Rayport and Sviokla (1998) is primarily based on the physical value chain driven by organizational business processes. The more virtual value creation activities are emerging through information processes. Virtual value creation then, clearly has a direct influence on actual activities through offering an information-supporting role.

Weiber and Kollman (1998) consider the new emerging virtual value chain and the changing role of information. The digital age has seen information functioning as a unique source of competitive advantage. Now virtual value chain activities in marketspace can operate completely independent of the physical value chain. Through the unprecedented speed of growth of the Internet a common value matrix is now emerging (see Figure 6.5) representing the interrelations between physical (marketplace) and virtual (marketspace) (Weiber and Kollman, 1998).

The online markets are creating a far more differentiated product and service offering. Interestingly many of the websites that may be viewed as market creators seem in many instances to transcend time related issues to typically accepted life cycles. A far more complex web structure of consumers is emerging due to global consumers with virtually real time information on product offerings and services. e-Bay represents an unusual phenomenon where both new and old are offered in a global marketspace. The auction environment provides complex interactivity and a 'flagship' for the development of interactive and dynamic websites. For further details on the emergence of online auctions as an emerging business model refer to Chapter 2.

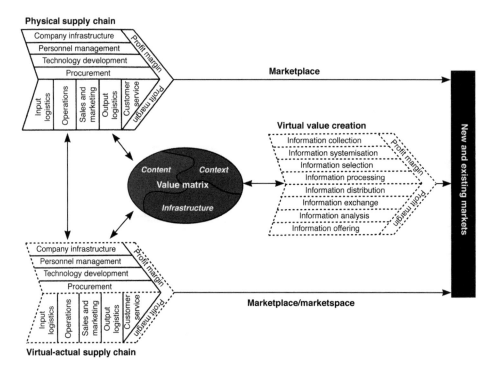

Figure 6.5   Emerging virtual value chain

Virtual marketing processes

The World Wide Web (WWW), with the adoption of hypermedia-based tools, is a superb method of communication. Already it is estimated that a WWW user has reference sources of phenomenal size at their fingertips. With such powerful search engines to locate information, this embryonic ultimate library is becoming an ideal and essential resource for business, consumers and researchers.

A pressing challenge for web users and developers is the need to move towards a more real time environment offering interactive communication rather than a more static traditional approach, which is being driven by broadcast marketing type principles. This is a view frequently proposed and seen as a natural progression – in the evolutionary principles of information – to the relevance to reality. Our ability to command and interact with information grows every day. Each day you are being presented with a mass of information via the news services such as radio, television, newspapers and in offices with computer systems providing internal information and more frequently also external information.

Successful virtual working requires the organization to adopt different approaches towards managing and leading in the following key areas: managing people, managing information, managing teams, managing processes, and managing facilities. The virtual community needs to adopt a central position of what is being viewed as a intermediary role in the Internet-based transaction (Figure 6.6; Kannan et al., 2000).

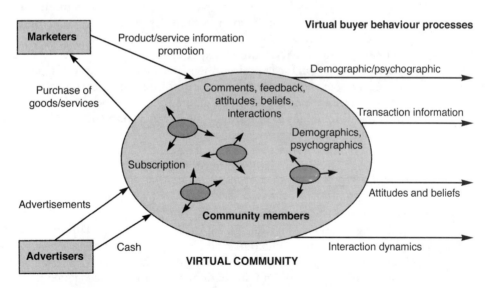

Figure 6.6   Virtual marketing processes (adapted from Kannan et al., 2000)

Evolution of buyer behaviour concepts on the World Wide Web

Transformation through B2B2C

The role of marketing thus moves from one of merely satisfying customer needs to a co-operative goal of facilitating the development of the market itself and which includes the consumer. Through the ever-increasing speed of product innovation, which is focused on the diversity and desire to purchase what is frequently perceived to be new products, the complexity of marketing solutions is increasing with the same vigour. The Internet, along with other computing technology, is increasingly viewed as a valuable and integral tool for the realization of such marketing activities to succeed. For example, the creation of strategic alliances is proposed to lead to the notion of an 'extended co-operation framework' (see Figure 6.8). The views proposed are intended to provide an interesting and possibly a broader perspective, which is focussed on changing buyer behaviour concepts through e-commerce. Table 6.1 provides an interesting comparison of the processes of buyer behaviour based on the traditional model and on the Internet.

The Web is a hypermedia environment that is incorporating interactivity with both people and computers and offering an alternative to real-world environments, where consumers frequently experience telepresence – the perception of being present in the mediated, as opposed to a real-world environment (Hoffman and Novak, 1996). Within virtual environments, both experiential (net surfing) and goal directed buying behaviours compete for consumer attention (see Figure 6.7). Consumer capabilities in such environments create new challenges and pose the issue of competency. This type of competency is related to 'flow' – the process of optimal experience. The optimal experience is achieved when a motivated consumer perceives a balance between their own challenges and the necessary skills for successful operational interaction in computer mediated environments.

The 'many to many' communications model proposed for the Internet creates fundamental changes to traditional one to many mass media advertising. For example, if one takes advertising approaches, which assume both passive and captive consumers, these are viewed in most instances as irrelevant on the Internet. Most marketing activities are still being driven by the 'one-to-many' mass communication model that presumes a 'passive mass audience' rather than a diversity of users seeking differing experiences. The role of marketing moves from 'satisfying the user' to one of 'explicitly including the user' through facilitating co-operation and integration (see Figure 6.8), e.g. strategic alliances. Through such an approach the evolution to 'mass customization' of products and services for various markets, is clearly around the corner for many homes and offices alike. For example, music will be delivered in unique individual styles for a heterogeneous consumer.

Reconstructing marketing for new buyer behaviour patterns

The Internet is being adopted by many organizations as a method of delivering new

Table 6.1 Consumer behaviour in the traditional marketplace and internet marketspace[a]

Buyer behaviour	Marketplace model	Marketspace model
Need recognition	Advertising presented in a strategically favourable way to relatively passive audiences as a means to stimulate demand	Advertising is accessed at the discretion of the consumer. The consumer is able to be integral to the advertising process and interact directly with the message
Information searching	Information searching in the traditional marketplace is time consuming and frequently expensive. The amount of effort put into the searching process is based on the risk levels involved in the purchase	In the marketspace information searching is extremely fast and inexpensive. Comparison shopping is simplistic and efficient with referrals easily available
Evaluation of alternatives	Being able to try products is critical for high risk products. Use of heuristics for many low involvement products	Products are frequently available on a trial basis through advances in technology. The internet has also seen the increase of free products
Purchase	The service encounter has a significant impact	Service encounter reduced and ease and functionality of e-commerce solution critical
Post-purchase evaluation	Post purchase experience affects consumer attitudes and as a consequence has an impact on the brand	The diffusion process is much faster in the marketspace due to the speed of communications and electronic communities driven by the Web and text-based newsgroups

[a] Adapted from O'Connor and O'Keefe (2000).

services and for many a means of bypassing intermediaries. Firstly, in developing such modes of delivery organizations are able to offer the same level of service to that provided through your traditional methods such as a salesperson or from a retail outlet. Secondly, Internet technologies are providing a distribution channel that enables an organization to personalize their interaction with customers and as a consequence improve associated customer relations and loyalty. Thirdly, the Internet provides an opportunity to develop a valuable new service, which is inexpensive and fast in terms of set up. Amway illustrates a website, which is dedicated to developing existing skills and knowledge of sales management for harnessing the dynamics of Internet technology.

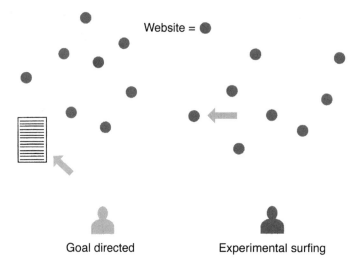

Figure 6.7   World Wide Web surfing

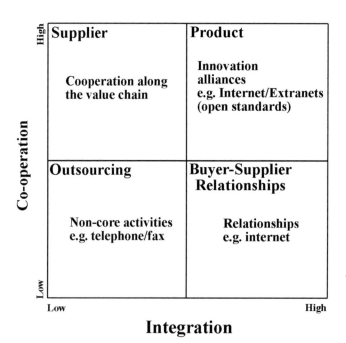

Figure 6.8   Reconstructing marketing networks

Many of the original structures that were constructed to facilitate e-commerce were characteristic of a basic community, bound by a very mechanical and linear perspective, with a common consciousness and set of values. These shared values primarily originated from the original core group of homogeneous Internet users, including academics, students and researchers. Today, the Internet is clearly a very different complexed web of people pursuing different goals that have evolved into more of a heterogeneous virtual community. This is currently transforming existing paradigms, creating new rules of co-operation and competition in the digital era.

Marketing professional need to focus on undertaking an active role in the construction of new organic paradigm forms for facilitating e-commerce, rather than perpetuating existing your mechanistic-type structures. Online services such Yahoo.com are becoming consumer gateways to the Web in meeting the needs of a very differentiated audience. Whatever form the new business models take, it is clear that the potential is enormous for marketing activities. This will be driven by the following:

- An infrastructure for e-commerce
- The medium's unique features
- Stimulating and exciting content rich environments.

As pioneering new companies in an industry begin to build electronic channels, such as Dell, CDNOW, Amazon Books, rivals will need to re-examine their value chains as indicated earlier. The computer industry is one of many examples where the success of businesses such as Dell computers is driving change in all the major competitors. For examples, organizations including Apple and Compaq have been forced to sell direct via the Internet, and this will clearly have direct implications on the established network of distributors. Many view such developments as necessary for their continued success and efficiency, but in many industries this will be at the expense of established distribution channels. The value chain is changing in many industries at an unprecedented speed for both distributors and manufacturers. There will be manufacturers who have the ability to engender speed and cost efficiency by going direct on the Internet, but in some industries the traditional distributors will be able to utilize their core skills in offering a flexible approach towards the pursuit of mass customization. Distributors, for example, in the electronics industry, could source components and in principle gather the parts overnight, deliver them to an assembly plant, pick up the assembled product, and deliver it to the customer. This raises further strategic implications where competition is even coming from outside the value chain.

The Web has increased the change in balance between the consumer and firm – a shift in the balance of power towards the consumer. The most effective forms of interaction between buyer and supplier tend to be collaborative in nature. E-business reflects a shift away from broadcasting a single communication to many consumers through adopting a more personalized approach to communications, which reflects more the consumers' diverse interests and needs. Customer interaction on the Web can be utilized in various ways, including:

- The design of new products

- The development of product and marketing strategies
- Innovative content.

The Internet provides a fast and efficient channel for enabling direct communication with customers or any participant on the value chain, but for the best practice organizations it is perceived as a communication driven by innovation and creativity management utilizing diverse and complex skills. Internet technology is driving the emergence of new forms of trade through fast and more complexed forms of sales management programs.

This is particularly relevant for information intensive products and frequently those products that are transferable across the Internet, for example software, music and the publishing industry. These types of industries in particular are in a position to create highly immersive virtual communities based on a framework of co-operation and integration. The case application of Groovetech provides an important illustration of a company that has developed a core service offering streaming music, which is totally market driven. The behaviour of consumers in dance clubs across the US and on the Internet is determining the streaming service which illustrates both integration and co-operation throughout the supply chain.

CASE APPLICATION

GROOVETECH: PORTAL TO THE UNDERGROUND MUSIC COMMUNITY

Groovetech is an *Internet-only* music station that provides listeners with live DJ mixes all around the world. They have created a centralized, global online community that represents all aspects of underground electronic dance music. It all began in 1995, as a local Internet site providing information on local clubs, events, as well as real audio mixes by local DJs. By 1996 Groovetech recognized the potential to provide a similar service to a global audience. The resulting website focussed on broadcasting underground dance music to dance music lovers across the digital world.

While many traditional radio stations already broadcast online, simultaneously streaming their regular programmes on the Internet, a new breed of pure web entities like Groovetech is growing.

Rather than just streaming music over the Internet, Groovetech has also embraced the endless possibilities to sell music over the Internet and to create a virtual community of dance music enthusiasts across the globe.

The listening lab

Groovetech aims to allow visitors the opportunity to browse through the Groovetech catalogue of dance music and listen to samples through RealPlayer. The listening lab is equipped with a searching utility to look for specific labels, genres, artists, song titles etc.... Visitors are able to purchase CDs through the browsing facility on the site.

As Groovetech's website has no advertising, and its webcast plays commercial-free sets, the only revenue stream stems from sales of hard-to-find dance music through the Groovetech store. This is also the Internet business model anticipated for the foreseeable future. Jon Cunningham, Groovetech's president did indicate that:

Groovetech may consider adding some sponsorship in the future.

Live streaming

Dance music consumers can access real time music over the web through Groovetech. Dance clubs throughout the US have registered with Groovetech, providing live 24 h webcastings of DJs from specialist clubs. Utilizing RealPlayer streaming capabilities visitors are also provided with a schedule of DJs for a number of US radio stations and clubs, allowing them to choose whom they would like to tune into. Groovetech not only streams real time broadcasts but also displays on a web cam, the DJ mixing the music. As Groovetech broadcasts real time performance from DJs, visitors globally can tune in, in different time zones to the 2-h sets.

The Groovetech community

The success of Groovetech is highly dependent of the community it creates, in order to encourage interaction between members; a bulletin board and chat room can be found on the site. The bulletin board allows members to display notices regarding concerts, comments on other members' concerts, etc. To display a notice on the bulletin board no membership is required, however to gain access and chat in the chat room with other members, membership to the site is required.

Areas of concern within the online music industry

While the number of audio content providers is growing, online listenership remains relatively small. Groovetech will not disclose the size of their audience, but the figure is estimated at less than 10 000. A direct competitor of Groovetech, Seattle's KING-FM, a pioneer in Internet broadcasting, claims only to have 8 000 webcast listeners a day. Groovetech however appear undeterred with this statistic and continue to broadcast to a global audience.

Such a small listenership can be contributed to the accessing capabilities across the Internet of the audience and substitute competitors. In addition many potential listeners, a large percentage of dance music fans, lack the fast computers and dedicated high-speed Internet connections needed to enjoy Groovetech and web radio.

There's a glaring dichotomy: old-fashioned radio is 'free and accessible to everyone' while web radio has a somewhat exclusive audience, those who can afford the latest computer technology.
Cathy Valentine-McKinney, The Puget Sound Radio Broadcasters Association

Without innovators such as Groovetech who provide an invaluable service for dance music consumers around the globe, regardless of market size, catering to the needs of a minority and retaining their originality of vision, new emerging markets and specialist global communities would never be realized.

Hypermedia support for new media based buyer behaviour

We will now consider the relevance of hypermedia software tools in the development and evolution of interface design for marketing solutions. It is evident that hypermedia supports collaborative working practices and in principle is viewed as integral to the success of interactive marketing or what is frequently called 'one-to-one' marketing. The Internet, as with internal computer networks, is process driven and as a consequence is viewed as an enabler of collaboration and improved communications. As intra- and inter-organizational boundaries shift, the Internet will adjust to reflect the changing working practices. More than that, it appears these collaborative axiomatic hypermedia tools, such as the World Wide Web can be used to augment heterogeneous communications for personalized buyer behaviour. For the purpose of this chapter, Figure 6.9 outlines a hypermedia support framework that considers Internet applications in the context of the exchange process and the level of interactivity from specific software applications. The proposed framework provides a useful overview for evaluating the impact of Internet applications on buyer behaviour patterns. Developing one-to-one marketing with consumer technology needs allows a business to focus on the top half of the framework.

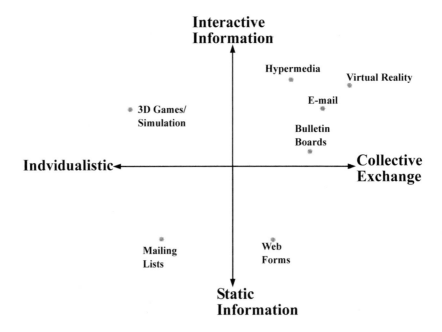

Figure 6.9   Hypermedia support framework

First, it is important to clarify our basic understanding of the term hypermedia support tools. In a broad sense hypermedia support tools are viewed as incorporating multimedia applications in the pursuit of a fluid and dynamic approach to retrieving and presenting information. The term hypermedia is the principle approach adopted by current Internet browsers such as Netscape Communicator and Microsoft Explorer. Wide ranges of hypermedia applications are currently available and viewed to be integral to traditional business information systems applications. Hypermedia is the primary medium for global communication dispersion driven primarily through the late 1990s to current times.

One of the biggest challenges arising from the dramatic growth of the Internet and the World Wide Web is to enable effective interactive online commercial trade and global communications. In addition to technological developments, emerging online communities are driving the development of Internet technology, which supports the needs of participants. Hypermedia, offering a fluid and dynamic approach, is clearly an outcome of such developments, which supports the need for organizations to be flexible and responsive to volatile and turbulent market conditions. The fundamental outcome of online communities is the disappearance of geographical boundaries. The Internet offers a unique medium for communications, with no geographical boundary or "tyranny of distance" to overcome. The evolution of Internet communications has developed through e-mail, newsgroups and now into a hypermedia-based approach which will continue to progress with the addition of 3D virtual space.

Traditionally, product innovation specialists for example use a variety of media (drawings, models, text, specifications, and verbal) for communications and documenting new and incremental developments in design. Advances in information technology, such as high-resolution screens, digital compression, memory capacity, microprocessor speed, and international standards, offers the potential for true integration and manipulation of information. The use of hypermedia support tools is becoming integral to the development of CAD applications, allowing designers to potentially create hypermedia files. Hypermedia files have the potential to document design instances and as a consequence support task oriented business processes. In the context of R&D the use of media-rich documents can aid designers to understand abstract concepts but also provide a mechanism for improved communications between functions and with the consumer (see Figure 6.10).

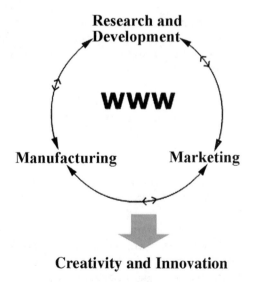

Figure 6.10   Process of innovation and creativity on the Web

How can such hypermedia support tools enable organizations to utilize effectively value added information from the Internet for improved communications in the decision making and control processes undertaken throughout a diverse range of roles? The use of hypermedia documents allows the user to address such a question in terms of two important aspects of collaboration and communications. First, the specialization associated within many decision support roles, which makes collaboration a necessity, contributes to difficulties encountered in communications. Such a proposition illustrates the tension, for many, between integration and differentiation. The use of hypermedia-based documents, via integrated networks both internally and on the wider Internet, offers the opportunity to overcome cultural differences between functional specialists in assisting users to understand abstract concepts. Secondly, hypermedia offers the opportunity for the integration of software tools used during business processes, for example in the design processes. The processes involved in product design for example require a complex system which incorporates the use of CAD packages, specialist analysis software, scheduling software, plus financial programs. The complexity of such systems makes it desirable to establish links to these documents from one single hypermedia-based interface, providing a balance between attaining some degree of integration but maintaining a level of specialization. Typically via the use of a company's Extranet the consumer can also follow and participate in every stage of the development process of a product. As a consequence buyer behaviour patterns are being driven in many industries through the emergence of collaborative marketing networks.

Applying such principles to the wider sphere of business process management and the Internet is taking a somewhat simplistic view, but it does illustrate the need for research into the relevance and potential importance of hypermedia as a serious business tool. Some challenges and opportunities can be drawn out in the pursuit of new buyer behaviour directions through virtual communities. The key issues identified for success are: computer infrastructure, internationally recognized standards, shared working environments, and new software applications for community building.

Computer infrastructure and bandwidth: most 3D-based computer networks can currently support large numbers of users. This in principle this seems more than adequate but consider educational environments or interactive news services, as typical examples of 3D applications, which constantly demand more bandwidth for higher resolution visuals and unprecedented growth in users. Understanding computer network architecture, scaling, and bandwidth (amount of information a network can transmit from one point to another) trade-offs is clearly very important to sustain an Internet environment that can meet consumer needs and expectations.

Acceptance of international information technology standards: the Internet's viability and current success has been based on accepted international standards and increasingly open source solutions. The speed and direction of a wide-ranging mix of information technology developments, in particular the open source movement, is anticipated to shape hypermedia and communications development.

Shared working environments: as online communities mature, the demand for shared state (space/rooms, objects) will increase significantly and drive both inter-activity processes and hypermedia tools.

New applications for online communities: current e-commerce will shift towards more information rich consumer groups or what is frequently being called virtual communities. The specialist hypermedia-based communities, will develop with the computing technology and gradually evolve into more 3D oriented space.

Conclusion

The creation of new buyer behaviour patterns through virtual communities is being realized – in both consumer and industrial markets – through the wide use of hypermedia-based software applications across the Internet. As a consequence one-to-one marketing is now becoming a reality for many organizations. The Internet has speeded up many existing marketing initiatives in an attempt to meet individual customer demands, such as direct marketing through database applications. A global e-commerce infrastructure has enabled online ordering to become a reality in both consumer and business-to-business markets with individuals and organizations being able to customize products and services to meet individual offerings. New hypermedia support tools through the World Wide Web are providing a dynamic but most importantly user-friendly interface to the Web.

Checklist

1. Unique forms of interaction including machine-interaction and human-interaction, respectively, have contributed to the rapid diffusion of the Web as a commercial medium for trade.
2. While for traditional media it is frequently said, 'the medium is the message' with the Web it is true that 'the medium is the market'.
3. Market segmentation is central to interactive marketing activities of the Web if organizations are going to realize one-to-one marketing.
4. The Internet continues to evolve into complex heterogeneous virtual communities which through organic growth is viewed as being fluid in nature.
5. Marketing needs to undertake a proactive role in the construction of new organic paradigms for facilitating commerce in the emerging electronic society.
6. The Web increases the power of the consumer and decreases the power of the firm, compared to traditional channels of distribution along the supply chain.
7. The new model underlying marketing in a hypermedia CME (Computer Mediated Environment) like the Web is a many-to-many mediated communications modelling with which individuals can interact with the medium.
8. The Web is a virtual hypermedia environment incorporating interactivity between people and computers. The Web is not a simulation but an alternative communications driven environment.

References

Chepaitis, E. (1997), Information ethics across information cultures. *Business Ethics, A European Review*, 6 (4), pp. 195–200.

Engel, J.F., Blackwell, R.D. and Miniard, P.W. (1990), *Consumer Behaviour*, Drydon Press.

Hagel, J. and Armstrong, A. (1997), *Net Gain: Expanding Markets Through Virtual Communities*, Harvard Business School Press, Boston, MA.

Hoffman, D.L. and Novak, T.P. (1996), A new marketing paradigm for electronic commerce. *Journal of Marketing*.

Kannan, P.K., Chang, A. and Whinston, A.B. (2000), *Handbook of Electronic Commerce*, Springer, New York.

O'Connor, G.C. and O'Keefe, R.O. (2000), *Handbook of Electronic Commerce*. Springer, New York.

Rayport, J.F. and Sviokla, J.J. (1994), Managing in the marketspace. *Harvard Business Review*, Nov–Dec, pp. 141–150.

Weiber, R. and Kollman, T. (1998), Competitive advantages in virtual markets – perspectives of information-based marketing in cyberspace, *European Journal of Marketing*, 32 (7/8).

Further reading

Borgmann, A. (1995), Information and reality at the turn of the century, *Design Issues*, 11 (2).

Davenport, T.H. and Pearlson, K. (1998), Two cheers for the virtual office. *Sloan Management Review*, Summer.

Watson, R.T., Akelsen, S. and Pitt, L.F. (1998), Building mountains in the flat landscape of the World Wide Web, *California Management Review*, 40 (2).

PART 3

Managing your customer through e-commerce

CHAPTER 7

Supply chain management for Internet commerce

After studying the chapter you will be able to:

- Identify the changing trends and directions of web-based supply chain management.
- Understand the different supply chain applications of the Internet.
- Describe new forms of buyer–supplier interactivity emerging from virtual sourcing.
- Critically evaluate the implications of new virtual supply chain initiatives.

Recently, physical distribution has been expanded into the broader concept of supply chain management. Supply chain management starts earlier than physical distribution, attempting to procure the right inputs (raw materials, components and capital equipment); convert them efficiently into finished products, and dispatch them to the final destinations (Bowersox and Closs, 1996). An even broader perspective calls for studying how the company's suppliers themselves obtain their inputs all the way back to the raw materials. The supply chain perspective can help a company identify superior suppliers and help them to improve their productivity in the supply chain, which ultimately would bring down the company's costs (PRTM Consulting, 1994).

The task of companies, who are managing information and product flows from suppliers to ultimate users involves the co-ordinating of activities of suppliers, purchasing agents, manufacturers, marketers, channel members and customers (Harland, 1996). Information systems play a critical role in managing the supply chain. Major gains in supply chain efficiency have resulted from information technology advances; particularly computers, point-of-sale terminals, uniform product codes, satellite tracking, Electronic Data Interchange (EDI), and Electronic Funds Transfer (EFT).

Structural and supply chain redesign issues

A supply chain encompasses all activities associated with the flow and transformation of goods from the raw materials stage (extraction), through to the end user as well as the associated information flows (Handfield and Nichols, 1998).

The design of a supply chain involves four design decisions. These decisions are the choice of actors in the supply chain, governance mechanisms in the chain, structuring (i.e. sequencing order) of the activities in the chain, and the choice of co-ordination structures in the chain. While some of these decisions are the result of natural production and delivery processes (e.g. beer cannot be brewed unless the barley is grown, or it cannot be loaded on a ship unless it has arrived on the dockside) or are strategically fundamental to the chain(e.g. for brand image reasons, unlike Carlsberg which is brewed close to destination, Heineken is brewed only in the Netherlands), other decisions are a matter of design and thus, theoretically at least, under the control of the designer of the supply chain. Moreover, these decisions are interrelated. For example, the choice of a totally vertically integrated governance structure precludes free choice of actors outside the ownership of the firm, while the choice of a market mechanism at every supply chain link would limit the design to 'dyadic co-ordination' at the buyer–supplier interface.

The first design dimension is the level of dynamism in the choice of actors in the chain. Static chains are chains where the partners in the chain are relatively established. On the other hand, in a completely dynamic chain, the partners in the chain can vary from one market opportunity to another market opportunity. While a vertically integrated chain indicates a high level of inflexibility in the choice of the actors (you only get to choose from whom your company owns or is willing to acquire) markets provide the ultimate flexibility in the choice and deployment of actors. In between, different levels of relationships (Lambert et al., 1996) provide intermediate levels of flexibility in the choice of supply chain partners.

The need for co-ordination

The governance decision deals with the ownership of various actors in the supply chain. A different actor (or organizational unit) performs each activity or step in the chain. If all the actors belong to the same organization, the chain is vertically integrated. On the other extreme, each actor performing a different activity may be completely independent from the others operating at an arm's length relationship. In between are different grades or levels of relationships that may exist between the various actors in the chain (Lambert et al., 1996).

Transaction cost economics (Williamson, 1981) suggests that, in those cases where co-ordination costs between the actors are likely to be high, organizations tend substitute co-ordination by hierarchy, thus creating vertically integrated chains. On the other hand, vertical integration implies that not all activities in the chain may benefit through economies of scale and specialization, thereby increasing the production costs associated with the entire chain. The governance of the chain thus depends on the balance achieved between the transaction costs and the production costs inherent in the chain. In those situations where high co-ordination costs are of primary concern, chains tend to be vertically integrated and governance is through hierarchy. On the other hand, when high production costs are unacceptable and need to be reduced, the governance is by procurement through markets. Use of Internet technologies can influence both production costs and co-ordination costs.

The structure of the supply chain (i.e. its sequencing) is usually determined by the natural sequence of processes inherent in the manufacturing process (Lee et al., 1997). The structure is often a consequence of chance, previous history, habit, limitations of the communication media, and limitations of the co-ordination mechanisms. Finally, co-ordination in the supply chain is based upon the flow of co-ordinating information:

> One important mechanism for co-ordination in a supply chain is the information flows among members of the supply chain. (Lee et al., 1997).

Co-ordination occurs through the communication of orders for goods and services, and notifications that the goods ordered are being shipped. Through long-established convention, information flows in traditional supply chains have been primarily dyadic (i.e. between the supplier and the buyer) and follow the same path as the physical supply chain flows (for a recent example of dyadic co-ordination information flows following the same path as the supply chain. Thus, orders flow upstream from buyers to suppliers, while notifications of shipments flow downstream from suppliers to the buyers, usually together with the physical shipment itself. Again, owing to long established custom, as in the cases of bills-of-lading, loading manifests, or airway bills, the information flows are normally bundled together with the physical flows and travel on the same carrier as the physical shipment.

However, these customary information flow paths may impose delays, limitations, and constraints that may reduce the efficiency, effectiveness, and the responsiveness of the supply chain. For example, a shipping manifest that arrives with the ship means processing delays in the wharf, while the shipping manifest documents are delivered and processed by the various authorities before the unloading sequence can be planned and unloading proceed. Or consider a co-ordination situation where each actor in the supply chain orders its requirements from its immediate upstream member of the chain. In this situation, dramatically illustrated by the famous 'beer game' (Forrester, 1961) inbound orders from downstream members serve as a co-ordination input to system inventory and production decisions. Lee et al. (1997) show that information transferred in forms of sequential orders tends to become distorted and can misguide upstream members in their production and inventory decisions. This distortion increases and variance accumulates as one moves upstream, creating a 'bullwhip effect'. This effect is a consequence of the sequential communication and co-ordination structure inherent in the chain and can easily be avoided if alternative communication and co-ordination paths are designed and implemented.

The potential role of the Internet

The Internet has the potential to transfer complex (i.e. design) information accurately and to reduce the delays as information passes up and down the supply chain. Given that individual suppliers have established rapid design response capabilities networked systems provide the ability to give a concerted and rapid response to the client.

Existing models of electronic commerce tend to focus on catalogue publication and retail (or retail-like) sale of products and services. Although this has been a very successful area of development there are a myriad other ways in which businesses interact and models of open electronic commerce need to develop to address these other relationships (Riggins and Rhee, 1998).

Catalogues and brokering

A 'web presence' seems to be incumbent on any organization that does not wish to be seen as backward or out of date. This inevitably involves laying out one's wares for inspection in some sort of corporate profile or presentation of goods and services. However, the maintenance of an up-to-date catalogue showing the full range of products or services on offer is a non-trivial task for all but the smallest and most stable of enterprises. At present, many just give a showcase or selection of their best work and products, relying on more conventional communication to display their full capabilities and close a deal.

General product catalogue services are also developing. In retail business, there has been a movement to trading via the network using simple purchase and payment models (O'Connor and O' Keefe, 1997). This deceptively simple change seems to be little more than that which occurs when one changes to using catalogue shopping instead of visiting the store. However, the limited and transient nature of the human computer interface violates the analogy, significantly inhibiting the customer's cognitive process when choosing a product. Morar and Patel (1999) discuss the impact of this change and through simple case studies, argue how its negative effects may be overcome with appropriate virtual environment models.

Internet trade is not without its problems for the supplier. Baldwin and Currie (1999) explore several issues of interoperability, building trust, confidence and security, and the need for a regulatory and legal framework. These must be forced by organizations that accept the challenge of developing supply chain management in an Internet environment. Although complex business networks already exist these issues arise because the Internet has no single owning or regulating body, unlike the earlier networks with limited access where one body had the power to resolve many of these issues by fiat.

Much of this work is well under way. The basic brokerage architecture has been expounded in projects like ABS (ABS, 1997) and CORBA (Infowin, 1996) and specific issues are being addressed. For example, secure payment (Asokan et al., 1997a; Abad-Peiro et al., 1998) and fair transaction models (Asokan et al., 1997b) have been developed in the SEMPER project (Lacoste, 1997) which has also addressed issues such as contract signature. These issues are important in the re-engineering the supply chain but they form a backdrop rather than the focus of the research.

Trading in marketspace

Virtual commercial environments are operating in cyberspace, where information is the 'life blood' of business processes, and through which virtual supply chains have emerged. Venktrannan and Henderson (1998) talk of an evolution from marketplace to marketspace. The internet for many offers new modes of commercial trade and communications. In considering the elements of value creation in marketspace, it is important to note that the context of transactions is fundamentally different to marketplace transactions. AOL along with many other internet-based organizations, such as Netscape, have a much more disaggregated content, context and infrastructure for trading than that often associated with the marketplace.

Virtual organizing on the Internet

The Internet increases the richness of communications through greater interactivity between the firm and the customer (Watson et al., 1998). There is a diverse range of possibilities, via the emergence of online Internet-based environments, which create unprecedented change bringing both product and market uncertainty and as a consequence new market challenges. As we approach the millennium there are radical web-based changes that are transforming many industries: from publishing to computing; from financial services to airlines, and from car manufacture to education (Hamel, 1998). The revolution in trading is no more profound than in the supply of music, which is the subject of discussion in the next section.

Case illustration of supply chain management for music

A traditional supply chain for music is shown in Figure 7.1. The power and control of the supply chain is very much in the hands of the record company. The company is in control of much of the distribution and also supplier selection. This is very much based on the quality of the music, past reputation and contract fee (price). The artist is very much under the control of the record

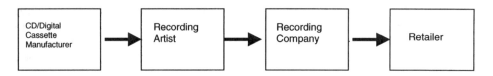

Figure 7.1   Traditional music industry supply chain

company for promotion, merchandise and the distribution of CDs and digital cassettes.

Recently, computer fans have been downloading music from the Internet on to home computers via a controversial technology called MP3, a method for creating compressed digital audio files. Developed by MEPG or Moving Picture Experts Group (http://drogo.cselt.stet.it/mpeg/), MP3, or MPEG 1 Layer 3 as it is technically known, is a way of compressing audio tracks, resulting in an incredible reduction in the original size of the track with minimal loss of quality. This makes it possible to take CDA files off a CD, convert them to MP3 and make them available for downloading. The threat of piracy and loss of royalties has outraged the music industry, so much that they are currently working on MP4, which is a new format that offers equivalent compression and quality benefits to that of MP3 and we return to evaluate both later in this chapter.

Figure 7.2 highlights the way the Internet (MP3) is changing the design from a tiered supply chain to a network. The artist has become more independent of the record company. The artist can negotiate the supply of CDs and digital cassettes directly through the website of a manufacturer. The development of MP3 and MP4 also provides an artist with the opportunity to deal directly with the customer

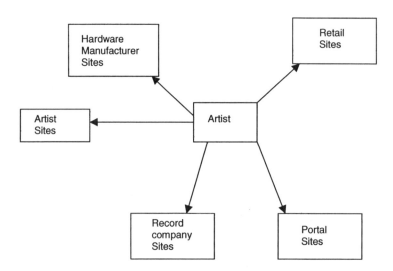

Figure 7.2   The modern music supply chain (dynamic supply web)

(e.g. Public Enemy are using the technology to release their latest recording tracks).

Retail sites (cdnow.com, amazon.com, samgoody.com) offer the supply of digital song files directly to customers. Record companies partner with e-commerce sites to sell music in proprietary formats or via approved third-party copyright-friendly codes, including Liquid Audio, a2b, or MS Audio. Playback devices are now compatible with all the major codecs.

Portal sites like iuma.com bypass the traditional record companies by offering pop fans the chance to download free music by independent artists from its website iuma.com which are featured in Figure 7.3 hope to vastly increase the number of musicians, who are able to make a living from their creativity and to liberate the next generation of artists from the dominance of big record companies. These artists will not receive income from the sale of recordings, but from a variety of other sources including publishing, fan clubs, merchandising and touring.

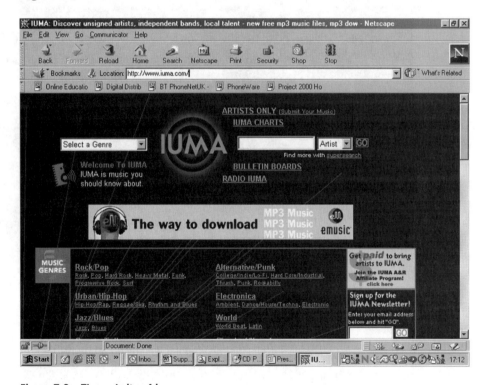

Figure 7.3   The website of iuma.com

Hardware manufacturers (Diamond, Saehan, Samsung) produce portable audio and video players that can connect directly to the Net – side-stepping a PC. As bandwidth gets better and codecs improve, consumers will have the facility to download full-length feature films (clickmovies.com) to home theatres, portable devices, and audio entertainment systems.

Major labels (polygram.com, bmg.com, and virginrecords.com) offer 'memberships' – for a fee; consumers can download a fixed number of songs for playback on a PC or a portable device or to be burned onto a CD. The website of virginrecords.com is presented to illustrate this 'membership' emphasis in Figure 7.4. Audio files are distributed in proprietary codecs that include watermarking to track piracy and encryption to limit the number of times a song can be copied and played.

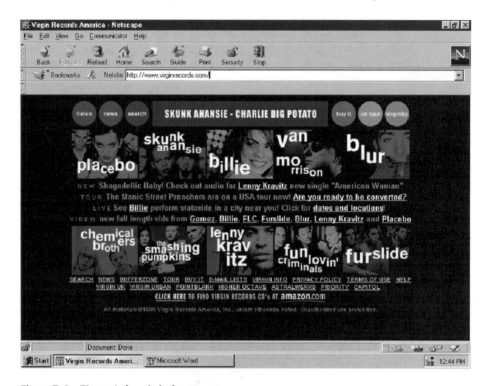

Figure 7.4   The website of virgin.com

Artists (beastieboys.com, aerosmith.com, therollingstones.com) sell CDs and singles as digital files directly to consumers who can download music in several formats, including MP3, Liquid Audio, a2b, MS Audio, or G2. The website of 'The Rolling Stones' presented in Figure 7.5 is a good illustration of a proactive group on the Internet. Copyright protections are built in with watermarking, and songs can be played on several new hardware and software devices. Customers can also listen to samples in streaming audio before buying.

The proliferation of ways in which people can buy music is likely to substantially increase the size of the music business. This increase will come in part because the

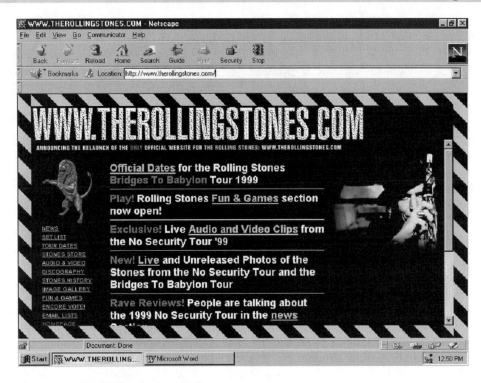

Figure 7.5   The Rolling Stones website

Internet opens up music publishers' back catalogues. Currently, people frequently leave record shops empty-handed because the music they would like to buy is either out of stock or deleted. With virtual inventory, music will be always available to be manufactured for the customer.

Even with the expansion of the music market, retailers and publishers face uncertainties, not least through piracy. The computer industry is attempting to protect publishers from the abuse of copyright by sophisticated surveillance of the Internet and by the development of MP4, which is licensed by Global Music (http://mp4.globalmusic.com) and a2b technology (http://www.a2bmusic.com), The real problem with a technology like MP4 as far as the Internet community is concerned is that there is no open development – it is a locked technology. For the music industry this obviously eradicates the piracy issue but for the Internet community, who are now used to the openness of MP3, this is a major shortfall and may be directly responsible for the much anticipated demise of MP4.

Virtual sourcing

Effective contracting for complementary capabilities going through a network of suppliers and subcontractors is a characteristic of virtual organizing. Quinn et al.

(1997) describes Nike as a model for effective sourcing of manufacturing competencies: 'Nike is basically a research, design, and marketing company – outsourcing 100 per cent of its athletic footwear manufacturing to numerous production partners abroad'. As corporations refocus on their core competencies and move away from vertical integration, they will aim to obtain complementary assets through interfirm relationships. For example, confectionery companies like Nestle, Mars and others get their packaging from leading packaging and printing companies. Nike and Reebok get their shoes, based on their proprietary designs, manufactured by leading Asian contractors. Dell's success is attributed to its superior sourcing strategy.

For more than a decade, the power of Electronic Data Interchange (EDI) has supported the ability to efficiently source products and services. Wal-Mart pioneered a new retail model by leveraging a sophisticated EDI network with its suppliers to radically lower its inventory level. EDI has had a significant role in reducing inventory levels in supply chains within consumer products (Proctor and Gamble, Kraft General Foods), athletic shoes (Nike, Reebok), apparel (Gap, Benetton) and computers (Dell, Gateway). The Web is enhancing the ability of the buyer to source standard products even further. Boise Cascade Office Products (www.bcop.com) has deployed an extranet for its largest 600 corporate customers. Dell is selling more than $3 billion in computers over the Web mainly to corporate customers like Shell and Boeing.

In the US General Electric's Trading Process Network (TPN) started as a service to streamline GE's procurement of standard products within GE Lighting. It has now expanded to cover a broader range of business units. The network links more than 2500 GE trading partners and accounts for more than $1 billion of procurement in 1997. By initial estimates, TPN has reduced the procurement-cycle time by 50%, procurement process costs by 30%, and actual material costs by 20%. GE is expected to source more than $5 billion of procurement annually through TPN by 2000.

Companies, irrespective of their line of business, have always relied on their suppliers for providing components and parts in terms of services, goods and products on time every time at the right quality and cost. Throughout the last few decades new philosophies like Just In Time (JIT), Total Quality Management (TQM), 5Ss and others have increased the level of dependency of (client) companies on their suppliers. This can be observed in the manufacturing sector in terms of early supplier involvement in developing new products, the on-site and in (assembly) line delivery of products with virtually no defects allowed and the continuous strive for reduced prices.

The creation of organizational integration mechanisms on the Internet such as discussion groups, web forums, video conferencing, and virtual multi-functional teams encourages the adoption of a more integrated approach throughout the supply chain. The globalization of industries, is making it imperative for a supplier, to have access to a wide range of external technological services, such as the Internet and other complimentary online networks, in order to operate effectively. They must have access to electronic capabilities using fibre optics, high-speed digital switches, satellite downlinks and compatible EDI ensuring reliable, efficient information flows among suppliers, manufacturers, and distributors while protecting proprietary data. Shared resources, such as harmonized electronic transfer across transportation modes and onsite education and training facilities, will also help companies improve their supply chain management in the emerging marketspace. Even small and medium-sized enterprises increasingly now relying on international networks of suppliers, distributors, and customers, frequently via the Internet in order to improve global competitiveness by reducing fixed and operating costs.

Clearly, with the passage of time additional sourcing possibilities may emerge through the Internet medium. Online sourcing of digitized information lends itself to the Internet. Info-Search, a prepaid library service, is a prime example. This service permits the user to access and search numerous periodicals in a variety of ways. Security and copyright infringement issues notwithstanding, other possibilities include various types of raw and processed data, market research information, designs and prototypes and quotation proposals.

CASE APPLICATION   ### LEADING AIRLINES IN WEB VENTURE

Nine of the world's largest airlines said yesterday they would link up with MyAircraft, the trade exchange owned by three of the biggest aerospace suppliers, to create the industry's leading procurement site potentially handling up to $75 billion worth of business.

The airlines including the three big US carriers – American Airlines, United and Delta – and British Airways and Air France, will merge their proposed Internet procurement venture with the existing MyAircraft exchange, set up by United Technologies, Honeywell International and BF Goodrich. The new site, which will be jointly owned by the 13 participants, plans to offer products ranging from aircraft spares and engineering fuel to in-flight meals and stationery. This is thought to be the first time that buyers and sellers have joined forces in a trade exchange in any industry. The move was widely expected, as analysts have predicted a shake-out of the various exchanges to create a single electronic marketplace in each industry.

The two other main procurement exchanges in aviation and aerospace are Exostar, centred around four of the big primary contractors – Boeing, Lockheed Martin, Raytheon and BAE Systems – and AeroXchange. AeroXchange is made up of 13 airlines, including Lufthansa, FedEx, Japan Airlines, Cathay Pacific and Singapore Airlines.

The new site could ultimately handle the 13 companies' combined $75 billion annual procurement budget, putting it slightly ahead of Exostar's potential $71 billion spend.

The venture, which is due to be named later this year, is expected to go live with initial offerings in the first quarter of 2001.

Source: Mark Odell. Financial Times, Friday October 27, 2000, p. 16.

CASE APPLICATION

SIEMENS TO LAUNCH $1 BILLION NETWORK

Siemens, the electronics and engineering group, yesterday announced a $1 billion (£600 million) investment programme that will put all its operations, from procurement to marketing and development on a single electronic network.

The move envisages the use of auctions in the procurement process mirroring a development that has taken place among e-commerce marketplaces in the US. Investors welcomed the news as evidence that Siemens was accelerating its transition from a mainstay of Germany's 'old economy' into a company concentrating on value-added, high technology products and services.

The switch to e-business will initially save Siemens about 1–2% in annual sales volume, growing 3–5% in the medium term, according to Siemens chairman (Mr von Pierer). About 70% of the group's activities are already electronically networked.

Analysts expect Siemens to report revenues of about £74 billion in the year ended on September 30. That suggests initial savings could amount to about £1 billion. Siemens intends to increase the volume of electronically processed procurement from 10% to more than 50% of the group's total procurement spending of £35 billion.

SBS, one of the group's fastest growing units, is Europe's third largest provider of IT consultancy services behind IBM and Cap Gemini, according to analysts at Goldman Sachs. It is expected to achieve sales of about £5.8 billion in the 1999–2000 business year, up 61% from £3.6 billion in 1998–1999). Shares in Siemens were 1.4% higher in Frankfurt, trading at £143.48.

Source: Tony Barber, Siemens to launch £1 billion network. Financial Times, Wednesday October 11, 2000, p. 27.

Supplier sourcing decision

In the traditional approach to supplier sourcing it is highly unlikely that every potential candidate supplier will be considered. There are two main reasons for this. First, organizations do not have perfect market information and hence cannot be aware of all the potential suppliers who may be best able to fulfil a particular order requirement. Even if near-perfect information were available the process of mutually selecting the most appropriate from a pool of thousands would be overwhelming. Second, there is a tendency for organizations to deal with suppliers with whom they have had satisfactory dealings in the past. While this is understandable, it can mean the most appropriate supplier for a particular need is overlooked. With customers demanding better quality, lower cost products, organizations must be prepared to be more dynamic in the process of supplier sourcing if they are to remain competitive.

While the number of suppliers having a presence on the Internet is growing rapidly, buyers have an enormous global supplier base accessible through a single computer connected to an Internet Service Provider (ISP). With many ISPs, particularly in the UK now offering free connection (e.g. www.freeserve.co.uk (BT's Surftime), www.ntl.com), the cost implications for using the Internet as a medium for supplier sourcing is negligible. There are however several difficulties with this approach which will to be discussed in the next sub-section.

Practical difficulties of web-based sourcing

There is first, the issue of training procurement personnel to navigate the Internet effectively. The most common way to find information on the Internet is to use one of the many search engines specifically designed for this purpose. To find relevant Web sites a user has to construct a string which is used by the search engine to examine its index of key words. In the case of supplier sourcing such a string would typically include the type of product sought and the quantity required. Constraints such as the maximum delivery lead times and the highest price payable would also need to be included. Many 'novice' Internet users find difficulty in constructing a search string which returns all possible candidate sites whilst leaving out irrelevant sites. The reasons for this include a lack of formal training in information science and an unfamiliarity with the use of Boolean operators to construct search strings. Furthermore, it is estimated that even the most powerful search engines cover only about 35% of all documents available on the Internet (Nwana, 1996). Hence, for maximum coverage, the buyer would have to perform the same search using several different engines. This is time-consuming and will also return duplicate sites. The problem can be partly resolved using a meta-search engine which is effectively a 'search engine of search engines'. These, however, do not guarantee 100% coverage and many will return duplicate sites. Even if it were possible to construct near perfect search engine strings and a search engine could guarantee 100% coverage, there would still be practical difficulties. Thousands of potential supplier sites could be returned as the result of a single query and finding the most appropriate supplier would be practically impossible, particularly if the buyer used multiple criteria to rank suppliers. It is in addressing these key issues that Internet-based intelligent agent software shows significant promise and this will be discussed at a later stage in the chapter. Now we introduce the area of buyer–supplier relations which are the basis of supply chain management. The relationship issues raised here have been discussed in much more depth in Chapter 5.

Developing partnerships on the Internet

As companies search for opportunities to improve, a major focus has been placed on developing web-based partnerships. On the delivery side of an operation, it is possible for companies to work with their customers more closely on the Internet in order to better understand their needs. For example, a retail store could share remote 'point of sales' data on actual customer purchases with their suppliers. The feedback on consumer buying would allow the supplier to better prepare operations to meet sudden shifts in market demand. As a result, the supplier can improve asset utilization and operational efficiency and then share these savings with others in the supply chain, including the end-consumer.

On the 'source-side' of the operation, companies using the Internet would work closely with suppliers to ensure an adequate flow of raw materials. For example, suppliers might analyze their customers' production needs and deliver the raw materials just in time for production use. Suppliers may be able to keep inventory in warehouses and bill the customers only when they actually use the material.

While these services appear to cost a supplier more money, both customers and suppliers achieve potential web-based benefits through a virtual supply chain partnership. The customers would free up valuable internal resources, since the supplier is performing certain activities for them. Correspondingly the supplier would save money, since their web-based contracts provide a competitive barrier to rivals and which potentially leads to fewer lost sales and lower marketing costs. Such a proposition provides a compelling reason for developing a virtual partnership.

Purchasing processes

It is noteworthy that firms have been using private networks, intranets, and conventional computer linkages to co-ordinate there contract negotiations, purchasing, and supply delivery for some time. This capability has enabled firms ranging from The Limited, Inc. to Wal-Mart to purchase, manage inventories, and deliver a customized mix of merchandise to designated locations. The Internet simply widens the application of this capability on a broader scale.

However, the development of extranets to include both clients and suppliers is much more complex. These need to be highly customized to specifically meet the various parties' communication and operating needs. Obviously the manner in which firms operate varies widely, such that extranet-driven business processes for dealing with both internal or external constituents need to be developed that address very specific firm-level circumstances. Carrefour and General Electric provide examples of extranet-driven purchasing processes. The former is discussed in more detail in the next section while the latter has been discussed in the section on virtual sourcing.

Performance measurement on the Internet

Supply chains have tended to utilize two different performance measures: (1) cost and (2) customer responsiveness. Customer responsiveness includes lead time, stockout probability and fill rate. There are examples of successful uses of the Internet in supply chain trade. General Electric, estimates that it has lowered its cost of goods between 5 and 20% simply because it has made it easier for the buyer to contact a supplier. Carrefour, the French multinational retailer, is testing new software in order to develop a link with its suppliers. The pilot programme in Italy links 30 suppliers to their Milan buying office (Carrefour has six stores in Italy and 308 stores in 17 countries). Proprietary software developed by QCS is used to negotiate contracts over the Internet. Firewalls and data encryption developed by IBM are used to secure negotiating parties' privacy. Carrefour's challenge will be to convince smaller suppliers to invest in the appropriate software and hardware and to convince smaller suppliers to get away from the traditional patterns of doing business (often by fax). Carrefour buys a great deal from smaller firms because they offer competitive deals. As such they cannot simply ignore their views. Their exclusion merely increases Carrefour's cost of merchandise.

The Internet can improve the ability of the buyer and supplier to respond to a changing customer demand and also allow a higher level of customer service. The supplier unencumbered by the need to go through the different levels of the supply chain can go direct to the customer. In turn the buyer is able to deal with the manufacturer rather than a reseller or retailer. The Web makes it easier in terms of the time to change an operation. For example, the Internet permits a reduction in system resources and enables the supply chain to adjust to changes in, for example, product demand, manufacturing unreliability, the introduction of new products, or supplier shortages. Thus Internet-based responsiveness is an important consideration in supply chain performance. The potential role played by intelligent agent software is discussed in the next section.

The use of intelligent agents

It is not our purpose to discuss the technical details of intelligent agent software (refer to Chapter 11 for more technical detail), however, it is useful for you to have some appreciation of the nature of Internet-based agents and their uses. There is no agreed definition of the term agent, as used within the information technology community (Nwana, 1996). Yet, most dictionary definitions of the word 'agent' indicate that it is someone or something acting on behalf of someone or something else, for example, literary agent, travel agent or an estate agent. The complexity of the Internet environment demands a new style of human–computer interaction where the computer plays an intelligent and active role (Maes, 1994). The type of software agent, which is able to perform supplier sourcing must be both intelligent and mobile.

Mobility refers to the ability of the agent to act independently, to wander the Internet searching for other agents or websites which can move it towards its goal. Also known as travelling agents, these programs will transport their being, code and state over the Internet. This often improves performance by moving the agents to where the data reside instead of moving the data to where the agents reside. To act as supplier sourcing agents the software needs to possess some degree of artificial intelligence. Although no agents yet exist for the specific purpose of business-to-business supplier sourcing, the technical infrastructure is already well established. For example, the Internet Softbot (software robot) is a fully implemented artificial intelligence (AI) agent developed at the University of Washington. It uses the WWW to interact with a wide range of Internet resources (Etzioni and Weld, 1994) and could form the ideal platform for a supplier sourcing agent.

Two other prototype agents have been developed at the media lab of the Massachusetts Institute of Technology. These are 'Tete-a-Tete' and 'Kasbah'. Tete-a-Tete is designed to help both the retail consumer and the retail merchant by enabling the shopper to perform searches for products based on criteria other than just price, such as performance, brand, delivery times and extended warranties. Kasbah is different from Tete-a-Tete in that it is an agent-based marketplace that closely resembles an online classified advertisements system (Chavez and Maes, 1996).

Kasbah automates both the search and negotiation processes. When selling an item, the seller creates a software agent and provides it with the knowledge necessary to negotiate a price, i.e. the selling agent is told what price the seller would like to get for the item, the minimum acceptable price, and some bargaining strategy for lowering the price over the course of a negotiation. Similarly, buyers create a software agent with its own strategies for finding the products they require and provide it with acceptable target prices. When created, these agents then exist in this virtual marketplace, seeking agents of other organizations who are buying or selling the required items and then negotiating. This initial phase of the negotiation process is completely handled by the buyer ad seller agents and it is only when negotiations have been completed successfully that the human buyer or seller is notified. Tete-a-Tete and Kasbah are regarded as intelligent applications because of their ability to act autonomously. That is to say they operate with little or no direct intervention from humans and have control over their own actions (Wooldridge and Jennings, 1995).

From the above description it can be seen that these agents have characteristics that are very similar to that required for establishing buyer–supplier relationships in a business-to-business environment. A buyer would specify appropriate primary criteria, which a potential supplier must be able to fulfil. These would include the product required, delivery lead times and costs. Additionally, the agent would be provided with a bargaining strategy. The agent would then search the Internet looking for suppliers that appear to be able to meet the primary criteria. Initial negotiations between the buyer and seller agents will result in the discarding of those sellers that cannot comply with the buyer's bargaining strategy. If the number of suppliers returned was still too great to be manageable, the buyer could define secondary criteria such as evidence of a total quality management policy and consistency of delivery performance (Tucker and Jones, 2000). This process may be repeated several times until the human buyer is satisfied.

By using intelligent agents for supplier sourcing, the bulk of the effort in finding the most appropriate supplier for a given product or service at a given time could be delegated entirely to the software. The intelligent agent application would handle the tasks of finding potential suppliers and of ranking them against the selection criteria as demanded by the customer. In this way the buyer could be presented with an on-screen list of the most appropriate suppliers with the minimum of human effort. Hence intelligent agents have the potential to automate the buyer–seller negotiation process (Fisher Centre, 1999). This can relieve a potential bottleneck in the supply chain as well as improving labour utilization rates.

The possibility of delegating most or all of the procurement process to software will impact greatly on the traditional relationships, the reliance on past experience, word-of-mouth recommendation, personal relationships and 'gut feelings' will be replaced by pre-programmed negotiation strategies. Undoubtedly, the tacit knowledge held by human buyers can and does have a significant impact on purchasing decisions. However, the complexity inherent in many sourcing decisions means that the selection process cannot be undertaken in a rational manner and buyers become subject to the phenomenon of bounded rationality. Bounded rationality means that decision makers are limited in their ability to make perfectly rational judgements by such factors as cognitive capacity, lack of perfect information and time constraints (Simon, 1955). The huge amount of data available over the Internet markedly increases the degree of information overload, extending the boundaries of the decision domain and increasing the complexity of the supplier sourcing process. Bounded rationality theory suggests that in these circumstances the human buyer will become increasingly unlikely to make the optimal purchase decision. It is important, therefore, to examine the basis of buyer–supplier relationships and to determine where and how agent technology is likely to have most benefit.

Conclusion

In conclusion it can be said the Internet, as a means of virtual organizing the supply chain, has become a central part of a commercial drive towards improved supplier performance and the re-evaluation, by many of value creation. A major shift in the communication between business organizations is taking place, which is actually redefining organizations and commercial transactions. The Internet has become a key element in moulding and propelling business into new directions from the traditional marketplace to emerging marketspace. The four categories of use of the Internet with relevance to supply chain management include the following: (1) communications (including contract negotiations), information access (including product specification and technical data), and advertising; (2) direct sales of existing products and services; (3) sales of internet-based products and/or services in which the Internet is integrated in the offerings itself; and (4) online distribution of digital information/data (e.g. software, music, process-related information, and marketing research). The Internet is facilitating an unprecedented level of integration across the supply chain in the pursuit of increased competitiveness. However, given the lack of control of any one firm or nation over the event and the activities on the Web, security and piracy issues are likely to be unresolved in the intermediate term.

Checklist

1. Internet environments are reshaping the ownership, control and value creation of supply chains.
2. Web-based communication is improving the richness of information between the buyer and supplier in the supply chain.
3. It is enabling new forms of commercial trade among the different supply players, respectively.
4. New forms of organizational integration mechanisms – discussion groups, web forums, video conferencing – are emerging.

5. SMEs are realizing the potential of the Internet for improving global competitiveness.
6. Marketspace transactions permit much greater autonomy and control over customer activity.
7. Web-based communication through the supply chain is driven by the pursuit of more efficient and effective buyer–supplier interaction and integration.
8. Virtual forms are beginning to replace vertically oriented supply chain structures and management styles.

References

Abad-Peiro, J.L., Asokan, N., Steiner, M. and Waidnar, M. (1998), Designing a generic payment service, *IBM Systems Journal*, 37 (1), pp. 72–88.

ABS (1997), Architecture for information brokerage services, ACTS AC206, available at http://b5www.berkon.de/ABS/(accessed 6 July 1999).

Asokan, N., Janson, P., Steiner, M. and Waidner, M. (1997a), Electronic payment systems, *IEEE COMPUTER*, September.

Asokan, N., Schunter, M. and Waidnar, M. (1997b), *Optimistic Protocols for Fair Exchange*, 4th ACM Conference on Computer and Communications Security, Zurich, pp. 7–17.

Baldwin, L.P and Currie, W. (1999), Key issues in electronic commerce in today's global information infrastructure, *Cognitive Technology and Work*.

Bowersox, D.J. and Closs, D.J. (1996), *Logistics Management: the Integrated Supply Chain Process*, McGraw-Hill, New York.

Chavez, A. and Maes, P. (1996), *Kasbah: an Agent Marketplace for Buying and Selling Goods*, Proceedings of the 1st International Conference on the Practical Application of Intelligent Agents and Multi-Agent Technology, April, London.

Etzioni, O. and Weld, D. (1994), A Softbot-based interface to the Internet, *Communications of the ACM*, 37, pp. 72–76.

Fisher Centre (1999), Available at http://www.haas.berkley.edu/~citm/nego-prog.html

Forrester, J. (1961), *Industrial Dynamics*, MIT Press/John Wiley & Sons, Boston, MA/New York, NY.

Hamel, G. (1998), The challenge today: changing the rules of the game, *Business Strategy Review*, 9 (2), pp. 19–26.

Handfield, R.B. and Nichols, E.L. (1998), *Introduction to Supply Chain Management*, Prentice-Hall, Englewood Cliffs, NJ.

Harland, C.M. (1996), Supply chain management: relationships, chains and networks, *British Journal of Management*, 7, pp. 63–80.

Infowin (1996), COBRA: common brokerage architecture, available at http://www.de.info-win.org/ACTS/RUS/PROJECTS/ac203.htm (accessed 6 July (1999).

Lacoste, G. (1997), *SEMPER: A Security Framework for the Global Electronic Marketplace*, IIR, London.

Lambert, D.M., Emmelhainz, M.A., Gardner, J.T. (1996), Developing and implementing supply chain partnerships, *International Journal of Logistics Management*, 7 (2), pp. 1–16.

Lee, H.L., Padmananhan, V. and Whang, S. (1997), Information distortion in the a supply chain: the bullwhip effect, *Management Science*, 43 (4), pp. 546–558.

Maes, P. (1994), Agents that reduce work and information overload, *Communications of the ACM*, 37, pp. 31–40.

Morar, S.S. and Patel, N. (1999), Electronic commerce within a virtual environment, *Cognitive Technology and Work*.

Nwana, H.S. (1996), Software agents: an overview, *Knowledge Engineering Review*, 11 (3), pp. 1–40.

O'Connor, G. and O'Keefe, B. (1997), Viewing the Web as a marketplace: the case of small companies, *Decision Support Systems*, 2 (3), pp. 171–183.

PRTM Consulting (1994), *Integrated Supply-Chain Performance Measurement: A Multi-Industry Consortium Recommendation*, PRTM, Weston, Ma.

Quinn, J.B., Bauch, J. and Zein, K.A. (1997), *Innovation Explosion*, The Free Press, New York.

Riggins, F.J. and Rhee, H.-S.S. (1998), Toward a unified view of electronic commerce, *Communications of the ACM*, 41 (10), pp. 88–95.

Tucker, D. and Jones, L. (2000), Leveraging the power of the Internet for optimal supplier sourcing. *International Journal of Physical Distribution and Logistics Management*, 30 (3/4), pp. 255–267.

Venkatrannan, N. and Henderson, J.C. (1998), Real strategies for virtual organizing, *Sloan Management Review*, Fall, pp. 33–48.

Watson, R.T., Akselsen, S., Pitt, L.F. (1998), Building mountains in the flat landscape of the World Wide Web, *Californian Management Review*, Winter, pp. 36–56.

Williamson, O. (1981), *The Economics Institutions of Capitalism: Firms, Markets, Relational Contracting*, The Free Press, New York.

Wooldridge, M. and Jennings, N. (1995), Intelligent theory and practice. *The Knowledge Engineering Review*, 10 (2), pp. 115–152.

CHAPTER 8

Consumer online payment solutions for e-commerce

- An integrated approach towards e-commerce
- Vital components for consumer online e-commerce
- Steps in processing online credit card transaction
- How to build a successful e-commerce site
- Products and tools for building your own e-commerce site.

- Identify the types of electronic payment systems.
- Understand the primary functions of e-commerce applications.
- Define the processes required for e-commerce.
- Evaluate the various options available in building an e-commerce site.

Commerce has been undertaken using various forms of advanced technology, since the 1960s with the most common implementation being within the organization. Through the 1970s and 1980s computer networks were established along the supply chain, in order to co-ordinate inter-organizational business processes and communicate more interactively. The most common transaction systems include:

- Order processing
- Materials requirements planning
- Airline reservation systems (Sabre system)
- Insurance applications
- E-procurement through trading hubs.

An integrated approach towards e-commerce

As the technology has changed, networked computing has become more of the norm, the types of applications and the level of usage has also adapted to the widening of possibilities. The number of companies doing business electronically via integrated networks has steadily increased over the past two decades. The majority of organizations now have electronic links with suppliers and buyers from the use of fax machines through to the emergence of the Internet. In addition, many businesses have deployed information technology to form virtual corporations. The development of a virtual corporation allows businesses to combine their core competencies to deliver products and services. The use of information technology is primarily the integration mechanism, which is facilitating business processes within and between organizations.

The communication technologies that we have become familiar with have continued to evolve to an extent that fax, EDI and e-mail have now become mainstream tools for many in their day-to-day business activities. For instance, during the 1980s and 1990s, EDI was gradually adopted by much industry including retail and many manufacturing sectors. Now EDI is a fully exploited technology driven by: (1) virtually private networks connecting computer systems between buyers and sellers and (2) VANs (Value Added Networks) allowing trading partners to connect indirectly through a dedicated network such as Advantis and IVAN. VANs for some companies are a means of plugging into an established system and as a consequence creates less development time for many. Figure 8.1 provides an over-

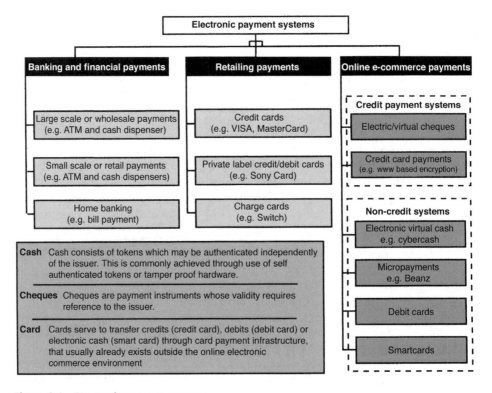

Figure 8.1   Electronic payment systems

view of the three broad categories of electronic payment systems: banking and financial payments, retailing payments, and online e-commerce payments (Kalakota and Whinston, 1996).

'Banking and financial payment' systems are based on Electronic Data Interchange (EDI) for inter-organizational commerce. EDI offers a structured approach towards electronic information transfer. EDI applications cover large scale bank-to-bank transfers and wholesale payments in addition to small-scale payments via Automated Teller Machines (ATMs). 'Retail payments' include a wide range of credit, debit and charge card payments types. Visa, MasterCard and American Express operate global systems for electronic authorization and settlement of card-based payments. The electronic clearing and global clearing network infrastructure is a valuable asset in the transition to online payment solutions. 'Online e-commerce payments' include all non-credit and credit payment solutions designed for online transactions (Langdon et al., 2000). Refer to the section on vital components for consumer online e-commerce for more detail on the types of online payment systems.

A range of other supporting facilities along the supply chain are also being widely adopted in support of improved supply chain management. Some of the services/applications currently being used include:

- E-mail
- Internet, intranets, extranets
- Electronic vendor/product directories
- Ordering and logistic support systems
- Management information and reporting systems.

An integrated model is now emerging that is accessible to companies of all sizes and this is based on internationally recognized standards. The integrated business models for e-commerce are now a reality through the unprecedented acceptance of the Internet and in particular, the World Wide Web as the commercial platform of choice in both business-to-business and business-to-consumer markets. Clarke (1993) proposed a five-phase process model for e-commerce, which have been adapted with a particular focus on the Internet applications below (Figure 8.2):

Pre-contractual phase

This phase is focused on the gathering of knowledge concerning the products and services being sought, and identifying potential sources of supply that may be from the marketspace or marketplace.

Contractual phase

The stage when a formal relationship between buyer and seller is created. This phase will include the establishment or acceptance of terms and conditions for transactions under the contract.

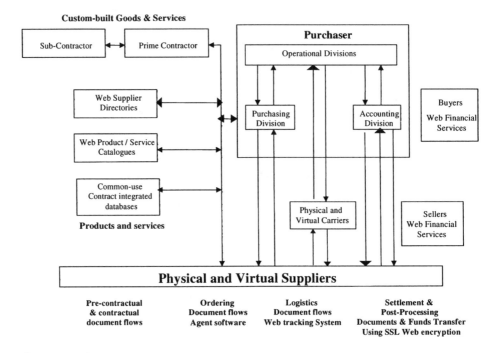

Custom-built Goods & Services

**Pre-contractual
& contractual
document flows**

**Ordering
Document flows
Agent software**

**Logistics
Document flows
Web tracking System**

**Settlement &
Post-Processing
Documents & Funds Transfer
Using SSL Web encryption**

Figure 8.2   Five phases of e-commerce

Ordering and logistics phase

For organizations operating in business-to-business markets, purchase orders are placed and processed and at this stage goods are transported physically or virtually to the customer. On arrival an inspection is followed by acceptance or rejection. In business-to-consumer markets this phase is probably part of the following phase. Settlement will be expected at the time of ordering.

Settlement phase

This phase will include invoicing, payment authorization, payment and remittance transmission. Through the acceptance of the Web as a means of buying and selling, the ordering, logistics and settlement have become integral activities for many organization especially in business-to-consumer markets.

Post processing phase

This phase involves the gathering and reporting of management information based on the analysis of trade information and statistics. The Internet has created far greater integration between the buyer and the seller and as a consequence virtually real time statistics can be view through Web-based management reporting tools.

The Web is facilitating a highly integrated approach towards online transaction systems between buyers and suppliers. Businesses are able to establish new electronic storefronts on the Web or move existing electronic transactions on to the Internet, through VANs. Establishing transaction systems on the Web will require both a technological understanding and also a new way of thinking about virtual markets. The global reach creates many new challenges as well as opportunities in terms of realizing cost efficiency, customizability, speed and quality of service.

Business transformation is inevitable when Web payment systems are used to automate business processes. Business-to-consumer (B2C) markets are synonymous with Amazon (http://www.amazon.com) and CDNOW (http://www.cdnow.com) models of online trading, while in business-to-business (B2B) markets Internet exchanges are becoming drivers of emerging industry trading hubs. The automobile industry provides an example, of how B2B is harnessing the Web for online trading with businesses such as Ford, General Motors and Daimler-Chrysler setting up an Internet e-procurement portal across which all their suppliers will trade.

Vital components for consumer online e-commerce

Online payment systems are central to the whole Web-based trading experience and are now readily available as integrated software packages from many e-commerce providers. The primary functions of e-commerce software include product information, order processing and tracking, payment transaction processing, order fulfilment, and shipping. Some of the popular suppliers of Web-based payment systems include Microsoft's suite of servers including Internet Information Server, iCat e-commerce suite, Oracle's Universal Server, IBM's Net.Commerce and Lotus Domino, Mira software plus many more. These software products provide a complete virtual shopping experience.

Electronic shopping cart

The principles of a Web-based shopping cart are similar to a traditional shopping cart in a retail outlet. While shopping on a website a buyer can browse and 'drop and store' in the virtual shopping cart. A web-based shopping cart is no more than an electronic storage medium which keeps track of the desired products. A shopping cart feature is now a standard function and is usually integrated into most e-commerce software

An electronic buying list

A potential or existing customer may want to create an electronic buying list for some future date or just as a useful wish list. A buying list is also standard functionality with e-commerce software and stores the desired list for future acquisition by the shopper. The main distinction between a buyer cart and a buying list is that the former stores items about what the consumer wishes to purchase while the latter is only providing as wish list that may or may not be purchased at a later date.

Order placement

At the end of the buying experience the consumer is ready to 'check-out'. In this electronic mode the buyer has completed the buying and is now in a position to order the items accumulated in the specific buyer cart. Most web pages supporting online ordering will have a button labelled 'check-out' to start the purchasing process. At this point the following web page will typically display the contents of the shopping cart, providing the consumer with the opportunity to drop items or maybe change some of the details, for example two of a particular item rather than one. The web page will normally provide details of the number of units, total price of each item, tax, shipping and handling charges and finally the grand total. The consumer at this point will be given the option to exit, therefore terminating the buying process, or submit the final order.

Shipping information

Some businesses trading online are now offering exposure to inventory and shipping information. Usually this can be accessed via some form of security code for regular customers. The consumers with an account are then in a position to reliably assess the availability and specific delivery of requested items. If an end user is not an account holder then the individual will typically be given an approximate date of delivery at the shipping address.

Payment information

Various methods of payment are currently available on the Internet with varying levels of success (see Table 8.1 for specific details). Electronic credit card payments are currently by far the mostly widely used, followed by digital cash and electronic cheque payments. Payment via the use of credit cards has become the generally accepted method of payment due to the development of the Secure Electronic Transaction (SET) protocol. The digital cash may become more popular over time especially for small purchases. Digital currency (see Figure 8.3) is equivalent to cash and will probably be used in a similar way in that it will be useful for small purchases. Electronic cheques have now been under development for quite a while but with limited use to date. An electronic cheque requires a digital signature and a certificate for an authorization method, such as an e-mail.

Security issues

Both individual and business perceptions towards security on the Web have changed significantly with confidence now becoming the norm. Concerns about security on the Web are generally unfounded and typically based on fear of the unknown.

Table 8.1   e-Commerce payment methods

Non-credit systems

Electronic/virtual cash: www.ecash.com, www.cybercash.com	Several payment systems have been established that replicate what is viewed as real cash (www.cybercash.com). Digital cash typically uses what is known as a bearer certificate system. Blank tokens are issued by the user but at the time of purchase need to be certified by the user's bank for availability of credit. This can make it difficult for small to medium sized organizations
Micropayments: www.ecoin.net, www.beanz.com	Micropayment systems have emerged due to the need for a method of paying for products and services that have minimal value. For example buying an electronic daily newspaper or an MP3 file for your mobile Rio player. Micropayment systems such as Ecoin have limited value and as a consequence minimal security. Loyalty tokens, such as Beanz (www.beanz.com), can also be included in this category that provide a form of digital cash that can be collected and then used to purchase items on the Web
Debit cards	Typically merchants trading on the Internet prefer credit cards, rather than debit cards, as they are secured by the bank. The Bank of Austria have allowed debit cards for teenagers who cannot have a credit card due to age restrictions
Smartcards: Mondex/MasterCard, Visacash	Smartcards are quite different from other payment methods in that a physical card is used The smartcard needs to be inserted into a smartcard reader and at this point items can be purchased. Across Europe smartcards are still being used on a trial basis. Visa Cash in the UK has been tested through issuing 60000 chip-based cards. Payments are cleared through the conventional banking system with payments being based on the bearer certificate system
Credit systems Electronic/virtual cheques: www.mkn.co.uk/bank	These are very similar in principle to a traditional cheque except that authorization is based on a digital rather than hand-written signature. BankNet in the UK is operating such a system. Encryption of the digitally signed checks is based on public key/private key cryptographic techniques

Table 8.1 (*continued*)

Credit cards: Visa/MasterCard, www.pay2see.com	As any online consumer will know, credit cards are the main means of purchase on the Internet. The credit card system overall fulfils payment requirements online. The only problem with this system is for micropayment, as the cost of transaction may be greater than the purchase cost. Credit card operation is also being streamlined to some extent through using a third party system (www.pay2see.com) that stores the credit card details and as a consequence credit card details in principle do not need to provided to retailers

The majority of website businesses offering web-based ordering generally use what is known as an SSL (Secure Socket Layer) server which provides an acceptable level of security for the financial information being transmitted over the Web (see Chapter 9). Browsers, in particular Netscape and Explorer, support secure trading by providing the buyer with some information about the level of security and encryption provided in the ordering process.

Shipments

Following the authorization of payment a message is automatically sent to the vender's shipping department, providing notification of payment. At this point the vendor is issued with a 'thank you' note to the purchaser and also typically displays on the web page an invitation for future shopping.

Steps in processing online credit card transactions

Processing credit card transactions online is relatively easy and many of the skills that businesses already have through the use of EPOS systems are valuable in acquiring what is required for web-based trading. Figure 8.4 provides an overview of the overall e-commerce process.

There are four basic steps in establishing a web store that can process credit card transactions across the Internet.

Hosting your website. You can either host your site on your own dedicated web server, within your organization, or with a third party Internet Service Provider (ISP). This will primarily depend on the volume of traffic anticipated, internal capabilities within a specific organization, and for many strategies towards alliances and collaboration. In choosing an ISP it is important to consider which e-commerce products are supported. If you choose to place your website with an ISP initially it is important to check the speed and technology of sites that are already hosted with the service providers you are considering. ISPs can primarily be cate-

Figure 8.3   Electronic/virtual cash provider

gorized into business-to-consumer and business-to-business types. It is particularly important to choose an ISP that has a backend infrastructure that is appropriate for your needs and that the necessary technical support is available to ease the process of getting your site 'up and running'.

Merchant account. Being an online merchant involves more than designing and hosting a website. The growing Internet population is becoming comfortable with ordering online and as a consequence online payment facilities will soon be a prerequisite for success. Therefore if you want to make money from the Internet through selling goods and services online then you need to become an online merchant. In simple terms you need to be a trader who enables customers to view, select, order, and pay with their recognized choice of plastic. The first step is to get a merchant account. if a business has already got a merchant account for terrestrial business, then the risk assessment will have already been undertaken and the merchant bank will consider the business a good risk. Internet Merchant facilities are different from a typical retailers merchant account and the Internet merchant facilities fall into the 'Cardholder Not Present' (CNP) classification of trading. This is similar to the requirements placed upon the mail order and telephone order market. The merchant services in the UK are typically from Barclays Merchant Services, NatWest Streamline Merchant Services, Midland Card Services

Table 8.2   Sample of merchant services in the UK[a]

Company	Datacash	Cyberstrider	Authority	Netbanx	Worldpay	e-banx	Secure Trading
Website (www.)	datacash.com	cyderstrider.com	radsgroup.com	netbanx.com	worldpay.com	ebanx.net	securetrading.com
Setup fee	N/A	N/A	£375	From £75 to £500	N/A	£795	N/A
Annual fee	£600	£75 (including setup fee)	£375	N/A	£125	N/A	£295
Monthly fee	N/A	N/A	N/A	N/A	N/A	N/A	N/A
Transaction fee (where applicable)	N/A	4–5% on cc £1 debit cards	3%	1–4%	4–5% including bank charges	3–10 p per transaction	Various – from 2%
Merchant fee (where applicable)	N/A	N/A	N/A	4%	4–5% including bank charges	5%	Bureau available (approx. 7–5% inc)
Setup time	2 days from acknowledgement from merchant bank	Within 24 h	4–5 weeks	Same day	Depends on aquirer	1–3 weeks, depending on bank; bureau service 1 week	Same day
Transaction partner	Amex, BoS, BMS, Girobank, NWS, RboS	Clydesdale/FDR	BMS	BMS, NWS, MMS, Lloyds, Cardnet RBoS, BoS	NWS, but with work with others including US banks	All UK High St. banks	NWS, BMS, Lloyds, RBoB, Amex. Dinners, etc.
Allow use of existing merchant agreement	Requires e-commerce Merchant ID	Sits alongside any existing agreement	Y	Yes – requires separate Internet	Y	Y	Dependent on bank
Multi-transaction	Y	N/A	N/A	N	N	N	Y
Multi-currency option	Y	N	N	Y – via NW or BMS	Y	Y	Y
Minimum transaction	£130	£10 preferred	£10	£10	N/A	N/A	N/A
Visa	Y	Y	Y	Y	Y	Y	Y
MasterCard (Access)	Y	Y	Y	Y	Y	Y	Y
Switch	Y	Y	Y	Y	Y	Y	Y
Visa Delta	Y	Y	Y	Y	Y	Y	Y
American Express	Y	N	Y	Y	Y	N	Y
Diners Club	N	N	Y	Y	Y	N	Y
Eurocard	N	N	Y	Y	Y	N	Y
Others	JCB, Solo	–	–	JCB, all Visa cards	JCB	–	JCB, Solo

[a] MMS = Midland Merchant; CNP = cardholder not present; MS = Barclays Merchant Services; NWS = Natwest Streamline, IdCard = Midland Bank Card Services; BoS = Bank of Scotland

or Lloyds Cardnet (Table 8.2). The merchant bank co-ordinates the transfer of funds between your bank, the seller, and the cardholders bank. The merchant banks in its third party role acts as a facilitator and to some extent a verifier of the specific online payment. Currently merchant services are difficult to obtain even for businesses that are allowed to take orders by credit card for mail order and telephone sales. Similarly if a business is relatively new with limited assets, it is unlikely that the acquirers will provide such a business with direct merchant facilities for face-to-face, terrestrial, CNP trading, and the most unlikely of all is Internet CNP facilities.

Small companies, who may not have a merchant account, can still trade on the Web through using a growing number of commercial organizations that provide small companies with a means of funnelling transactions through their merchant account. These organizations, Payment Solutions Providers (PSPs) are generally long established with a track record in trading online. A PSP can offer a starting point for organizations that are finding it difficult to open a merchant account. This option generally costs more and payment of cardholders' money is typically delayed which is a reflection of the level of risk associated with such a business. Even though a slightly more costly option if you compare it to not trading online it can be seen as a necessary investment.

Payment processing. The types of payment needs to be decided upon whether this will be solely a credit card transaction or whether to accept various payment methods including Cybercash and electronic cheques. Off the shelf software is available that can be used to create an appropriate web application to securely undertake transactions. The services provided by PSPs make online authorization a simple and relatively cheap process. PSPs have a relatively cheap charging structures for the merchant and PSPs will filter out 'faulty' and fraudulent transactions at source and as a consequence minimize Net administration costs. It is also important to consider security issues of trading online that fall into three main categories: cardholder, acquirer, and merchant. For the cardholder or consumer security is of prime importance through the transmission process and also when the credit card details are stored on the server within the merchant's organization.

The acquirer needs to be confident that the card details are not intercepted at the time of ordering online and are stored on secure servers that are seen to be safe from hackers. As a merchant you need to provide secure authorization and payment file delivery. For a merchant to offer such levels of security significant trading levels are required to justify the cost incurred. The concerns identified by all three groups can be met through working with an established PSP in the short term until trading levels are high enough to justify the necessary investment in computing equipment and the required human resources for implementation and maintenance.

Below is further detail on the main merchant service currently offered in the UK.

Build your product catalogue. You can use site builder software to add a product catalogue to your existing website or alternatively build a new web store. If an existing website has been created with the view to offering company information and general promotional information it may be easier to re-plan the website with the primary focus being the online transaction process. The design of the website will be dependent on its primary role. For example, is the website supporting a retail chain or is it the sole source of purchase? Quelch and Klein (1996) stated that new web-based companies are operating primarily in marketspace adopting a 'transaction-to-information' model, in other words the website is designed first and foremost for online trading.

How to build a successful e-commerce site

As with most new ventures or applications the easiest way of getting a realistic idea of the implications is to get some 'hands-on' experience. Not too long ago the Internet probably seemed quite an abstract concept to you, but through the use of a browser – the Internet and the Web soon becomes demystified. Trading on the Web is very similar in that it seems complex but after you have experienced the process it is quite simple in principle. There are two principle aspects to trading on the Web: first, getting people to visit your site; and secondly selling to them once they are browsing through the product catalogue. The two-step approach of trading online requires a combination of marketing and technical skills. Marketing staff require some technical understanding while technical specialists need some market awareness. Due to the complex nature of trading online e-commerce applications tools are far more reactive to marketspace, which is due to the speed of change and the level of technological integration on the Internet. Not surprisingly successful e-commerce sites are professionally marketed in a sense that they are very in tune with the customer. For example, if one considers bookacourse.com, here they adopt what they call a consumer-to-business model, in that the consumer directly determines developments in terms of product and service offerings, even in determining the price incurred.

As a starting point you need to consider whether specific products and services can be sold via the Web. First, consider their suitability for mail order and this will provide you with an indication of the relevance of certain products and services to the Web, as similar motivations and limitations apply. For example, the weight and price of some products can make the cost of delivery too expensive. For retailers it is a common assumption that there are three key factors to consider in opening a store: location, location, location. On the Web, one can likewise assume that this factor needs to be taken into account in developing your integrated marketing communications orientation, which is essential for sales volume. Promotion initiatives are the enabler of creating a location or what is more commonly termed a Web presence. For example, with many web-based companies, such as boo.com, sales leads are generated from conventional media including billboard and TV advertising. On the Web, you find that there are many ways of creating 'location, location, location' and this includes: registering with search engines, establishing mutual links, and participating in relevant newsgroup discussions. A trading site needs to sell the moment a visitor arrives and the design process of e-commerce applications will need to harness this viewpoint. For example, consider the following questions:

- Why should visitors buy from you?

- Are your prices constantly the lowest?
- Is your web service excellent?
- Is the purchasing process fast and easy?
- Is the delivery process fast and reliable?

As a consequence when you are building and e-commerce site consider the following:

- Keep the number of clicks to a minimum, especially through the ordering process.
- Get the 'add to cart' button in front of the consumer as quickly as possible which means faster sales.
- Consider consumers concerns. Some people will be concerned about credit card security plus general terms and conditions.
- Apply for quality assurance trading marks from organizations such as Uktrust or Webtrader.

In building your e-commerce site it is important to be aware of the various options available. A number of options are available from do-it-yourself to bespoke solutions. Some form of packaged solution is probably the most appropriate with various options available for all sizes of organizations. A business may build the e-commerce site, internally or through a partner, and possibly through a combination of both. For example, an organization may have very good web graphics skills but limited technical knowledge and as a consequence buy in skills from an e-commerce solutions provider.

Server-based solutions

A number of options are available on the Internet for server side solutions and these can be low cost options. Typical providers include IBM's HomePage Creator (www.ibm.com/hpc/uk) and BT Storefront (www.btwebworld.co.uk). Through the use of a simple web-based wizard and a simple browser you can create an e-commerce enabled site for your business in just a few hours (refer to the section on how to build a successful e-commerce site). The main issue of concern is that you would be leaving your customer and order information, on a third party's computer, which is at a remote location. The other option is to develop your own server side solution and host it on your own server. Clearly developing your own unique solution would be very expensive and typically undertaken for large e-commerce development projects. The main priority must be to remain in control and in particular control your online brand.

Software-driven solutions

Many software solutions are available as stand-alone applications, or they are integrated into larger web-based software tools, for building your e-commerce solution. Such solutions (refer to the section on how to build a successful e-commerce site) provide you with an opportunity to benefit from shared development in addition to benefiting from the learning experience, debugged code and lower cost. Typically these companies are partnered with web design and web hosting agencies which provide a potential supporting network.

Costs

A typical e-commerce solution should cost £1000–5000 for a site of 200–5000 different products. This will vary significantly depending on whether the solution is building on an existing website, with established graphics, or is starting from new and needs graphics to create an online brand and presence. In addition, annual costs for updates and changes for such a website will cost approximately £500–1000 per year plus the cost of hosting the site including naming registration which will cost a further £1000 per year. These prices will clearly vary based on the size of the product range and the scale of the underlying transaction system driving the website.

CASE APPLICATION   **BRITISH AIRWAYS (WWW.BRITISHAIRWAYS.CO.UK): ADDING EASE AND CONVENIENCE TO FLYING WITH ONE OF THE WORLD'S LARGEST AIRLINES**

The air travel industry is relatively saturated, with many airlines becoming stronger and more competitive. The $7 billion online travel selling industry is expected to see sales rise over 200% within 2 years. Travel purchases online are growing, according to an e-commerce survey by PhoCusWrite.com and for the first time. The number of online travellers usually using traditional travel agencies to buy their airline tickets for leisure travel has fallen to fewer than 50%, which indicates a significant loss of business. It is therefore imperative that online transaction systems continue to develop in complexity in order to fight for a competitive advantage.

British Airways online adds a new dimension to the flying experience, BA online provides consumers of the site the opportunity to use the site with ease and at their convenience. Many other airlines, in addition to BA, offer their services over the Internet including Virgin, QANTAS, CathayPacific. They are all attempting to distinguish their services over the Internet, but to some extent are governed by technological developments.

The facilities and services offered by BA online are diverse and encompass all aspects of overseas travel, not just flight related issues but a diverse range of other related information services. BA online is an information rich website, providing the user with detailed information regarding planning the trip, travel guides, details of airports, special offers, flight information including timetables and schedules and a membership lounge for frequent flyers.

The whole world is changing for us and I have never seen so much excitement, so much threat, so much intellectual invigoration as I have seen in this environment.
                                      Dale Moss, Director of world-wide sales, British Airways

BA has set a target to achieve 50% of all British Airways sales online by 2003. Such an ambitious target will represent a challenge for BA as they have yet to fully anticipate the online consumers needs.

When that happens, success is ours, … We don't just move people from point A to point B… On the leisure side it's about fun, and excitement and bringing people together, and that's what we sell – it's a relationship that's all about communication. People have to add value in this equation.

(www.britishairways.co.uk)

Online booking

As the actual tangible product of flying cannot be experienced online, the process leading to the tangible product can be. The core service of BA is online booking. BA has grasped the concept of an online booking facility and the increasing demand to make it easier for passengers to purchase their tickets online. The booking facility online provides the user with more than just a medium with which to purchase a ticket. In order to add value to the overall experience, BA enable the visitor to check availability of seats and flights, prices, travel insurance and the option to either pay online or to pay at designated travel agents, thus providing options to consumers concerned about payment fraud over the Internet.

The executive club

Frequent British Airways flyers are provided with access to a special online community 'the executive club'. Access to this community provides the user with speciality services such as dedicated reservation lines, 0% commission and air miles from partner airlines, hotels and car hire, the ability to choose an in-flight meal, priority wait listing on busy flights, the ability to pre-select a seat.

As BA have demonstrated, it is not just enough to possess technical literacy and offer a product or service over the Internet, agents must think creatively about how to offer value to customers.

Products and tools for building your e-commerce site

The first question you need to ask yourself is if you want to create customized solutions or be more inclined to buy an 'off the shelf' solution. Having web development skills in your company or being a merchant may in part determine this. We will now consider some of the many options available for both web developers and merchants.

e-Commerce solutions for web developers

A client requests you to build them an interactive e-commerce site, which includes a buying cart and online ordering system. As described above the buying cart is a script that keeps track of items ordered but most importantly the order is still stored if the customer begins to look at other products on the website. A developer with some programming knowledge could build a custom application using various platforms and applications development tools. Typically an e-commerce site will either be designed for a Microsoft Internet Information Server (IIS) platform or a Unix-based platform using, for example, Apache Web server software. The actual e-commerce application will typically be designed using Java script, Vbscript, Cold-Fusion or may be Drumbeat; along with an ODBC compliant database. For your larger applications, Oracle and IBM can provide their own proprietary-based development tools that mainly comply to open standards architecture. Now we have considered the various options available let us consider some of the options available with varying levels of expense, functionality, and effort required by developers.

JavaScript solutions offer a low cost option for the developer. There are several JavaScript solutions that may suit your needs, if you are searching for a relatively cheap option. If a developer is an expert in scripting then in principal a solution can be purely written for a specific need. A more common approach is to modify an existing JavaScript solution that has already been written. Many are available on the Web, which are either free or available for a license fee. Go to websites such as Ross Online (http://www.anweb.com/shopjs) or Motivational Marketing Associates (http://www.mmaweb.com/). Other useful sources of information include: (1) the JavaScript Weenie and (2) the JavaScript Source. It is important to remember that JavaScript solutions are frequently not appropriate and will depend on the intended market. A problem for many with JavaScript is that it involves the use of cookies; in other words storing a data string on the client's hard drive with the ability to retrieve it later. JavaScript is typically useful as an optional extra, but it is not always a main source of coding. Due to cookies storing information on the client side many websurfers object to JavaScript applications and as a consequence set their browser to reject any 'write-cookie' request.

For those who are interested in trading in the US then it is important to remember that AOL's browser is set to disable JavaScript and as we all recognize most users on the Web use a browser with the original settings. Typically, a web surfer will have limited interest in what is viewed as technical issues such as JavaScript. In the AOL community it is important to note that the JavaScript e-commerce solution is probably not going to be appropriate for you.

With CGI-based scripts, such as code that is written in Perl, the computation and data collection is undertaken on the server side. E-commerce solutions are driven by server side software applications and these are generally viewed as most appropriate. A typical product that generates CGI script is WebGenie Software (http://www.webgenie.com). WebGenie primarily generates CGI scripts, which you are then able to modify and adapt to your specific needs. The software clearly targets web developers rather than merchants. For your larger e-commerce solutions then Oracle (http://www.oracle.com) is clearly the leading supplier on the Internet. 'Oracle e-commerce' is a comprehensive suite of integrated e-commerce applications for internet marketing, sales, and service.

At the centre of the 'Oracle e-commerce' software is the transaction system that is offering secure methods of ordering plus all the typical other utilities such as buying carts and an ability to expand the store environment based on web traffic.

The software products from Oracle are grouped into the following applications: iMarketing, iStore, iPayment and iSupport. iPayment is a complete electronic payment system that applications developers, systems integrators and other software specialists can use as a 'payment enable' web application. For a large business looking to offer an integrated e-customer focused approach throughout the organization then you will find that Oracle provides a suite of excellent tools.

e-Commerce solutions for online merchants

In the previous sections we have considered the various options open to organizations with dedicated web developers, but fortunately for less technical experts there are various other applications available. If you need a fast means of becoming an online merchant without many technical hurdles then you need to consider software applications such as 'Shopsite' from Open Market Inc. (http://www.shopsite.com) or 'SoftCart' from Mercante Inc. (http://www.mercantec.com). ShopSite uses a template-based approach to building an e-commerce site. With this approach building an e-commerce site is a matter of filling in the blanks. The templates are designed to read product data from a database. SoftSite makes updates and new additions very simple and fast. SoftCart in contrast offers a more comprehensive approach. SoftCart e-commerce applications are driven completely from the server side. SoftCart offers different versions all written in ANSI C and compiled for different servers. As the software application is driven from the server side the consumer can bookmark the site and continue searching on the Web, for example, in checking competitor pricing, and on return (via the bookmark) the consumer will find their buying cart as it was before. Even though ShopSite and SoftCart offer applications primarily designed for online merchants, the products do also offer functionality for developers.

Conclusion

The overall atmosphere towards the creation and development of websites is changing both in the US and Europe. Investors are now expecting a return within the near future rather than in an uncertain and unpredictable 5 years time. As a consequence such a change in attitude by businesses and Venture Capitalists (VCs) asks the question, which websites are actually making a profit? A recent article in the US, by Barons (http://www.barons.com), indicated a changing trend. The results were from a survey of 207 Internet companies and it was indicated that approximately 25% were expected to run out of cash within the next 12 months. Many of the companies surveyed were household names in the US, such as the music retailer CDNOW (http://www.cdnow.com) and the grocery store Peapod (http://www.peapod.com). On a more optimistic note, a recent Boston Consulting Group (http://www.bcg.com) survey of 412 web retailers found that one-third of e-commerce businesses are making a profit.

The flag ship for online retailing must be Amazon (http://www.amazon.com) but it has publicly stated it does not expect to make a profit until 2002. The long awaited profits are primarily a consequence of massive expansion and more recently the growth into the sale of more diverse products such as CDs and toys. A company that is leading the way in the grocery sector, in profiting on the Web, is Tesco Direct (http://www.tesco.co.uk). Tesco Direct currently offers its service to approximately 40% of the UK population and is expected to grow, according to the finance director Andrew Higginson, to 90% by the end of 2000. Moving to the financial sector we must consider the unprecedented success of Charles Schwab (http://www.schwab.com) in online share dealing. The company reported that its first quarter profits for 2000 had risen from $143 million the previous year to $284 million this year. At the end of 1999 Schwab controlled 22% of online trading volume (*Web Developers Journal*, 19/05/00).

Evidently, one finds growth sectors on the Web. For example, even though travel websites are very popular very few are currently popular due to the very small profit margins. Volume appears to be the key to longer-term success for companies such as Lastminute.com (http://www.lastminute.com). The Gartner Group (http://www.gartnerweb.com) anticipates that the travel market will increase six-fold by the end of 2001. We also need to remember the potential of online gambling and the growth is expected to be enormous over the next 2 years. William Hill (http://www.willhill.com), Ladbrokes (http://www.ladbrokes.com), and Littlewoods (http://www.bet247.com) are all established with websites online and are all expecting significant profits.

Checklist

1. The development of a virtual corporation allows businesses to combine their core competencies to deliver products and services.
2. Information technology is primarily the integration mechanism, which is facilitating business processes within and between organizations.
3. Electronic payment systems: banking and financial payments, retailing payments, and online e-commerce payments.
4. Supporting facilities for electronic payment systems include: (1) e-mail, (2) Internet, intranets, extranets, (3) electronic vendor/product directories, (4) ordering and logistic support systems, (5) management information and reporting systems.
5. Vital components of online e-commerce include: (1) electronic shopping cart, electronic buying list, (2) order placement, (3) shipping information, and (4) payment systems (credit/non-credit systems).
6. Basic steps in establishing a website which need to be considered are: (1) hosting your website, (2) merchant account, (3) payment processing, (4) building a product catalogue.
7. Consider the two-step approach to trading online, that is, getting consumers to the website and selling to them once they are browsing.
8. In building a site you need to decide if your organization wants to build a customized solution or is more inclined to invest in a 'off the shelf' solution.

Having web development skills in your company or being a merchant may in part determine this.

References

Clarke, R. (1993), *EDI is but one Element of E-commerce*, Proceedings of the 6th International EDI Conference, Bled, Slovenia, June. http://www.anu.edu.au/people/Roger.Clarke/EC/Bled93.html.

Kalakota and Whinston (1996), *Frontiers of E-commerce*, Addison-Wesley, Reading, MA, p. 298.

Langdon, R. and Shaw, M. (2000), *Handbook on e-Commerce*. Springer, New York.

Quelch, J.A. and Klein, L.R. (1996), The Internet and international marketing, *Sloan Management Review*, Spring.

Further reading

Andersen Consulting. Our Point of View: Success in a Wired World. http://www.ac.com/ecommerce/.

Barling, C. (1999), How to build. *Internet Works e-Commerce Supplement*, July, pp. 28–32.

e-Commerce Research Forum. Center for eBusiness at MIT. http://ebusiness.mit.edu/research/papers.html.

Siegel, D. (1999), *Futurize your Enterprise, Business Strategy in the age of the e-Customer*, John Wiley & Sons, New York.

Timmers, P. (2000), *E-commerce, Strategies and Models for Business-to-Business Trading*, John Wiley & Sons, New York.

Thompson, B. (1999), Making it pay, *Internet Works e-Commerce Supplement*, July, pp. 28–32.

CHAPTER 9

Privacy and security issues for e-commerce

Key topics

- Electronic commerce safety and network security
- Authentication
- Securing data integrity, privacy and accountability
- An integrated approach – IBM's security solution.

After studying this chapter you will be able to:

- Identify the major e-commerce security areas.
- Understand the different confidentiality, integrity and authenticity issues.
- Describe the types of firewalls and proxies used in securing networks.
- Critically evaluate the implications of integrated security solutions.

In this chapter, we cover a number of important privacy and security issues. Although, this area is highly technical, our goal is simply to acquaint you with the basic concepts, such as cryptographic algorithm, digital signature, and firewall.

The popular impression that many people have of the Internet is of hackers and geeky students lurking around the net, recording your every transmission and trying to take possession of your bank account. The reality, of course, is less dramatic. The risk that you take if you send your credit card number over the Internet is probably no greater than the risk you take every time you hand the card over to a waiter in a restaurant or to tell someone over the telephone.

However, there is some risk involved, if only because of the open and anarchic nature of the Internet. If the promise of the Internet (and in particular its precocious offspring, the World Wide Web) is to be fully realized, it is important that users have confidence in it (Buggsang and Spar, 1996, pp. 125–133).

Our security objectives will fall into one or more of the following five categories:

1. Access control: assurance that the person or computer at the other end of the session is permitted to do what he asks for.

2. Authentication: assurance that the resource (human or machine) at the other end of the session really is what it claims to be.
3. Integrity: assurance that the information that arrives is the same as when it was sent.
4. Accountability: assurance that any transaction that takes place can subsequently be proved to have taken place. Both the sender and the receiver agree that the exchange took place.
5. Privacy: assurance that sensitive information is not visible to the eavesdropper, usually achieved using encryption.

These objectives are closely related to the type of information that is being transferred. The first example that people usually think about when considering that is credit card transactions. However, this is only one of many possible uses for web security. For example, imagine that we are going to open the first college of education based entirely on the Web. This venture will involve sending many different types of documents, with a variety of security objectives. Here are some examples:

1. We will want to ensure that the course materials are only available to registered students, so we will apply access control to them.
2. When the students take their online exams we will need to be sure that the papers really do come from the student and we will also want to protect them in transit to prevent cheating. This exchange will need both privacy and authentication.
3. Finally, the hard-working student of the web university will receive his online diploma from the dean of the university and will go out into the job market armed with this document. He will need to be able to prove that it really was signed by the dean and he really received it. This exchange would therefore have to be authenticated and accountable.

Electronic commerce safety and network security

The nature of the web application gives some additional areas for concern. The following list summarizes some of these vulnerabilities:

1. When the user clicks on a link, the system that he is connected to is determined by what is defined in the document stored on the server. If that server has been compromised, a hacker could misdirect the user to his own server.
2. CGI programs are often written ad hoc, rather than being properly designed. This means that they are likely to contain bugs, which may be exploited by a hacker.
3. HTML documents can imbed in many different types of data (graphics, sound, etc.). On the browser each data type is associated with a presentation program, called a viewer. These programs are, themselves, often large and complex, which means they may well contain bugs. Furthermore, some of the file formats contain some programmability (a good example of this is Postscript). A hacker could use these features to execute programs or install data on the client machine.

Firewall technologies

Firewalls are pieces of software or hardware allowing only those users, who are outside a system with specified characteristics to access that system (Figure 9.1). They protect a system or network or a section of the Internet from unauthorized use from both within and outside. Inside the system it is possible to implement an internalized firewall system. Firewall devices enable secured access and communications with external networks where the level of security and trust is not well established.

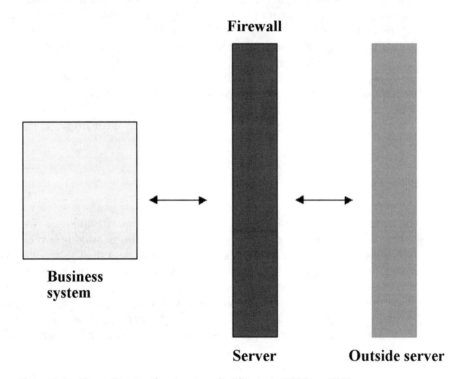

Figure 9.1   Firewall protection (source: Corbitt et al., 1999, p. 135)

Since their inception as simple bridges with access lists, Firewalls have become one of the most crucial components in any successful Internet initiative. They can provide a single "choke point' on a network in which traffic can be filtered, monitored and analyzed. Many organizations go further and implement Firewalls to the highest level currently possible and integrated virus and content scanning for web pages, e-mail and other types of internet traffic.

The majority of companies are using a software-based Firewall such as Firewall-1 by Checkpoint Software or Gauntlet Firewall by Network Associates. These Firewall packages run on top of a Unix or Windows NT server, and provide a very broad range of capabilities. Network Associates recently integrated their entire suite of products (PGP, VirusScan, CyberCop) into Gauntlet's capabilities. It seems that their hope is that by leveraging off to the large customer bases that already uses these products, they can increase market share on the Firewall stage.

Firewall limitations

Increasingly, the level of satisfaction with Firewall technologies has been diminishing. Customers want, need and demand more from the capabilities presented to them by Firewall vendors. Major issues to customers are ease of management, cost of ownership and learning curves. Companies either are pressuring vendors to create Firewalls that are easy to install and manage, yet highly secure and versatile. Companies require a Firewall solution that can grow and change quickly with their organization without significant cost or effort.

There is a danger in the over development of firewalls. As with all servers and the software loaded onto them, the more things that run on the server and the firewall, the more things that can be cracked open by a hacker. Thus, the more difficult it is to maintain and ensure security. The use of proxies with firewalls seeks to address these limitations.

The use of proxies

One of the more common forms of firewall is the use of a proxy (Figure 9.2). A proxy is a small program that is able to read messages on both sides of a firewall. Requests from outside users for information, files, transactions or communications from the web server are intercepted by the proxy, checked and then forwarded to the server machine. The response is eventually forwarded back to the requestor.

Proxies increase network security because they can strictly control authentication processes and check all logins on the server. Proxies can support high-level protocols that can enable and deny access to the server and thus to the organization's systems. Proxies also provide better network management and a higher level of

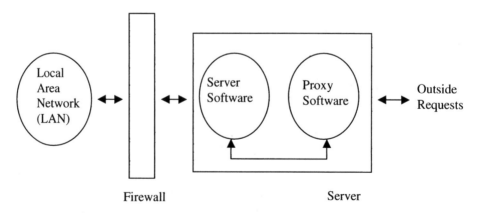

Figure 9.2 Protection through proxies (source: Corbitt et al., 1999, p. 135)

security because they add another level to the transaction process, which increases the potential for checking. However, one disadvantage of the use of proxies is that by having an additional level of activity in the process, there is a greater chance for viruses to infiltrate the system and escape detection until some damage has been done.

CASE APPLICATION   **LINES OF DEFENCE**

The hacking techniques used on e-Bay and others is known as Distributed Denial of Service (DDOS). It relies on embedded software on thousands of unsuspecting companies' servers which, on the hacker's command automatically begin bombarding target websites with requests until they crash. But it is only part of a spectrum of Internet crime ranging from electronic sabotage to disgruntled employees to computer viruses, fraud and, less commonly so-called 'cyber-terrorism'.

Information Week, the technology publication estimates total global losses from Internet crime reaching $1500 billion (£1027 billion) in 2000. Electronic crime is the fastest growing area of work for the FBI's international attaches. The Organization for Economic Co-operation and Development believes that unless crime is stemmed it will undermine consumer trust in e-commerce and the huge investments made by business and governments.

Companies such as BT and RSA Security, the world's leading Internet security firm, have backed moves for greater co-operation. But differences remain over whether crime or privacy is the more urgent issue. World-wide investment in information security services is predicted to increase from $4.8 billion (£3.3 billion) in 1998 to $16.5 billion in 2004, according to International Data Corporation.

Legislators on Internet security in the US, the UK and the Netherlands are aware of the fine line between protecting individual rights to data privacy and meeting law enforcement needs. Yet recent Internet surveillance bills such as the UK's Regulation of Investigatory Powers Bill (RIP) triggered a firestorm of controversy among privacy campaigners and business.

There remains a sceptical rump of companies that argue, privately, that the level of Internet crime is being exaggerated by security firms and police. They point to the lack of identified web incidents and hard data on Internet losses.

Despite the 'invisibility' of such Internet crime, the regulatory issue is not going to disappear. It is due to be discussed by the next meeting of G8 officials in Berlin, while the World Trade Organization is likely to focus on e-commerce when its next round of talks start in the spring.

The global nature of the Internet means that there will have to be harmonized security standards. Although the OECD is not lobbying for a new, global body, it does think it has a role in encouraging information sharing world-wide. The WTO tends to be focused on trade, and not security issues.

Source: adapted from Carlos Grande 'Crime wave has websites rushing to fill the breach'. Financial Times, Thursday October 19, 2000, p. 14.

Authentication

Authentication is the process by which you know for certain that the person or process with which you are carrying on a conversation is indeed the party they claim to be. Authentication can be accompanied by a number of different means. It can be based on a unique property possessed by the person or process. One example is fingerprints. Authentication can also be based on a knowledge possessed by the person or process. An example here is digital signatures, where the unique knowledge is the sender's private key: SSL provides an authentication service and this is discussed in depth in this part of the chapter.

One of the key safeguards in any system is user authentication. This is why you are assigned a username and password, which must be verified by the system before you are allowed to use it. The username and password files, however are a weak link in the system, and if they can be hacked and stolen, anyone possessing them can gain access to one system, and from there, possibly others. Other security loopholes have been discovered in popular Unix software.

One way to avoid some of these loopholes is to encrypt the password file. Other, more complicated authentication systems grant tickets to the user after he or she has signed onto the system. The tickets are time-stamped and are valid only for a specific time period. Someone 'listening' on the network may be able to grab the unsuspecting user's username and password as it entered a login. However, without the resulting ticket and means to decipher it, they cannot use services on the system.

Authentication systems can be expensive to install and maintain, and are by no means widespread. This makes the Internet a non-secure environment. Your first weapon against unauthorized entry is to observe standard safety precautions:

1. Change your password frequently.
2. Do not use simple English words as your password; add other characters or numbers so password sniffers cannot use automated programs to find your password.
3. Do not give your password to anyone.

Some more sophisticated systems and authentication precautions will be discussed in forthcoming sections.

Digital signatures

Digital signatures provide a means for the contents of a message and the identity of the sender to be verified. A digital signature is implemented using an asymmetric encryption cipher and a hash function. Digital signatures depend on the fact that asymmetric encryption ciphers are reversible. Digital signatures also depend on the fact that the original message, the signature, and the key pair are related so that changing any one of them will result in a failure to verify the signature.

Figure 9.3 shows how digital signatures work. The sender prepares a message digest (depicted in the upper left corner of the figure). The message digest is then

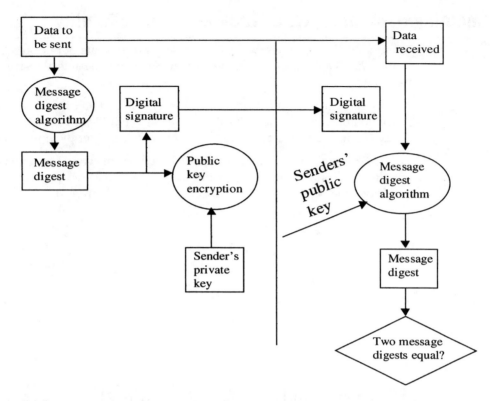

Figure 9.3 How digital signatures work (source: Adapted from Corbitt et al., 1999, p. 133)

encrypted using the sender's private key. The recipient receives the message and decrypts the message using the sender's public key. The recipient also computes the message digest, which should match the decrypted message digest. If it does, the signatures verify. If it does not either the message contents have been modified or the signature is a forgery.

RSA can be used for generating and verifying digital signatures. To sign a message, the sender encrypts the message using his or her private key. The sender transmits the message and signature. The recipient decrypts the message using the sender's public key and compares the result with the message already received. If the message was in fact signed by the sender, the two should match.

Note that when RSA is used for ensuring data privacy, the sender encrypts the message using the recipient's public key (instead of the sender's private key, as is done for signing (Naik, 1998)). The company's flagship product, the public-key cryptographic system, is also known as "RSA' (http://www.rsa.com).

Securing data integrity, privacy and accountability

In our security objectives, we listed access control as one of our objectives for the World Wide Web security. This means that we want to be able to restrict our server in two ways:

1. It should online deliver documents from within certain directories (for example, we do not want people to be able retrieve system files).
2. For certain restricted documents, it should only deliver them to specified users.

The latter point requires that we also address another one of our other security objectives, accountability, because the server must identify the client user in order to decide whether to deliver the document or not (Figure 9.4).

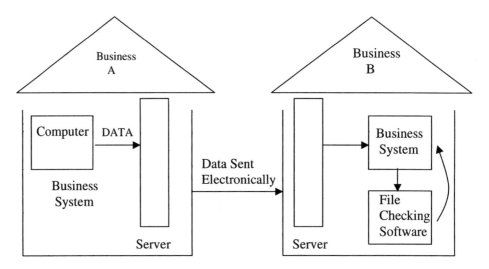

Figure 9.4   Changing data integrity in an electronic environment (adapted from Corbitt et al., 1999, p. 134)

Basic authentication is not a secure system, because the process it uses to send the user ID and password (base64 encoding) merely obscures them from causal view.

With basic authentication, your server has identified who the client user is by means of a user ID and password. How sure can you be that the user is really who he claims to be? To answer this you have to consider ways in which the ID and password may have been compromised:

1. The user may have voluntarily given the ID to another person.
2. The user may have written down the ID, and someone may be using it without his knowledge.
3. Someone may have guessed the password.

4. Someone may have intercepted the user's ID and password between client and server systems.

The first three possibilities are problems which occur in any password-based system. The normal response to such issues is to suggest better user education and rules. This is quite reasonable and effective within a single enterprise, where you have some control over the users of the system. It is much less effective in the Internet environment, where the users can come from many backgrounds and locations.

The last possibility is dependent on the level of protection given to messages by the HTTP protocol. The base64 encoding system is intended as a mechanism for converting binary data into a form that can be sent through the mail gateways, some of which can only handle 7-bit ASCII data. The result of this conversion is to mask the contents of any text string but, although it looks as though the data is encrypted, the protection that base64 provides is an illusion.

We will illustrate this with an example. In order to crack a message the hacker first has to be able to capture it. There are various ways to do this through hardware and software and none of them are very difficult. What is more difficult is finding a suitable point to make the trace. There are numerous techniques that a hacker can use to divert Internet traffic through his own tracing system, although they are becoming more complex as firewalls and routing controls become smarter.

Therefore it is good policy to only ever access the webadmin across a secure network connection, or to only use it for initial set-up and make subsequent modifications to configuration files by hand. As a user of the Web you will find cases where you will be prompted for a user ID and password. In some cases these are not used as a means of protection, but just to keep track of visitors to the site. Whatever the reason, you should never use a password that is the same or similar to any system password you have access to. The real solution to the fragility of basic authentication to enable accountability, is to use cryptographic techniques and these will be discussed in the next section.

Encryption schemes

An encryption scheme is a method of encoding information. An encrypted version[1] of transmitted normal text is called ciphertext and the encryption scheme is referred to as a cipher. If the plaintext

    Buy 1000 shares of IGCO now

is encrypted using a cipher, the resulting ciphertext is

    zabxyabc egtum pa wclfp

We cannot make sense of the ciphertext without knowing the cipher and the encryption key.

---

[1] This is using the ROT13 encryption scheme. This is a simple encryption scheme in which letters are rotated 13 positions further down the alphabet.

Because ROT13 is so simple, the plaintext is easy to figure out, given the cipher-text. That is, practically anyone could decrypt (or decipher) an encrypted ROT13 message. We can therefore say that ROT13 is not that a secure a system for encrypting information.

Because of the great interest in conducting business and other types of transactions over the Web, a number of technologies developed by computer scientists have been adopted or adapted for use on the Web. New technologies have also emerged. However, computer spies have also become more sophisticated in their decryption abilities.[2] Therefore, complex encryption schemes are necessary to ensure security. In the next sections, you will learn about several different types of encryption mechanisms. Our goal is to give you a basic understanding of the techniques employed in developing secure systems.

Private key cryptography

In private key cryptography, both the sender and receiver share the same private key. The key is used to encrypt the plaintext and also to decrypt the ciphertext. The key must be kept private (secret) to ensure system security. If a spy obtains the key they too will be able to decrypt encoded messages. In the encryption schemes currently in use, keys are often either very large prime numbers or the product of large primes.

A simple example, utilizing a cipher that is not secure, should clarify the idea behind private key cryptography. Suppose Alice wants to send the message

meet me at the roadhouse at noon urgent

to Bob. One cipher based on a shared private key, which in this case is a small number, simply 'wraps' the words based on the key's value. That is, you write the characters in lines, based on the key's value. The ciphertext is then constructed by listing the characters in the order in which they appear in the columns. For example, if Alice and Bob agree on a key of 5, the ciphertext of Alice's message will be

meehannearotutetounrttasogmhde3oe

When Bob receives the ciphertext, he decrypts it using the private key 5. First, bob counts the numbers of characters in the ciphertext, which in this case is 32. Since there are five characters per row, based on the agreed upon cipher and key, Bob realizes that the message is seven rows long – six full rows and one row containing two characters. Bob writes out the message in row format as follows:

Meetm
Eatth
Eroad

---

[2] The word 'hacker' is sometimes used to describe computer thieves or computer criminals. However, it is also used to describe clever programmers or people who program a great deal. Therefore, we prefer to use the word 'spy' to indicate illegal activity.

House
Atnoo
Nurge
Nt

Writing the text horizontally row-by-row, Bob obtains

Meetm eatth eroad house at noo nurge nt

Reading from left to right, Bob is able to determine the original message. If a spy knew the cipher and the private key, he or she could also decrypt the intercepted message.

In practice, both the cipher and private keys are much more complex than this simple example. Many other issues need to be dealt with as well, such as changing private keys periodically, distributing keys securely, etc.

Public key cryptography

Another security issue is the problem of authentication. When Bob receives a message, how can he be sure that Alice sent it? That is, how can he be sure that the message is authentic? Private key cryptography allows two parties to exchange messages and maintain confidentiality but not authenticity. If the ciphertext is intercepted, it will be difficult to decrypt without access to the private key and without knowing the encrypting cipher. Public key cryptography is useful for this purpose.

In public key cryptographic systems, every person who intends to send a message has a private key. In addition, every person has a public key that matches up with their private key. The private key is used to encrypt messages, and those messages can only be decrypted using the matching key, and vice versa.[3]

As the name implies, public keys are not kept secret. Suppose Alice sends Bob a message that she has encrypted using her private key. When Bob receives the ciphertext, he tries to decrypt it using Alice's public key, which is available to everyone. If Bob can decrypt the message, he knows that it must have come from Alice, because Alice's public key can only decrypt messages encrypted by her private key, and only Alice knows her private key. Notice that if Alice's message had been intercepted, anyone could have decrypted it using her public key. Privacy is not provided by public key cryptography, only authentication. Many other issues must also be dealt with when using public key cryptographic schemes, including creating secure keys, distributing public keys and so on.

Hashing algorithms

Suppose Alice sent Bob a message and it was intercepted. The person that inter-

---

[3] The computer science theorists Rivest, Shamir, and Adleman developed the public key encryption scheme that is most commonly used. It is called the RSA encryption scheme.

cepted the message might be able to alter its contents before passing it along. A way to verify that the message received is the same as the message sent involves the use of hashing algorithms.

A hashing algorithm takes a plaintext message as in-out and then computes a value based on that message. The length of the computed value is usually much shorter than the original message. While it is possible that several plaintext messages could generate the same value, hashing algorithms are designed such that this is very unlikely.

For illustration purposes, we will define a very simple hashing algorithm. The algorithms used in practice are much more sophisticated. Our hashing algorithm will multiply the number of as, es and hs in the message and will then add the number of os to this value. For example, suppose the message is:

the combination to the safe is two, seven, thirty-five

The hash or message digest of this message, using our simple hashing algorithm, is as follows:

$(2 \times 6 \times 3) + 4 = 40$

The message digest of the plaintext is sent to Bob along with the ciphertext. After Bob decrypts the message, he computes its hash using the agreed upon hashing algorithm. If the hash value sent by Alice does not match the hash value of the decrypted message, Bob will know that the message as been altered. For example, if Bob received a hash value of 17 and decrypted a message Alice has sent as

you are being followed, use back roads, hurry

he should conclude the message has been altered. This is because the hash of the message he received is:

$(3 \times 4 \times 1) + 4 = 16$

which is different from the value 17 that Alice sent.

These simple example illustrates the most common encryption schemes. Private key cryptography is useful for sending confidential messages; public key cryptography is useful for authenticating that the message came from the sender; and hashing algorithms are useful for verifying message integrity. In practice, some combination of these schemes is usually used.

Accountability and privacy: using Security Sockets Layer (SSL)

The Internet is a relatively anonymous technology. The security of data transmission by electronic form, whether online or not is a fundamental issue for all those businesses and individuals, who are engaged in electronic commerce. All businesses must ensure that the security and integrity of their data and the transmission of sensitive payment information is protected from data corruption and browser-side interference. This led to the development of software for online identification.

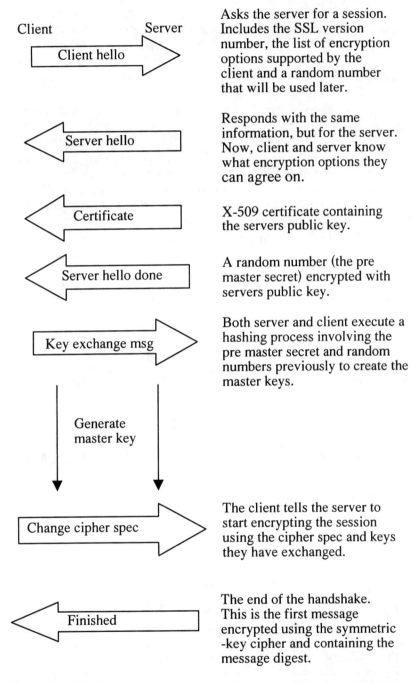

Asks the server for a session.
Includes the SSL version
number, the list of encryption
options supported by the
client and a random number
that will be used later.

Responds with the same
information, but for the server.
Now, client and server know
what encryption options they
can agree on.

X-509 certificate containing
the servers public key.

A random number (the pre
master secret) encrypted with
servers public key.

Both server and client execute a
hashing process involving the
pre master secret and random
numbers previously to create the
master keys.

The client tells the server to
start encrypting the session
using the cipher spec and keys
they have exchanged.

The end of the handshake.
This is the first message
encrypted using the symmetric
-key cipher and containing the
message digest.

Figure 9.5   How SSL works (adapted from McClure, S. SSL makes headway as an encryption standard. http://www.ne-dev.com/ned-01-1998/ned-01-security.html)

As its name suggests, the SSL provides an alternative to the standard TCP/IP socket API which has security implemented within it. The advantage of this scheme is that, in theory, it is possible to run any TC/IP application in a secure way without changing it. In practice, SSL is only widely implemented for HTTP connections, but Netscape Communications Corp. has stated an intention to employ it for other application types such as NNTP and Telnet, and there are several other such implementations freely available on the Internet.

SSL is a protocol that creates a secure connection to the server, protecting the information as it travels over the Internet (Figure 9.5). A website secured by SSL will have a URL beginning https instead of the usual http. It is available on several different browsers. As corporations discover the benefits of exploiting web technologies, they are also uncovering some of its corresponding perils. Inherent in the e-business transformation is the process of exposing valuable corporate systems and data to increased risks. Once a computer links to the Internet or even intranets and extranets, it becomes visible to a wide audience and vulnerable to the hazards associated with broad exposure. As this transformation occurs there is a subsequent increase in dependency on security, availability and manageability.

In the short-run, the commercial development of the Web will depend on giving consumers the opportunity to be anonymous or pseudonymous when they are

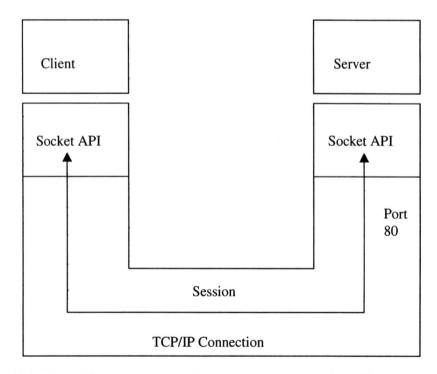

Figure 9.6   Standard SSL (adapted from adapted from McClure, S. SSL makes headway as an encryption standard, pp. 1–4. http://www.ne-dev.com/ned-01-1998/ned-01-security.html)

engaging in information exchanges and online transactions. At the same time, it depends on web providers receiving the minimum information necessary, in order to complete their exchange; for example, authentication, certification, confirmation, non-repudiation and payment in the case of transactions.

In essence there are two parts to the SSL standard (Figure 9.6):

1. A protocol for transferring data using a variety of predefined cipher; and authentication combinations, called the SSL record protocol.
2. A protocol for initial authentication and transfer of encryption keys, called the SSL handshake protocol (discussed in more detail in the next section).

An SSL session is initiated as follows:

1. On the client (browser) the user requests a document with a special URL which commences https instead of http, either by typing it into the URL input field, or by clicking on a link.
2. The client code recognizes the SSL request, and establishes a connection through CP port 443 to the SSL code on the server.
3. The client then initiates the SSL handshake phase, using the SSL record protocol as a carrier. At this point there is no encryption or integrity checking built into the connection.

The SSL handshake protocol

The objectives of the SSL handshake are:

1. To establish the identity of the server and, optionally, the client.
2. To establish symmetric key encryption for the remainder of the session.
3. To do these things in a secure way.

You will see that the server public key is transmitted in a certificate. A public-key certificate is a way in which a trusted third party can vouch for the authenticity of a public key.

Following the handshake, both session partners have generated a master key. From that key they generate other session keys, which are used in the symmetric key encryption of the session data and in the creation of message digests. The first message encrypted in this way is the finished message for the server. If the client can interpret the finished message it means:

1. Privacy has been achieved, because the message is encrypted using a symmetric-key bulk cipher (such as DES or RC4).
2. The message integrity is assured because it contains a Message Authentication Code (MAC), which is a message digest of the message itself plus material derived from the master key.
3. The server has been authenticated, because it was able to derive the master key from the pre-master key. As this was sent using the server's public key, it could only have been decrypted by the server (using its private key). Note that this relies on the integrity of the server's public key certificate.

The web document itself is then sent using the same encryption options, with a new set of session keys being calculated for each new message. This is a highly simplified version of SSL. In reality it contains numerous other details that counter different types of attack. Refer to the specification at http://home.netscape.com/newsref/std/SSL.html if you want to know more.

Obviously, the handshake and the many cryptographic processes it involves is quite an overhead to both client and server. To reduce this overhead, they both retain a session identifier and cipher information. If a subsequent document request occurs, they will resume the SSL connection using the previous master key.

We have said that SSL does define a process for client authentication (that is, a way for a client with a public key to prove its identity to the server). This is not currently implemented in any server or browser products.

However, one thing that SSL can do for us in this area is to make the basic authentication scheme more secure. In the previous section we have shown that basic authentication does not protect the user ID and password in transit. If we wrap the basic authentication flow in an SSL encrypted connection, this weakness disappears.

Limitations of SSL

SSL is not without its limitations. Certificates and keys that originate from a computer can be stolen over a network or by other electronic means. One possible solution to this weakness is to use hardware tokens, instead. Hardware tokens improve your security tremendously because they can be made to recognize only the person for which they were created. This recognition can be achieved, by biometric means like fingerprint or retinal scans matching.

Recent discoveries have proven that the technology is not infallible. The protocol has been found vulnerable to hyperlink spoofing, which is an attack on SSL server authentication. Also, weaknesses have been found in the hash algorithm used for SSL authentication and integrity. In spite of these vulnerabilities, when properly implemented, SSL is still a formidable means of securing a web-based application's data, which is found to be sensitive.

An integrated approach – IBM's security solution

This section explains how the IBM integrated security solutions approach the challenge of securing an e-business holistically. They offer an integrated set of solutions, organized around a 'Security Policy Director', which attempts to fulfil the security requirements of a dynamic global enterprise.

IBM's FirstSecure offers an integrated solution which provides a modular approach to a complex problem. In fact, the key security functions and focus areas within FirstSecure include:

1. Intrusion immunity
2. Public key infrastructure
3. Secure business server
4. Toolkit

and are organized around a secure policy director.

The focus of FirstSecure's intrusion immunity capabilities is on detecting security problems and on comprehensively reacting to these problems. It also integrates with the security policy director by accepting or requesting a component policy and sending security alerts/events. The potential benefits of combining intrusion immunity with a policy director are quite alluring. For example, if an alert comes in, the policy director will not just record the alert for someone to look at later but it will set right gears in motion to handle the situation. Depending on the alert, the response could be shut down to a particular resource, to re-route access to a dummy data set to obtain more information on the intruder or to perform a virus sweep on the affected area.

But this growth and business transformation does not come without pain. To benefit from web-based technologies running in a secure connected, many companies are adopting numerous proprietary technologies and installing many point products from multiple vendors. The result is an installation like that shown in Figure 9.7. The sheer number of security products is causing numerous problems.

Doing business on a web-based network means the customer must protect itself from many threats not present on a traditional network. Enabling a secure e-business requires new products such as digital signatures. Integration of all the security products required for both protection and enablement is extremely difficult. Lack of integration leaves the enterprise exposed to significant risk, and ill-equipped to deliver new business solutions in today's web-based world.

For public key infrastructure, the focus is on certificate authentication, secured communications, and validation of signed policy. It would be the policy director that sends out the changes to the affected areas of the system. For the secure business server, the policy director integrates access control with the gateway functions of a firewall and firewall content filters. And finally, the toolkit enables customers to build and deploy secure applications within their enterprise for policy management.

Implementing an e-business strategy can benefit from the accumulated wisdom and experience manifest in the latest set of security solutions from IBM. The architecture of these new solutions will allow them to integrate with the OS/390 or OS/400 security schemes that protect data and transactions. The IBM integrated security solutions accommodates the various e-business environments:

1. Intranet, contained entirely within an organization;
2. Extranet for business-to-business transactions; and
3. Internet for communicating and doing business with consumers.

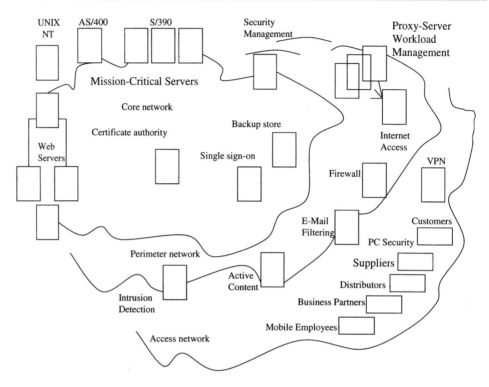

UNIX
NT

AS/400

S/390

Security
Management

Proxy-Server
Workload
Management

Mission-Critical Servers

Core network

Certificate authority

Backup store

Internet
Access

Web
Servers

Single sign-on

VPN

Firewall

E-Mail
Filtering

Customers

PC Security

Perimeter network

Suppliers

Active
Content

Distributors

Intrusion
Detection

Business Partners

Mobile Employees

Access network

Figure 9.7   IBM's integrated security solution (source: IBM integrated security solutions: comprehensive security solutions for enabling e-business, www.ibm.com)

Figure 9.7 shows the offerings of IBM ISS to address the security risks that organizations face in the course of their e-business evolution. The end-to-end design, which dovetails well with OS/390 and AS/400 security, satisfies business in the various stages of transformation:

1. Securely deploying e-business applications.
2. Strengthening the security of existing operations.
3. Integrating a security solution with the legacy IT environment.
4. Helping companies in leveraging the potential of e-business.

A holistic security solution must reduce risk, but it must do so without introducing overwhelming complexity and cost. Creating the right security for the e-business environment is more than piecing together point products, it is facilitating the continual monitoring and adjusting of solution elements according to corporate-wide policies. Policy needs to be the focal point of an integrated security solution.

The integrated solution includes SecureWay, FirstSecure, Trivoli User Administration, Trivoli Security Management and Trivoli ADSM. This combination of function covers the set of five high-level security requirements that serve as the conceptual base of IBM's security architecture for e-business, namely:

1. Authorization
2. Accountability
3. Assurance
4. Availability
5. Administration

SecureWay FirstSecure covers authorization, accountability and assurance from a corporate-wide perspective. FirstSecure includes virus protection, access control, content traffic control, encryption, intrusion detection, digital certification, firewall technology and a toolkit. FirstSecure also offers service solutions to speed and simplify its installation as well as validate that the operational environment is secure, with no back doors inadvertently left open.

And finally, Trivoli User Administration and Trivoli Security Management help ensure the security mechanisms are being managed efficiently and effectively. These solutions provide a simplified, single point of control by providing the mechanisms to manage a complex security environment. These include functions that deal with security policy, identities, privileges, and auditing, for both users and programs.

IBM's integrated security solutions are organized around a policy director. The initial integrated security solution, which includes IBM SecureWay, FirstSecure, Tivoli User Administration, Tivoli Security Management and Tivoli ASM, set the stage for a comprehensive security system that reduces complexity and facilitates the quick deployment of e-business applications, which help manage your profits and cost base.

Securing payment

Ultimately, the most effective way for commercial web providers to develop profitable exchange (payment) relationships with online customers is to earn consumer trust. Without doubt it is the confusion over laws of encryption and confidentiality that are holding companies back from implementing e-commerce payment systems. This is dealt with in more detail in Chapter 8. At this stage it is suffice to say that with the aid of a voluntary licensing programme for providers of cryptographic services and the legal recognition placed on digital certificates, the organizational challenge of creating an e-commerce friendly community may not be too far ahead. The Office of Fair Trading in its paper 'Widening the Net', is broadening the range and number of bodies to secure and protect the rights of consumers trading (www.oft.gov.uk/html/trading/fr26-03.htm).

Conclusion

Security of networks and systems operating in business organizations is of paramount importance to all businesses engaged in electronic commerce and Internet commerce. Systems can function very effectively and improve the efficiency of businesses to a significant degree. However, if the confidentiality of the data transacted, communications sent or the files stored cannot be assured, then the system is of little value to the organization. Business done electronically relies on the integrity of the data being sent. If data is corrupted by poor systems, poor systems management, inadequate or incompatible software and hardware, or by viruses, then the business transacted is of no value whatsoever. Business organizations need to be able to protect the goodwill and value of their business. They need to be assured that their data and their files are not stolen or made accessible to those who have no right of access. Network systems must be made secure from prying computers and the eyes and intelligence gathering of hackers. Business systems must ensure that the identity of both the sender and receiver of information or transaction desired. It is only with the development and implementation of proper IT policy and the establishment of an IT audit that business will gain proper and thorough security in the operations of their networks.

CASE APPLICATION   **G8 SEEKS TIGHTER INTERNET**

The world's Internet industry should select national representatives to help authorities in the fight against cybercrime, according to Internet experts from the leading industrial nations. Government and industry representatives of the Group of Eight countries also used a meeting in Berlin to step up calls for international agreement on minimum Internet security standards on the Internet.

They received backing from Gerhard Schroder, the German chancellor, who used a speech in Hanover yesterday to argue that the global character of Internet crime 'requires global countermeasures – better international co-operation and, above all, binding international minimum standards'.

Cybercrime has been estimated to cause DM100 billion (£29.5 billion) damage annually. Yesterday's Berlin meeting did not reach formal conclusions but Michael Niebel, the European Commission representative, said one 'one concrete proposal' was for national contact points 'to which you can turn for information' when pursuing crime. He suggested national representatives could link-up, further strengthening their effectiveness.

The G8 and other countries already operate a round-the-clock communication system for combating cybercrime. But there was widespread agreement that representatives in industry could further aid crime prevention.

Internet businesses in some countries have resisted such proposals because of the suspicions that law enforcement agencies were simply expecting industry to do their work for them. Despite agreement on the need for minimum security standards, there remains no clear view on what should be included.

Michael Sussman, a senior counsel at the US Department of Justice, said a priority was to ensure countries enacted laws that ensured cybercrimes were offences to which extradition laws could be applied.

Source: Ralph Atkins and Tobias Buck. Financial Times, Friday October 27, 2000, p. 16.

Checklist

1. Security is an essential feature of the Internet, if the promise of the Internet (and in particular its offspring, the World Wide Web) is to be fully realized.
2. There is a need for e-business to control access through firewalls and proxies, into and around their websites.
3. Authentication mechanisms such as digital signatures act as a secure means of verifying users operating in the digital environment.
4. SSL through public and private key cryptography enables data to be encrypted for secure transmission over the Web.
5. There are a number of limitations to SSL, which is leading to continual refinement and technological innovation of web-based data transmission mechanisms.
6. To benefit from web-based technologies running in a secure connected environment, many companies are adopting numerous proprietary technologies and installing many point products from multiple vendors.

References

Buggsang, J. and Spar, D. (1996), The net, *Harvard Business Review*, May–June, pp. 125–133.

Corbitt, B., Lawrence, E., Tidwell, A., Fisher, J. and Lawrence, J.R. (1999), *Internet Commerce – Digital Models for Business*, John Wiley & Sons, New York.

IBM Integrated Security Solutions: Comprehensive Security Solutions for Enabling e-Business. http://www.ibm.com

Macgregor, R., Aresi, A. and Siegert, A. (1996), *How to Build a Secure World Wide Web Connection*. IBM/Prentice Hall PTR, NJ.

McClure, S. (1998), SSL makes headway as an encryption standard, http://www.ne-dev.com/ned-01-1998/ned-01-security.html.

Naik, D. (1998), *Internet Standards and Protocols*, Microsoft Press, Washington, DC.

Office for Fair Trading, *Widening the Net*. www.oft.gov.uk.

CHAPTER 10

Marketing ethics on the Internet

Key topics

- Emergence of accountable marketing
- Working towards a code of ethical conduct on the Web
- Main issues of ethical concern
- Rules of ownership
- Enforcement and operationalizing ethical codes

After studying this chapter you will be able to:

- Understand the ethics of information gathering.
- Evaluate the individuals right to privacy.
- Describe the major ethical issues relating to online exchange.
- Explain possible mechanisms of ethical enforcement.

Ethics is the moral dimension to business activity (Velasquez, 1998). The firm embracing the Web has to define clearly the rules of ethics it intends to follow in its relationships with the market. If, in recent years one has observed improving marketing conduct, it is largely due to strong countervailing powers, like the consumerist and environmentalist movements, which in a way forced companies to improve their ethical conduct. Nothing is more convincing than the fear of punishment to induce good citizen behaviour. The ethical firm must go beyond this and publicly confirm its commitment to promote ethical web decisions and to create a corporate culture conducive to ethical web behaviour.

In e-commerce, marketing is the most visible functional area because of its interface with the different marketspace players: consumers, distributors, competitors and public opinion. Web advertising and selling activities are the most noticeable and close to the public view and, therefore, it is not surprising that marketing on the Internet is the subject of considerable societal analysis and media scrutiny. Web-based marketers, more than any other functional practitioners, are likely to be confronted with ethical dilemmas at some point in their careers.

Emergence of accountable marketing

The consumerist and environmentalist movements have forced some marketing theoreticians to widen their classical marketing concept in a way that puts the emphasis on the necessity to develop an increased consciousness within the firm of the socio-cultural side-effects of its economic and especially its marketing activity. Thus Kotler (1997) proposed the adoption of the societal marketing concept: this societal marketing concept holds that the organization's task is to determine the needs, wants and interests of target markets and to deliver the desired satisfactions more effectively and efficiently than competitors in a way that preserves and enhances the consumer's and society's well-being (Kotler, 1997, p. 27).

This concept is based on three implicit assumptions:

1. Consumers' wishes do not always coincide with their long-term interests or those of the public at large.
2. Consumers prefer organizations that show real concern for their satisfaction and well-being as well as the collective well-being.
3. The most important task at the organization is to adapt itself to the target markets in such a way as to generate not only satisfaction, but also individual and collective well-being, in order to attract and keep customers.

Defining ethics

The field of business ethics has traditionally been the domain of philosophers, academics and social critics. Consequently, much of today's literature about business ethics is not geared toward the practical needs of leaders and managers – the people primarily responsible for managing ethics in the online marketspace. Simply, put, ethics involves learning what is right or wrong, and then doing the right thing – but 'the right thing' is not nearly straightforward as conveyed in a great deal of business ethics literature.

Many ethicists assert there is always a right thing to do on the Web based on moral principle, and others believe the right thing to do depends on the virtual situation – ultimately it is up to the individual. Many philosophers consider ethics to be the 'science of conduct'. Many ethicists consider emerging ethical beliefs to be 'state of the art' legal matters, i.e. what becomes an ethical guideline today is often translated to a law, regulation or rule tomorrow. Values which guide how we ought to behave are considered moral values, e.g. values such as respect, honesty, fairness, responsibility, etc. Statements around how these values are applied are sometimes called moral or ethical principles.

The concept of 'business ethics' in the virtual context, has come to mean various things to various people, but generally it is coming to know what is right or wrong in the marketspace and doing what is right – this is in regard to effects of products and services and in relationships with shareholders. Online business ethics is critical during times of fundamental change – times much like those faced by virtual companies, both profit and non-profit. In times of fundamental change, values that were previously taken for granted are now strongly questioned. Many of these values are no longer followed. Consequently, there is no clear moral compass to guide business through complex dilemmas about what is right or wrong. Attention to online ethics sensitizes employers and employees to how they should act. Perhaps most importantly, attention to ethics in the marketspace helps ensure that businesses when struggling in times of crisis and confusion, they retain a strong moral compass. However, attention to online business ethics provides numerous benefits that will be discussed later in the chapter.

There are two broad areas of business ethics. First, you have managerial mischief. Velasquez (1998) explains that 'managerial mischief' includes 'illegal, unethical, or questionable practices of individual managers or organizations, as well as the causes of such behaviours and remedies to eradicate them'. There has been a great deal written about managerial mischief, leading many to believe that business ethics is merely a matter of preaching the basics of what is right or wrong. More often, though, business ethics is a matter of dealing with dilemmas that have no clear indication of what is right or wrong. Second, there are 'moral mazes'. This includes the numerous ethical problems that managers must deal with on a daily basis, such as potential conflicts of interest, wrongful use of resources, mismanagement of contracts and agreements, etc.

Business ethics as a management discipline

Business ethics has come to be considered a management discipline, especially since the birth of the social responsibility movement in the 1960s. In that decade, social awareness movements raised expectations of businesses to use their massive financial and social influence to address such social problems such as poverty, crime, environmental protection, equal rights, public health and improving education. An increasing number of people asserted that because businesses were making a profit from using our country's resources, these businesses owed it to our country to work to improve society. Many researchers, business schools and managers have recognized this broader constituency, and in their planning and operations have replaced the word 'shareholder' with 'stakeholder', meaning to include employees, customers, suppliers and the wider community.

The emergence of business ethics is similar to other management disciplines. For example, organizations realized that they needed to project a more positive image to the public and so the recent discipline of public relations was born. As commerce became more complicated and dynamic, organizations realized they needed more guidance to ensure their dealings supported the common good and did not harm others – and so business ethics was born.

Today, ethics in the marketspace can be managed through the use of codes of ethics, codes of conduct, the role of ethicists and ethics committees, policies and procedures, procedures to resolve ethical dilemmas and ethics training. Internet marketing ethics, in other words, is a form of applied ethics. It includes not only the analysis of moral norms and moral values, but also attempts to apply the conclusions of this analysis to the assortment of institutions, technologies, transactions, activities and pursuits which we call 'e-commerce'.

Working towards a code of ethical conduct on the Web

The ethical e-business will need to balance the drive for profits with ethical considerations. Garrett and Klonoski (1986) proposed an ethical model which has been widely accepted by the marketing academic community. They have identified five types of organizational ethical behaviours forming a hierarchy, from the lowest to the highest level of corporate moral development.

Stage 1 Amoral. It is the lowest level. Owners and managers are the only important stakeholders. The prevailing philosophy is to maximize profit at almost any cost.

Stage 2 Legalistic. Being ethical means simply obeying the law. The only obligations that a firm of this type recognizes are legal obligations.

Stage 3 Responsive. The firms having reached this level begin to develop some ethical concern. They recognize that a good relationship with the community is important. The responsive firm usually behaves ethically, if only for self-serving reasons.

Stage 4 Emerging ethical. These firms make explicit recognition that the cost of being ethical may sometimes involve a trade-off with profits. Concern for values is explicitly mentioned in the corporate mission statement or in a code of ethics.

Stage 5 Developed ethics. The organizations have clearly articulated value statements communicated, accepted and implemented by everyone in the organization. These companies are at the peak of the ethical hierarchy.

The AMA (2000) indicates that most physical and virtual companies have reached Stage 3 of the hierarchy. The number of e-businesses, at Stages 4 and 5 is growing, however.

Code of ethics: The American Marketing Association (AMA)

1. All members of the AMA are committed to ethical professional conduct. They have joined together in subscribing to this Code of Ethics, which embraces the following guiding protocols:
2. Support of professional ethics to avoid harm by protecting the rights of privacy, ownership and access.
3. Adherence to all applicable laws and regulations with no use of Internet marketing that would be illegal, if conducted by mail, telephone, fax or other media.
4. Awareness of changes in regulations related to Internet marketing.
5. Effective communication to organizational members on risks and policies related to Internet marketing, when appropriate.

6. Organizational commitment to ethical Internet practices communicated to employees, customers and relevant stakeholders.

Source: AMA, Code of Ethics for Marketing on the Internet 2000.

There are three main areas of ethical activities covered by the AMA's ethical code and each will be discussed in turn:

Privacy

Information collected from customers should be confidential and used only for expressed purposes. All data, especially confidential customer data, should be safeguarded against unauthorized access. The expressed wishes of others should be respected with regard to the receipt of unsolicited e-mail messages.

Ownership

Information obtained from the Internet should be properly authorized and documented. Information ownership should be safeguard and respected.

Marketers should respect the integrity and ownership of computer and network systems.

Access

Marketers should treat access to accounts, passwords, and other information as confidential, and only examine or disclose content when authorized by a responsible party. The integrity of others' information systems should be respected with regard to placement information, advertising or messages.

Any AMA member found to be in violation of any provision of this Code of Ethics may have his or her Association membership suspended or revoked.

Main issues of ethical concern

Drawing on the work of Garrett and Klonoski (1986), Velasquez (1998) identifies two types of privacy – psychological and physical:

Psychological privacy is privacy with respect to a person's inner life. This includes the person's thoughts and plans, personal beliefs and values, feelings and wants. These inner aspects of a person are so intimately connected with the person that to invade them is almost an intrusion of the very person. Physical privacy is privacy with respect to a person's physical activities. Since people's inner lives are revealed by their activities and expressions, physical privacy is important in part because it is a means for protecting psychological privacy.

The focus here is on informational privacy in e-commerce – the right of individuals to exercise control over information about themselves. It can be derived from Klonoski's right to privacy. From the authors' perspectives, there is nothing inherently unjust or unethical in gathering information on customers when appropriate procedural justice safeguards are put in place to protect them. What has irrevocably altered this information gathering process is the growth of sophisticated computer technology, which enables the collection, dissemination, and combination of information at previously unprecedented levels. Technology has substantially altered the relationship between customers and retailers, and tipped the balance in favour of online merchants' commercial interests versus the customers' privacy interests. This change leaves online consumers particularly vulnerable, subject to harm, their right to psychological and physical privacy compromised. Just as our legal conceptions of the right to privacy lag behind in adapting to rapid technological change, so do our ethical conceptions of privacy in contemporary social conditions.

The online consumer market is growing quickly as more and more consumers access the Web. In September 1997, some 10 million people in the US and Canada had made a purchase online. It is predicted that by June 1999, some 92 million people in the US and Canada were reported to be online (Commerce.net and Nielsen, 1998).

The explosion in electronic commerce has been accompanied by an ever-increasing ability of web merchants to gather, compile, and sell personal information on consumers. CMG Information Services, Andover, MA is working with some of the largest commercial sites on the Web to compile data about their customers' reading, shopping, and entertainment habits. According to Hansell (1998), CMG is already tracking the moves of more than 30 million web users, often without their knowledge. Information-gathering techniques and the amount of individualized information gathered are varied. The info-gathering and profiling techniques of online bookseller Amazon.com are so refined that returning customers are given a suggested list of books and videos based on their previous buying habits and similar profiles built from other customers. In addition to web merchants compiling data about their own customers, web-tracking and analysis services such as Media Metrix Inc., will soon offer a wealth of data about competitors as well.

Web merchants employ a variety of techniques to gather information about customers and visitors to their sites. The following are examples:

1. Voluntary dissemination. Customers may voluntarily provide personal information to web merchants when buying goods online. Typical information provided would include names, addresses, credit card numbers, phone numbers, and merchandise ordered. This information allows merchants to develop highly detailed, personalized profiles on customers that can be used to aim promotions at them in the future.
2. Free merchandise and gifts. Free-PC.com in 1999 announced it would give away 10 000 personal computers to people in exchange for extensive details on their personal lives and online activities. Once online, Free-PC.com will track which Internet sites the recipients visit, the time spent on each site, and the ads viewed. In addition, ads appeared non-stop on the computer screen. Free-PC earns revenue by selling on-screen advertising space.

3. Anonymous profile data. A first time anonymous user on the Web can reveal a certain amount of data about themselves. Web merchant's can determine the types of browsers visitors are using, their operating systems, countries of origin, and Internet Protocol (IP) addresses, which betray the identity of the Internet Service Providers (ISPs) or the companies from which they have access to the Web. For individuals arriving at sites through hypertext links on other sites, the originating website addresses are transmitted to the new site. This allows merchants to measure the number of visitors to the different sections of a site, determine what links drive the most traffic through, and make the site more useful to its visitors.

4. Cookies. These are devices that track visits to websites by storing information on visitors' hard drives. Websites subsequently use this information to keep track of when users visited the site before, what they viewed, and the amount of time spent viewing the site. Information collection via cookies is often not obvious to consumers. If people have registered by name at websites, the servers can track their online actions and use previously deposited cookies to link these data to their names and addresses. The information collected can then be sold by web merchants to advertisers and other interested parties. Cookies give virtual retailers certain advantages over their physical counterparts. The information collected can be used to change the layout of a virtual store and target merchandise tailored to the previous preferences expressed by web visitors. Both Netscape and Microsoft Explorer web browsers can be set to notify computer users when websites want to deposit cookies, and the users can accept or refuse.

5. Newsgroups and chat rooms. It is possible to collect e-mail addresses and IDS in newsgroup postings or chat rooms and create demographic profiles based on participants' online habits and postings. Moreover, e-businesses can buy e-mail addresses and information on customer preferences from other merchants, much like direct marketers currently do.

CASE APPLICATION   **ETHICAL ISSUES RAISED AND ADDRESSED BY THE FTC**

The Federal Trade Commission (FTC) surveyed 1402 commercial websites during a 2-week period in March 1998. It concluded that the industry's efforts at self-regulation had fallen short of what is needed to protect consumer privacy. Survey results revealed that upwards of 85–97% of commercial websites in all samples surveyed collected personal information from consumers. The type of information collected most frequently included: e-mail address, postal address, telephone number, fax number, and credit card number. Of those sites collecting personal information, only 14% provided any notice to consumers of information collection practices.

   The FTC was particularly disturbed by the nature and amount of information gathered from children. Of the 212 children's sites surveyed, 89% collected personal identifying information directly from the child including such things as name, e-mail address, social security number, and date of birth. Websites used a variety of techniques to solicit personal information from children including registration, eligibility to win prizes using imaginary characters to solicit information, having them sign guest books, invitations for electronic pen pal programs, and free home pages.

On completion of its 3-year study of industry guidelines and actual online practices, the FTC concluded that effective industry self-regulation with respect to online collection, use, and dissemination of personal information has not yet taken hold. In its report, the FTC stated that unless the industry could demonstrate that it could develop and implement broad-based and effective self-regulatory programs, additional government authority in the area would be necessary.

Unlike in the US, information privacy is considered a fundamental right in Europe, and the right to privacy is legally codified. In October 1995, the European Parliament enacted guidelines on information privacy called the 'European Community Directive on Data Protection'. Member states must adopt national legislation ensuring protection of personal information and prohibit any company doing business in Europe from transmitting personal data to countries that do not guarantee privacy protection. Currently the US is considered one of those countries. The EU directive prohibits the sharing of consumer data with other companies and provides consumers with a bill of rights. Leibowitz (1999) notes that consumers have the 'right to be informed about the processing of personal data, such as where the data originated and the purpose for which information is processed; the right to access or review personal data and correct errors; and the right to deny use of the data'

e-Commerce businesses should plan that they will at some point be subject to regulations consistent with the FTC report and EU privacy directive. Under the EU directive, the requirements for notice, consent, access, integrity and security are similar to the principles stated in the FTC report to Congress and implemented in the Geocities consent order. The following steps should be taken to prepare for possible future regulation: (1) implement a notice and consent procedure, by which users are provided with clear notice of the uses of their personal information and may consent to or opt out of such uses; (2) the procedure should permit the user to correct inaccurate information and an option to revoke consent to use; and (3) develop a technical capability to inform users of all the personal information collected about them, where and how that information is stored and to whom it is disclosed.

At this point, the US government is still pursuing a policy of self-regulation with regard to online privacy information. However, in its privacy report the FTC expressed clear reservations about the industry's ability to develop a workable privacy protection plan. In 1998, FTC chairman Robert Pitofsy testified before Congress in support of S.2326 'Children's Online Privacy Protection Act' of 1998, which was subsequently passed as part of S.442 Internet Tax Freedom Act.

The legislation directs the FTC to prescribe regulations requiring commercial website operators to obtain verifiable parental consent before collecting personal information from children under 13. They must also provide opt-out options to parents, and maintain the confidentiality and security of collected data. Website operators must also obtain verifiable prior parental notification and consent to use any information gathered for marketing purposes, or to list a child's name or e-mail address on a home page, pen pal service, message board, or chat room. The Child Online Protection Act of 1998 imposes fines and/or imprisonment on website operators who commercially disseminate information via the web and fail to restrict access to material harmful to minors.

WORKPLACE SURVEILLANCE

The government bodies regulating employers' snooping on staff e-mails and phone calls have given conflicting expectations of how two overlapping sets of new rules will interact. The Department of Trade and Industry's surveillance rules which come into force next week, give employers a largely free hand to snoop. The main proviso is that staff are warned their personal e-mails and calls may be monitored

But a draft code on surveillance, issued by the Data Protection Commission within days of the DTI's announcement of the new rules is markedly more restrictive. It warns that blanket monitoring of e-mails is unlikely to be justified and that employers should not open personal messages received at work.

Business groups are frustrated by the apparent contradictions. 'We had hoped for some joined-up thinking between the DTI and the commission' said Rod Armitage, Head of Legal Affairs at the Confederation of British Industry.

The rules allow surveillance to prevent the abuse of the employer's computer systems by staff. Monitoring which meets this broad parameter – and has therefore crossed the first hurdle of being lawful under the rules – could still fail at the second hurdle of the data protection code.

When an employer suspects there is no abuse of the system, it would be unfair processing (of data) to just go on a fishing expedition (trawling all employees' e-mail accounts). The Data Protection Act requires a proportionate response.

Mr Trower (Strategic Policy Manager at the Commission)

This two-tier approach means that employers who meet the law set by the DTI nevertheless find themselves open to enforcement action, including potentially unlimited fines, from the commission.

The DTI reject this view. 'As far as we are concerned it is not a double hurdle at all', the DTI said. 'Businesses will have to observe the Data Protection Act just as they do now. Any monitoring must be proportionate and related to business needs... the two will sit seamlessly side by side', the DTI added. This seamless fit may require some concessions from the commission. Lawyers point out that the draft code was based on an earlier version of the DTI's rules which would have imposed significantly tighter restrictions on employers. The DTI changed its stance after intense business lobbying.

Whether industry can pull off the same trick with the draft code is more debatable. The CBI points out that the draft code says the data protection law does not require an employer to allow staff to use their phone, e-mail or Internet systems for personal calls and messages. While the wrangle goes on, lawyers advise businesses to take a pragmatic view.

Source: adapted from J. Eaglesham, Financial Times, Monday October 23, 2000, p. 4.

Rules of ownership

Developed over decades or even centuries, property rights set out to clarify the basis of ownership or exchange. They provide a consistent way of defining who owns what and how possessions can be transferred from one owner to another.

Property rights reduce the costs of exchange by clarifying ownership and providing a means for punishing thieves, thus they defined not only possessions but also theft.

The connection between property rights and commerce applies with full force on the Internet. The advent of e-commerce does not eliminate the basic need for an infrastructure to clarify ownership and thereby allow owners to reap economic rewards. But at the moment, online property rights are imprecisely defined, the Net remains a virtual free-for-all where information is seen as a public good and ownership is up for grabs.

Copyright law will do a lot to protect the property of companies that transact in cyberspace, but they will not do nearly enough. First, copyright is already one of the most intricate and esoteric areas of law. Courts vary widely in their interpretation of existing statutes and even in their understanding of a given law's intent. The extension of those laws into a new realm of commerce is almost sure to create ambiguity and uncertainty leaving courts and litigants to fumble toward new definitions of private property and property rights. Second, because the laws are national, they will have little influence on the Internet's international transactions.

This implies that even if the laws stop a company based in London from covertly downloading a competitor's software, textbook, or database, they may not stop that company from routing the material through a computer in Thailand or the Netherlands. Finally, even if the laws were applied at the global level (and there is some talk of doing so under the new World Trade Organization), they still would not provide the means for businesses to determine if their information has been altered or copied in cyberspace.

Let us consider, for example, the services provided by America Online (AOL). AOL sells access to the Internet. It gives users an easy way to enter cyberspace and a new forum in which to advertise products or disseminate ideas. When new subscribers join AOL, thought they get much more than a pathway to the Internet. They get a well-regulated, well-maintained road. AOL offers a user-friendly environment and direct access to commercial services. In return, it regulates all users and demands that they comply with explicit rules. Likewise when a content provider signs on with AOL, it does not simply transmit its information into the vast reaches of the Internet. Rather, it provides content – news stories, photographs, flight schedules – directly to AOL, which then redistributes the content to its own subscribers, a discrete and identifiable customer base. By intermediating the transaction, AOL converts the Internet form an open, lawless realm into a secure community where access is controlled and rules enforced. As a result, AOL can assure its content providers that their sales will be controlled, identified, and reimbursed. In effect, AOL creates and enforces the property rights of its customers. Even without a well-defined legal infrastructure, AOL is writing the rules of commerce.

Access rights

Web-rule enforcement poses the most obvious problems for e-commerce. Online communities are necessary because individual security precautions have only a limited value on the Web. Value lies, instead, in a wider, protected community of users, who can communicate among themselves confidentially and thus confidently. The value of the community is created by the entities that run and manage it. They are the ones who determine its size, choose its members, implement security provisions, and punish violators. If the Internet is the lawless frontier, then these service providers are the new marshals in town.

For online communities to form, content providers need to feel confident about whom they are dealing with and how the material is being used, and how they are receiving payment. What they need, in short, is an entity to transform the anonymity and anarchy of the Web into a market with identifiable customers and recordable transactions. That entity would manage a corner of the Internet where explicit rules and norms would prevail.

Microsoft Network is one example of this trend toward online communities. Originally conceived as another proprietary online service, MSN has recently been repositioned as an Internet community with well-ordered rules and value-added services. Other online services, such as AOL, Prodigy, and Compuserve, are similar reinventing themselves as full Internet communities. Also, there is Time Warner's popular pathfinder site – which offers rich content form across the media giant's empire – which requires users to register, tracks their subsequent usage and plans soon to offer accompanying transaction services. Several other telecommunication and media companies have also announced plans to launch their own communities on the Internet.

While the shift toward communities of commerce is most evident in consumer-oriented services, the logic of communities extends even further than that. A computer manufacturer could easily create an Internet community with its key distributors, just a s a large clothing company might reap the benefits of establishing a secure transaction infrastructure with its suppliers. Universities could choose to distribute their own course catalogues only with their own corners of the Internet, and banks could dedicate separate, secure lines for their own internal transactions.

In all of these examples, the companies managing the online transactions of their users would have created privately ruled communities, just as developers in some areas have built private 'towns' in the LA district, complete with strict rules, security forces, and gates to keep outsiders away. To build these communities, service providers would employ encryption, firewalls, and other evolving technologies to control access in the same way as developers control it in physical communities. These themes are discussed further in Chapter 9.

THE REGULATION OF INVESTIGATORY POWERS ACT

Serious ethical concerns regarding online privacy were brought to light in 2000 by the Government's proposed bill to allow the interception of e-mails. The Regulation of Investigatory Powers (RIP) bill will require ISPs to allow authorities to intercept and decrypt electronic communications such as e-mails. However Simon Davies (The Daily Telegraph. 'dotcom.telegraph', Thursday June 15, 2000 p. 1), who is an LSE academic believes that 'the bill is a substantial invasion of privacy. It puts the Internet under mass surveillance. It is getting to the point where amendments are not sufficient and the bill should be scrapped'.

The Foundation for Information Policy Research says the RIP bill is likely to breach the European Convention of Human Rights, as it violates the presumption of innocence, infringes the right to silence and does not provide adequate safeguards against abuse.

Business organizations object that the powers are so sweeping the law might force Internet companies abroad and damage the government's stated ambition to become a world leader in e-business. A study by the LSE for the British Chambers of Commerce guessed the bill could lose 20–30% of e-commerce investment over the next 5 years and a corresponding volume of trade, which it reckons – on Government figures – would lose the UK £55 billion.

CHILDREN

As the Internet was evolving, significant fears rose with the scale and type of content that was being published. A major concern regarding the context of the Internet was particular children and adult pornography, the latter of which is illegal, can be extremely graphic, violent and desensitizing. An innocent keyword typed into a search engine or the misspelling of a website's name can lead children and adults into sites that are both shocking and often difficult to leave.

In order to combat such content being accessed by children, the marketplace has witnessed an influx of online safety software companies. New Nanny is a world leader in online safety software that gives parents and others a tool to provide a safe and positive online experience for kids. The software is purchased by concerned parents and installed limiting the availability of the Web to children.

THE INTERNET AND THE WORKPLACE

There are an increasing number globally of employees gaining access to the Internet. A new issue is now raised concerning corporations dealing with issues such as productivity, bandwidth usage, and legal liability that are associated with Internet usage.

Controversially, organizations in the UK have recently been allowed to screen Internet usage of their employees through technology similar to Net Nanny to ensure responsible Internet usage. The ethics alone regarding privacy of employees within the organization and Internet monitoring or restrictions is by some not ethical, the results of recent research have yet to be witnessed.

Enforcement and operationalizing ethical codes

In his chapter in the *Companion Encyclopaedia of Marketing*, Smith (1999) concentrates on operationalizing those ethical issues which he considers specific to marketing, namely:

1. Product policy
2. Promotions
3. Distribution
4. Pricing
5. Marketing research

Here we have followed Smith's guidelines, but operationalized in a web-specific context.

Product policy

There are a number of ethical concerns with the disclosure of all substantial risks associated with product or service usage on the Web. It needs to be emphasized that many of the products are not physical in nature, but are information intensive. This includes those products which are 'questionable' and those that might be deemed to be harmful – 'me-too' products and product counterfeiting. Some concern is needed in regard to the identification of any product component or substitution that might materially change the product or impact on the buyer's purchase decision. Finally, there is the issue of the identification of extra cost-added features which need to be considered by the marketer trading on the Web.

Promotions

The basic issue here is the truth in advertising. This may involve a deliberate intention to deceive (deception) or may be unintentional (misleading). In most countries, the advertising profession have sought to retain responsibility for self-regulating the Web, preferring this to excessive regulation through legislation. To this end, the AMA have recently published detailed codes of practice and have formal procedures for receiving and dealing with complaints.

The two main areas of concern to the AMA in the area of web-based promotions are:

1. Rejection of high-pressure manipulations, or misleading sales tactics.
2. Avoidance of sales promotions that use deception or manipulation.

Distribution

Most issues in distribution relate to the exercise of channel power whereby the larger and more powerful members on the Web use this power to exact an unfair advantage from their suppliers and/or their customers. A particular topic here is the power of multiple e-tailers. The type of issues of particular significance include the manipulating of the availability of a product for the purpose of exploitation. Then, there is the use of coercion in the marketing channel. Also, the exerting of undue influence over the reseller's choice to handle a product.

Pricing

Like product issues, pricing is subject to regulation by UK Trust and which questions issues such as price fixing, the practice of predatory pricing and the disclosure of the full price associated with any purchase.

Marketing research

In a Business Week survey in 1998 it was found that the privacy and confidentiality of personal information (61%) was more important than cost reduction in influencing the individual's decision to start using the Internet. There are clear rules of ethical marketing research conduct. The Web should be prohibited from selling or fundraising under the guise of conducting research. The maintaining of research integrity is essential, by avoiding misrepresentation and omission of pertinent data. Bearing this in mind there is a need to treat outside clients and suppliers fairly.

Ethical guidelines

The following guidelines should be considered when evaluating the extent to which an organization may be deemed to be pursuing ethical conduct on the Web.

1. Do their values adhere to relevant laws and regulations. If the organization is breaking any of them then it might be better to report this violation than for the organization to try and hide the problem. Often, a reported violation generates more leniency than outside detection of an unreported violation. Increased priority on values needs to be given to help the organization to avoid breaking these laws and to follow the necessary regulations.

2. Review those values which are the top three or four traits of a highly ethical and successful organization. For example, for accountants: objectivity, confidentiality, accuracy, etc.

3. Identify those values needed to address current issues in the marketspace. Appointments of key staff to collect descriptions of the major issues in the marketspace. Collection is needed of the behaviours that produce these issues. Consideration will be required of those issues ethical in nature, e.g. issues with regard to respect, fairness and honesty. Identification is required of the behaviours needed to resolve these issues. Also, which values would generate those preferred behaviours. These may be values included here that some people would not deem as moral or ethical values, e.g. virtual team-building and promptness, but for the online manager, these practical values may add more relevance and utility to a code of ethics.

4. Identify any values needed, based on findings during strategic planning. Review information from the SWOT analysis. What behaviours will be needed to build on strengths, shore up weaknesses, take advantages of opportunities and guard against threats.

5. Consider top ethical values that might be prized by stakeholders. Some consideration needs to be given to the expectations of employees, clients/customers, suppliers, funders, members of the local community.

6. Examples of ethical values might include:

   - Trustworthiness: honesty, integrity, promise-keeping, loyalty.
   - Respect: autonomy, privacy, dignity, courtesy, tolerance, acceptance.
   - Responsibility: accountability, pursuit of excellence.
   - Caring: compassion, consideration, giving, sharing, kindness, loving.
   - Justice and fairness: procedural fairness, impartiality, consistency, equity, equality, due process.
   - Civic virtue and citizenship: law abiding, community service, protection of environment.

Key business phenomena such as: profit, market share, corporate strategy, productivity, balance sheets and so forth are often at the forefront of the physical business with ethics taking a very much 'add-on' role, but with the digital business with radically new and very business models in the exploratory stage (Chapter 3), there is an unparalleled opportunity to place ethics on an equal strategic footing with financial and operational objectives.

Conclusion

In the long run, the Internet will not transform business into a friction-free realm in which millions of anonymous buyers and sellers meet for one-shot instantaneous transactions. Nor will the Net remain unregulated and uncensored for commerce. Commerce will migrate to areas where rules prevail and responsibility can be assigned. Some of those areas probably will appear unorganized, and transactions within them will take place much faster and more cheaply than in the physical world. But increased speed and reduced costs will not lead to the disappearance of rules, communities, or intermediaries. On the contrary, the real move to electronic commerce will demand several layers of intermediaries to form new communities and support new rules. Electronic commerce requires those changes, which will also provide companies with the greatest opportunity for profits in cyberspace, the real power will lie with those that make the rules.

Checklist

1. The speed of change in e-commerce is leading to the need for new standards of ethical practice in both the domestic and global marketspace.
2. Copyright and patent law has acted as an early guide to developing ethical standards.
3. Preliminary activity is initially focussing on the means and rules of web-based exchange.
4. Community enforcement is emerging as a powerful mechanism where set norms and rules are followed and prevail.
5. Concern is being expressed on the ethical rights to individual and organizational privacy and information protection.
6. New ethical agent technology is emerging to assist the end user for protective purposes.
7. Ethical conduct transcends nations to encompass the global user community.

References

AMA (2000), *Code of Ethics for Marketing on The Internet*, AMA, Chicago, IL.

CommerceNet and Nielsen Media Research (1998), The number of internet users and shoppers surge in United States and Canada, August 24 www.commerce.net/news/press/19980824b.html.

De Bra, P.M.E. and Post, R.D.J. (1994), *Information Retrieval in the World-Wide Web: Making Client-Based Searching Feasible*, 1st International Conference on the World Wide Web, Geneva, Switzerland, May 25–27, pp. 137–146.

Dejoie, R., Fowler, G. and Paradice, D. (eds.) (1991), *Ethical Issues in Information Systems*, Boyd and Fraser, Boston, MA.

Eichmann, D. (1994), *The RBSE Spider – Balancing Effective Search Against Web Load*, 1st International Conference on the World Wide Web, Geneva, Switzerland, May 25–27, pp. 369–378.

Fielding, R.T. (1994), *Maintaining Distributed Hypertext Infostructures: Welcome to MOM Spider's Web*, 1st International Conference on the World Wide Web, Geneva, Switzerland, May 25–27, pp. 147–156.

Garrett, T. and Klonoski, R. (1986), *Business Ethics*, 2nd ed., Prentice-Hall, Englewood Cliffs, NJ.

Hansell, S. (1998), Big websites to track steps of their users, *New York Times*, August 16, p. A1.

Hasel, J. (1999), Net gain: expanding markets through virtual communities, *Journal of Interactive Marketing*, 13(1), pp. 55–65.

Huff, C. and Finholt, T. (1994), *Social Issues in Computing*, McGraw-Hill, New York.

Johnson, D.G. (1994), *Computer Ethics*, Prentice-Hall, Englewood Cliffs, NJ.

Joint Report on Data Protection Dialogue to the EU/US Summit, June 21, 1999, www. ita.doc.gov/ecom/jointreport2617.htm.

Kotler, P. (1997), *Marketing Management*: *Analysis, Planning and Control*. Prentice-Hall, Englewood Cliffs, NJ.

Leibowitz, W. (1999), EU extends its privacy protection, *National Law Journal*, January 18, pp. B1–B2.

Mcbryan, O.A. (1994), *GENVL and WWWW: Tools for Taming the Web*, 1st International Conference on the World Web, Geneva, Switzerland, May 25–27, pp. 129–135.

Oz, E. (1994), *Ethics for the Information Age*, William C. Brown Communications, Dubuque, IA.

Smith, N.C. (1999), Marketing ethics, in: Baker, M.J. (ed.), *Encyclopaedia in Marketing*, International Thomson Business Press, London.

Spar, D. and Bussang, J.J. (1996), Ruling the net, *Harvard Business Review*, May–June, pp. 125–133.

Velasquez, M. (1998), *Business Ethics: Concepts and Cases*, 4th ed., Prentice-Hall, Englewood Cliffs, NJ.

PART 4

Internet tools for wired marketing

CHAPTER 11

Advanced web technology for interactive marketing

Key topics

- Intersection between marketing and open-source solutions
- Intelligent agent software for personalized information and e-commerce
- Mobile push and pull technologies
- Web-to-database integration
- Broadband applications across the Web.

After studying this chapter you will be able to:

- Understand emerging intelligent software technologies and their ability to personalize a website.
- Have a viewpoint on the relevance of intelligent agents for interactive marketing.
- Describe the relationship between push and pull technology for marketing on the Web.
- Evaluate the role and importance of database integration.
- Understand the implications of the emerging broadband applications.

The rapid explosion of the Web has created an immediate need for businesses to leverage the potential of the Web to enable a successful web marketing future ahead. Advanced web marketing technology provides a means of building closer relationships with customers and markets. The purpose of this chapter is to illustrate to you the relevance and potential importance of advanced emerging web technologies and techniques to increase the return on your web-based marketing investment. In our description of advanced web technology we also identify the three main hurdles to overcome in the implementation and development process, which are expense, technology and privacy.

The expense of initiating one-to-one sales, marketing and services come at a premium for business and consumers. Historically one-to-one marketing has been an expensive option and this is also the same on the Web. Such a personalized approach can pay significant dividends over time through website and company loyalty, being able to stretch your marketing budgets by focusing on targeted marketing, improved response rate to targeted advertising, having a greater understanding of individual customers and so on. The technology allows many great ideas to become reality through the more mainstream arrival of advanced technology that is both affordable and also easily accessible.

New emerging technologies for the Web are changing our interaction with websites with a shift to push approaches in addition to a pull perspective. For example we view the Web primarily as a means of sourcing information and using the Web as windows for e-business activities in general. The arrival of push technologies is forging new forms of web–client relationships. As an active web user you most certainly receive various e-mails on supposedly areas of interest which may be pure interest or in terms of desirable items to purchase. Such interaction is gradually shifting the balance towards more push marketing and away from pull strategies. The new emerging technologies can be seen to be creating this shift through various web-based technologies. WAP technologies for mobile phones for example are currently in the process of providing a window to the Web through an every day device. WAP technology provides an ideal platform for two-way one-to-one marketing 'on the move'.

Technologies and the massive investments into one-to-one marketing immediately raises important privacy related issues. For successful one-to-one marketing trust is essential and can be helped through empowering users with control over there own personal information and encouraging them to practice self-regulation. Many organizations through 'codes of practice' adopt a transparent approach and undertake an independent information-based audit through organizations such as Anderson Consulting.

Now we will describe the main web technologies driving the developments at the intersection between marketing and technology and provide an insight into their application in a business context. Advanced web technologies considered in detail in this chapter include: open-source solutions, intelligent applications, mobile applications, web-to-database integration, and broadband applications.

Intersection between marketing and open-source solutions

The emphasis on establishing open standards through information technology applications has been of prime importance from the 1980s and at the dawn of a new millennium internationally recognized standards for integrated technology is now the norm. This has provided a platform for a new wave and style of development that has seen the unprecedented rise of open-source solutions. You may be thinking what is this open-source software that I have never heard of before. It is FREE software solutions that are gradually becoming integral to many diverse applications including computer networks but also ATM machines, mobile technology and is expected to have significant impact on household appliances. Leonard (1999) stated 'the concept of the business model for open-source software is a contradictory feat of legerdemain'. Open-source refers to a model of software development in which the underlying code to the program, the source code, is freely available to the public for modification, alteration, and endless redistribution. For software organizations this is still traditionally viewed as giving away the 'crown jewels' and poses the question to shareholders and venture capitalists of where is the profit? The answer lies somewhere at the intersection of the open-source creative community and technological change. The dynamics of technological development and creative thought across a wired community provides a unique opportunity for a form of relationship marketing and a challenge in having the vision to adopt new organizational forms. Typical open-source products having great commercial success include: Linux, Apache, Sendmail, Scriptics plus many more. Just as importantly the open-source entrepreneurs who are committed to the brand of the free have realized a new support industry and as a consequence allows the community to tap into multiple revenue streams (see Table 11.1). Such revenues provide various avenues such as support services, supporting products, plus the

Table 11.1   Free software movement through open-source solutions (adapted from Patricia Krueger. Toure de Source. Wired, May 1999)

Caldera Systems	One of the top ranking companies in sales of Linux servers and client systems globally. Develops and markets a line of applications based on the Linux operating system such as Internet/intranet servers, networking and desktop systems. ← ↑ → ↓ ° ± ″ ≥ × ∝
LinuxCare	An organization dedicated to Linux providing 24/7 technical support. Focused on providing support for Fortune 4000 companies plus related consulting and educational services. ↓ ± ″ ≥ × ∝
Penguin Computing	Dedicated to building Linux workstations and servers with support and training for engineers. ↓ ° ± ″ ≥ × ∝
Scriptics	Develops open-source development tools plus provides consulting services on the open-source scripting language Tcl. ← → ↓ ± ″ ×
Sendmail Inc.	The company emerged from the ubiquitous e-mail transfer agent Sendmail which is still widely used across Unix servers. The creator of the code for Sendmail, Eric Allman, founded the company to develop commercial tools for ISPs and the e-mail market. All new developments are in open-source. ← → ↓ ± ″ ∝
Arsdigita	Uses open-source tool kits to build and operate online communities. Provides free support via bulletin boards. ↑ ↓ ± ″
C2Net	Focused on its secure, commercial version, of the Apache based web server, the leading web server software application. ← ↓ ± ″ × ∝
Red Hat Software	The leader in commercial Linux distribution. Various strategic alliances with leading computing organizations such as IBM, to customize systems and support. Distributes over 50% of Linux servers. Investors include Oracle and Compaq. ← ↓ ± ″ ≥ × ∝
Cyclades	Markets Linux networking products including routers, serial cards for remote access connectivity. One of the leading Linux hardware brands. ↓ ° ± ≥ × ∝

demand for creative technical thinking. A dynamic open-source environment, alliances of organization and individuals with similar vision can easily coalesce for open-source project nodes to collectively provide software solutions.

Key business processes

←	Shrink-wrapping and marketing open-source software
↑	Developing new open-source software
→	Developing new applications for open-source software
↓	Developing and releasing enhancements to existing open-source software
°	Developing new hardware that incorporates open-source software
±	Customizing open-source software or systems
//	Providing consulting services for open-source users
≥	Distributing non-English versions of open-source software
×	Providing technical support for open-source software developers
∝	Providing technical support for open-source software end users

Open-source solutions have become central to the development of software applications on the Web and as a consequence can be fuelled further by new forms of marketing initiatives. For instance the emergence of anarchic organizational modes of working, in meeting the needs of a 'frenzie' to develop innovative solutions faster and faster, also demands new forms of marketing initiatives at the intersection point with technology. This in a sense is a new wave of relationship marketing for the Web and is evolving through what is viewed as collaborative marketing networks. Open-source solutions are allowing closer access with the customer through the open technological software developments phases and as a consequence are stimulating innovation.

Intelligent agent software for personalized information and e-commerce

There simply are too few hours in the day! Information overload is now becoming the norm for Internet users. This viewpoint seems so realistic that any help in handling at least some simple tasks is usually appreciated.

Many say that in the future there will not be a need for online outlets because personal agents will connect the consumer to the distributor. This view proposes it will be the branded agents that will be of importance rather than retailers. Or probably more likely, the agents will be directly branded and integral to portals such as Amazon, especially in consumer markets. Industrial markets will probably be directly driven through personal agents across the supply chain. Firstly, lets clarify exactly what we mean by agent technology and its relevance to B2B and B2C markets.

We also need to consider the ability to meet the fast changing demands through backend web-based systems becoming more intelligent. Consider the following quote:

> The catalogue – not the lack of transaction processing software, not the lack of bandwidth to the home, not the lack of robust security, and not the lack of an appealing shopping experience – is what I believe is blocking the growth of the Internet commerce today. Until businesses can easily produce and manage online catalogues, I do not think we will see any of the dramatic growth forecasted

Being able to personalize both information and e-commerce solutions allows tremendous revenue and profit opportunities, whether trading directly online, via interactive TV, through a kiosk, or telephone centre, by automatically tagging and hyperlinking catalogue information. Software by organizations that specialize in intelligent software applications, such as Autonomy, provides the opportunity to create a compelling online buying experience by automatically profiling individual buyers by analyzing there purchasing behaviour and product or brand preferences. This enables personalized recommendations to be made and as a consequence opens up cross selling opportunities. Even more importantly, it enables companies to target individual customers by featuring special banner advertisements or splash pages, via the Web and e-mail. The 'splash' pages are ideal for suggesting products and brands that match their shopping experience. Software companies such as Autonomy provide solutions that make this viable commercially with a high level of automation. At the heart of Autonomy software is the ability to extract the meaning from any text. The technology driving Autonomy automatically:

- Aggregates all internal and external information, for example internal documents, e-mails and external feeds and websites. The information is then organized into easy to navigate directories.
- Tags and categorizes all types of information based on the actual ideas in each piece of information.
- Inserts hyperlinks to other relevant information.
- Accesses relevant information based on natural language queries.
- Provides profiles based on user behaviour in terms of ideas in the information read or written.
- Routes information to individuals and organization most likely to be interested based on behavioural patterns.

Learning through intelligent agents

When different people come together without centralized rules and acceptable procedures, many creative and interesting, while many less pleasant, aspects emerge. The result in the digital age is a distributed global information source that contains non-homogenous data organized according to different human association models and value systems. This today has become known as the World Wide Web. Novel solutions are now becoming available in aiding users to quickly select the information they want. Such solutions are emerging at the intersection of information retrieval and machine learning, plus work into intelligent agents and intelligent user interfaces. We need to consider three criteria for the success and current development of intelligent agents: representation of what the particular application uses for documents, how it selects users, and finally what learning algorithm it uses.

There are various definitions of the term intelligent agent but for our purposes I will focus on systems such as user assistants and recommendation systems that employ machine learning and data mining techniques. Such systems assist users by finding information or performing some simpler tasks on their behalf. For example, such tools may help in web browsing through retrieving documents similar to already requested documents. Two frequently used methods for developing intelligent agents are *content based* and *collaborative approaches*. Either or a combination of the two can help users find and retrieve relevant information from the Web. We will now consider some of the general trends in terms of development.

A content-based approach to text classification searches for items similar to those the user prefers based on a comparison of content the user retrieves. Some of the difficulty with this approach is in capturing different types of objects integral to the Web content, for example audio, movies, and images. Figure 11.1 provides a simplistic representation of the basic approach adopted by content-based intelligent agents. This approach orientated around text learning is the most common approach currently being used.

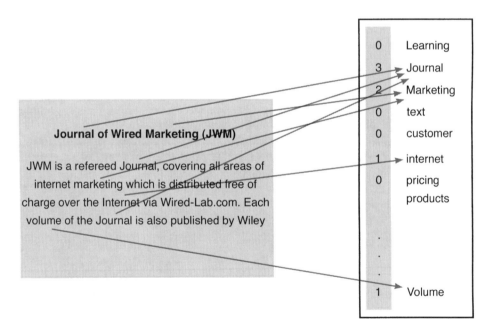

Figure 11.1   Content-based intelligent agents

Table 11.2 provides a listing of content-based intelligent agent applications plus their intended purpose.

The collaborative approach, compared to the content-based approach, assumes

Table 11.2   Content-based approaches (adapted from Mladenic, 1999)

Agent	Where developed	Goal	Publication
Antagonomy	NEC	Personalised newspaper	Kamba et al. (1997)
Contactfinder Krulwich and Burkey (1996)	Andersen	Consulting	Finding experts
FAQFinder	Chicago University	Answering questions	Burke and Hammond (1995)
Internet Fish	MIT	Finding information on the Internet	LaMacchia (1996)
Letizia	MIT	Browsing the WWW	Lieberman (1995)
Portal-in-a-Box	Autonomy	Browsing the WWW	http://www.autonomy.com
WAWA	Wisconsin	Browsing the WWW	Shavlik and Eliassi-Rad (1998) http://www.cs.cmu.edu/ ~conald/conald.shtml

there is a set of users using the system rather than an individual. In a collaborative approach the advice provided by the intelligent agent is based on the reaction to other users. The system, or frequently the Web, searches for users with similar interests and recommends the items based on user preferences. With such a collaborative approach there is no content analysis and as a consequence objects can be handled with equal success. Each item is given a unique identifier and a user rating derived through group usage. The similarity rating is specifically based on comparison of the ratings they assign to the same items.

For example consider the imaginary music ratings given by web users in Table 11.3; 8 represents the highest score while 0 is the lowest. The collaborative approach would find user 1 similar to user 3, while user 2 would be found different from user 1.

Table 11.4 provides a listing of collaboration-based intelligent agent applications plus there intended purpose.

Table 11.3   Collaborative-based approach

Music	Prodigy	Apex twins	Tip records	William orbit	Neil Young	Bob Dylan	Nick Drake
User 1	7	8	6	8	2	3	8
User 2	2	1	1	0	8	7	4
User 3	8	7	7	8	0	6	7

Table 11.4 Collaborative applications (adapted from Mladenic, 1999

Agent	Where developed	Goal	Publication
Firefly, Ringo	MIT	Finding music, movies, books	Maes (1994)
Referral Web	AT&T Labs	Finding experts	Kautz et al. (1997)
Siteseer	Imana	Browsing the WWW	Rucker and Marcos (19xx)

Table 11.5 Both content-based and collaborative approaches (adapted from Mladenic, 1999)

Agent	Where developed	Goal	Publication
Fab	Stanford	Browsing the WWW	Balabanovic and Shoham (1997)
Lifestyle Finder	AgentSoft	Browsing the WWW	Krulwich (1997)
WebCobra	James Cook University	Browsing the WWW	Vel and Nesbitt (1998) http://www.cs.cmu.edu/ ~conald/conald.shtml

Table 11.2 provides an outline of software applications, plus a basic description of their intended purpose, that adopt a hybrid approach through using both content and collaborative methods in the development of intelligent agents.

CASE APPLICATION

SFGATE DEPLOYS AUTONOMY'S PORTAL-IN-A-BOX: AUTOMATICALLY AGGREGATED CONTENT FROM VARIOUS SOURCES INTO A CUSTOMIZED VERTICAL PORTAL

SFGate, is a leading Internet portal that uses Autonomy's online information portal technology to stay ahead of the competition by cost-effectively and automatically providing SFGate visitors with updated and highly relevant news coverage from the local community together with global coverage. SFGate combine content from The San Francisco Chronicle, KRON-TV and the Associated Press with its own original material.

SFGate looked towards Autonomy to provide automatically generated hyperlinks as a means of collating and distributing high volumes of information and to make SFGate's vision of personalized portals a reality. SFGate's use of Autonomy reflects a growing trend toward smaller more focused vertical portals. Many businesses that offer content, products and services through portal giants are looking for alternative sites that are more relevant to their customers' needs whilst advertisers are looking for sites that target particular groups.

The reality for online publishers such as SFGate has been that once they decide to build their vertical portal they are faced with the labour intensive process of designing, building and maintaining the portal. Many existing portal sites are faced with the manual categorization, tagging and hypertext links of all the information and many cannot devote the resources required to handle all the incoming information.

They want a system that automatically organizes information from a diverse range of sources and delivers it to users quickly, accurately and dynamically. A main consideration of creating such a personalized service is the expense of handling the large amount of content aggregated from other sources such as newsfeeds, and articles. Publishers need to look at technology that will enable them to create and maintain personalized portal sites without incurring large overhead costs in the form of labour, in addition they require a system that dynamically and continuously understands individuals' needs in order to deliver truly personalized information on demand.

Autonomy's portal-in-a-box is a system that fully automates the process of delivering information to visitors based on their interests and creates an easy to navigate portal that seamlessly adds vast amounts of information to the site. Portal-in-a-box enables publishers to cost effectively create and maintain an information rich portal.

The future of portal-in-a-box

The personalization capabilities of Autonomy's portal-in-a-box will open up new revenue opportunities through the automated delivery of personalized e-mails and personalized start pages, in terms of employees being free to create new content channels, etc. Personalization of content and the ability of target delivery in a timely fashion are keys, in the continued move towards one-to-one marketing on the Internet.

Mobile push and pull technologies

The international consultancy firm The Strategist Group estimates there will be more than 530 million wireless subscribers by the year 2001. Wireless Internet Today forecast the number of wireless subscribers will break the 1 billion mark by 2004, and it is expected that a large proportion of the phones sold in this coming year will have multimedia capabilities. The multimedia applications will include e-mail, push and pull information services from the Internet. The major application for WAP in the future is anticipated to be for e-commerce as identified in Figure 11.2.

As a means to guide the developments in the telecommunications industry open standards were developed primarily through what is now recognized as the WAP Forum (www.wapforum.org). The Wireless Application Protocol (WAP) is now the de-facto world standard for the presentation and delivery of wireless information and telephony services on mobile phones and other wireless terminals.

Wireless devices represent the ultimate in constrained information technology including limited CPU, memory, battery life, and the need to design a simple user-interface. *Wireless networks* are constrained by relatively low bandwidth, high latency, and irregular availability and stability of communications. WAP tech-

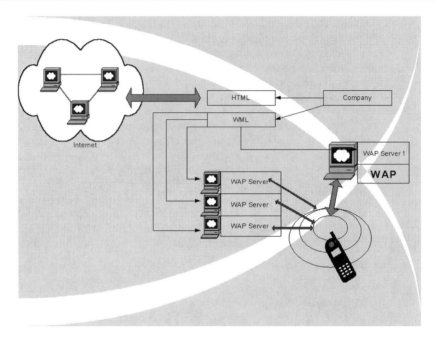

Figure 11.2.   Mobile commerce through a WAP handset

nology has pitched itself to leverage the phenomenal investment in web servers, web development tools, web programmers, and web applications while dealing with the unique problems inherent with the wireless domain.

The overall goals in the continued development of WAP are as follows:

- Pull and push Internet content through advanced data services to wireless phones and other wireless devices.
- Creation of a global wireless protocol specification that is used across all wireless network technologies.
- Creation of flexible content and applications that scale across all wireless networks and devices.
- Embracing of existing standards for web technology and extending further the pursuit of wireless multimedia applications.

Market dynamics

The market conditions of wireless technology are quite unique and strikingly different from the desktop or even laptop market. Convergence in technology is anticipated in Personal Digital Assistants (PDAs), maybe not in terms of use and application but definitely in the common use of wireless applications protocols. This is currently happening the US with the launch of the Palm VII and the imminent launch in Europe. We also only need to look at current developments in the

PDA market with organizations such as Handspring. The recent product launch of Visor by Handspring is expected to shift the PDA into a mass market product and more into the B2C market in addition to the B2B. How do these wireless devices, in particular mobile phones, differ from the traditional desktop and laptop products? Some of these differences include:

- Ease of use: mobile devices, such as mobiles, are viewed by the mass market as far more intuitive for the user. This is primarily driven through a task orientated design perspective.
- Market size: the growth to date has been unprecedented with Nokia forecasting over 1 billion subscribers by 2005.
- Price sensitivity: after many years of subsidized handsets by mobile phone companies the market has become very price sensitive, especially when compared to the desktop PC market.
- Usage patterns: wireless data access is expected by the consumer to be as seamless and easy as all the other handset functions. Seamless and intuitive applications are essential based on the type of user and the type of use.
- Essential tasks: wireless internet users will not want to surf the Web but will be far more task specific with a desire for information that meets the needs of the moment.

Dynamics of the network and handheld devices

Wireless data networks, as opposed to wired networks, create different constraints on the transmission because of fundamental limitations of power, available spectrum and mobility issues. Wireless data networks typically used for handheld devices, such as mobile phones, tend to have:

- Less bandwidth
- More latency
- Less connection stability
- Less predictable availability.

Although similar to differences in networking handheld devices they also are significantly different in terms of functionality and purpose to a desktop or mobile. They present a more constrained computing environment relative to desktop computers. The fundamental differences are primarily through product design and also battery life. Mass market handheld devices typically have:

- CPUs with limited power
- Less memory (ROM and RAM)
- Limited power consumption
- Small displays
- Various input devices including phone pad, voice input, fold-up keyboard.

Due to these constraints the user interface of a wireless handheld is fundamentally different to a desktop computer or laptop. The constraints are based on relative comparisons but we must also remember the far greater focus on task specific applications.

Building on existing web standards

WAP standards have been designed around complementing existing standards. This is best illustrated when considering how WAP specification does not for example specify the means of data transmission but is intended to sit on top of existing bearer channel standards. This means any existing wireless communications standards and infrastructure can use the WAP protocol as a natural extension enabling a complete product solution. The WAP Forum, the main standards body, will also be working alongside other Internet standards organizations, such W3C and IETF to ensure future convergence with HTML-NG (Next Generation) and HTTP-NG specifications and provide input on future requirements of wireless network technologies. The key elements of WAP specification are illustrated through the WAP programming model that is very similar to the WWW programming model.

Wireless Mark-up Language (WML) is a mark-up language adhering to XML standards but also designed to run powerful applications within the constraints of handheld devices. WML and WMLScript, which are enablers of WAP applications, do not assume a QWERTY keyboard or a mouse and are typically focused on handheld devices with their own constraints and opportunities.

Applications development through extending existing tools

For both the client and server end, illustrated in Figure 11.3, developers will find it easy to support WAP applications due to the WAP programming model being closely related to the WWW development model. WML is a tag-based document language but specified as an XML document type. As a consequence existing XML authoring tools, in addition to HTML development environments, can be used to create the WML applications. Because WAP uses HTTP 1.1 standard protocol as a means of communicating between the WAP gateway and web servers (see Figure 11.3), web developers can deploy their applications on any off-the-shelf web server. WML developers can use technical web tools such as Cold Fusion, CGI, Perl, PhP, ASP and many more in creating dynamic applications. In creating the pages for the web developers can use separate URLs for their HTML and WML entry point, or use a single URL to dynamically serve HTML or WML content that depends on the browser type. The ability to be able to serve HTML or WML, depending on the browser and indirectly the computing device, creates endless opportunities. Direct marketing can then push applications to both office bound individuals and people on the move.

WAP gateway and proxy technology

The specification, agreed by the WAP Forum, for WAP applications uses standard

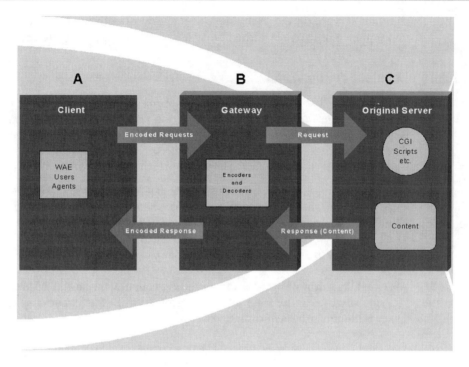

Figure 11.3.   WAP programming model

web proxy technology to connect the wireless domain (the wireless location) with the Web. Through the use of WAP gateway (refer Figure 11.3) computing resources the WAP architecture enables handset devices to be relatively simple and inexpensive. A WAP gateway for example will typically take over all DNS services to resolve domain names used in URLs, thus shifting the computing task away from the handset and onto the gateway. A WAP gateway typically has the following functionality:

- Protocol gateway – the protocol gateway translates transmissions from the WAP protocols to the WWW protocols (HTTP and TCP/IP). These are frequently termed the WAP protocol stack and the WWW protocol stack which illustrates that there are many defined standards or layers within each.
- Content encoders and decoders – the content encoders translate web content into more compact encoded formats. This reduces the size and number of packets transmitting over the wireless data network.

The structure outlined ensures that handheld users can browse a variety of WAP content and applications regardless of the wireless network that is being used. This means that applications developers can build tools and applications that are both network and terminal independent. The WAP proxy design enables both content and applications to be hosted on a standard web server using proven web technologies such as CGI scripting. The WAP gateway is then able to aggregate data from different servers on the Web and also catch frequently used information and as a consequence improve both flexibility and response time for the user.

The future of content on the Web

The future will develop content that is more flexible and in tune will a greater variety in computing devices from desktop computers to mobile handsets. XML with become the norm and will be used to deliver content to various devices through the use of WML and HTML style sheets (Figure 11.4).

What will this mean to you? The widespread adoption of the WAP specification is yielding the following benefits:

- A common user interface that is being used by all industry participants. WAP will be the de-facto standard.
- Ubiquitous service through WAP enabled devices.
- A wide selection of devices including PDAs, mobiles phones, pagers that are all WAP enabled.
- A vast selection of applications will be available via handheld Internet devices. Primarily due to the Internet being received as both a cheap and flexible option for both consumers and businesses alike.

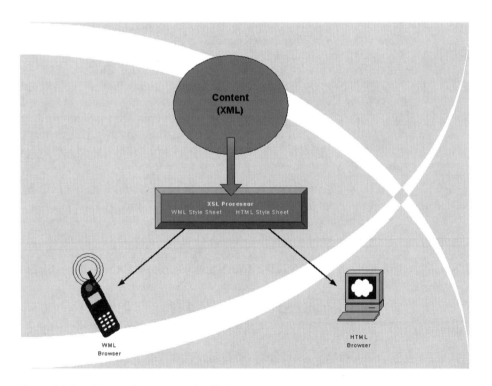

Figure 11.4.   Future of content on the Web

Web-to-database integration

Most activities we seem to do day to day go into some type of database, whether this is going into a local shop or banking on the Internet. Our lives are being logged at an ever increasing rate. This is particularly true in developed and developing countries and through the potential of wireless communications could soon become a global reality. When used to their best potential databases can make our time more fulfilling and productive in both B2B and B2C instances. Consumers are becoming an integral part of the marketing process and this is primarily being driven by database driven marketing and commerce in general. The mass acceptance of the Web has driven the consumer into 'centre stage'. Most medium to large websites are now database driven and all e-commerce sites use database applications. This trend is expected to become the norm with content becoming separate from format. The focus of this chapter is to help you and your organization integrate your one-to-one web marketing activities with other marketing systems and understand the main issues of importance. We also guide you through some of the new database technologies that are now available.

Many company websites are still driven by 'static' content in the sense that there is very little change from week to week. These are typically sites providing basic information on a company and promotional content. For more high traffic media sites content typically changes daily and generally on-going day and night. twenty-four hours a day and 7 days a week is becoming the norm for high traffic sites. Such sites are only manageable through web-to-database integration. The database integration allows truly dynamic websites that are typically updated through both internal and external information sources. Many of the traditional database software companies, such as Oracle and Sybase, have added additional functionality to their core products to allow direct integration with their website into a traditional internal client-server environment. For example both Oracle and Sybase provide advanced web development tools to support the integration process.

Types of systems and processes for web integration

We will now consider the many ways of using databases and supporting real time connectivity technologies for on-to-one web-based marketing. Web-to-database integration supports the process of managing web content through to taking orders and providing specialized services for customers. Database technology for the Web has evolved from the 1970s and as a consequence offers very stable and diverse solutions from companies such as Oracle, Sybase, Microsoft, plus many more. The main applications for web-to-database integration are:

- Content management
- Customization
- e-Commerce
- Customer service

The process of providing and gaining information from your web audience is very similar to traditional marketing and sales activities except that it is much faster than could have been anticipated. One-to-one marketing on the Web requires the use of three technologies working together to form relationships with customers: customer databases (CRM), interactive media, and systems that support personalization of information. We will now consider each of the applications identified above in more detail with consideration towards utilizing the three technologies.

Content management

Content management is driven primarily through customer databases and interactive media and is particularly important as a website becomes large, especially when considering the work involved in site maintenance. As indicated earlier the separation of content from format is now accepted, especially with the growth of e-commerce. Typically you create the content (text, graphics, etc.) in a database, via some type of web editor, and this is then dynamically up-loaded into a preformatted template(s) to create complete web pages. This content management is typically becoming a mix of both internal sources and external information providers, such as I-syndicate (www.i-syndicate.com). As the content and format are separate you can change them independently. The main benefits of such an approach include: consistency in format through standard templates, more focused due to being able to concentrate on core skills, through using standard templates it is far easier to change the overall look and feel of a site.

Customization

Being able to offer customized options or a complete consumer specific website to an individual is certainly a future trend. Currently most websites only offer limited customization, for example Yahoo and similar sites allow you to personalize your web experience by choosing to receive specific information. Even though the information is being customized to meet an individuals requirements the format of the pages typically remains consistent. As a consequence it is ideal to use a database application with templates to offer dynamic information. From the perspective of the website's owner gathering information you are also at the same time gathering valuable customer profiling information and as a consequence building a greater understanding of your customer. Currently the most effective means of customizing web content for a specific consumer is through sites that prompt for a user ID and password. By identifying a user in such a way the site can then easily customize content. This will develop in a similar direction to Computer Integrated Telephony (CIT) where the receiver of the call can automatically load customer details on a PC through the telephone number. Using a similar approach websites will also gradually automate the identification process to some degree through an Internet IP address.

e-Commerce

As discussed in detail in Chapter 8 one of the most widely publicized issues currently in the media is ordering online and e-commerce in general. The most recent significant change in the area of e-commerce is for smaller organizations, who frequently do not have the technical expertise or resources in general to establish a website, but can now process customer orders. Such companies can now plug into or share resources through using a third party website that seamlessly links into the smaller firms' website. For example many portal websites are diversifying into the area of providing ordering and payment facilities that can be used by their customers, for example Supanet.co.uk. In addition there are many more specialist broking type services that also offer the ability to plug into e-commerce applications. Specialist database applications, along with other software applications, are what make e-commerce across the Web possible. Beyond the technical issues in being able to trade online, the challenges in conducting commerce on the Internet are very similar to business in the physical world. In particular this involves having a recognized identity, being creditworthy, and issues of security. For more detail refer to Chapter 8.

Customer service

Providing customers with access to diverse information as a free service is one of the most effective uses of one-to-one web marketing. Information services generally come from databases across the globe. Just as importantly the ability to search for information sources typically via search engines are all database driven. For example consider all the search engines and directories you can remember such as Yahoo, lycos, netcentre, google and so on. Many firms now also take the opportunity of linking a search engine typically one of the large recognized ones directly into there own website. This clearly adds value to customers but is also a form of relationship marketing for the search engine website.

Broadband application across the Web

The majority of access to the Internet as been controlled by Internet Service Providers (ISPs) such as Demon and Freeserve in the UK for example. These companies offer access to the Internet via the use of traditional telephone lines that are leased from telecoms operators. This is all about to change through the introduction of new technologies. Broadband is one of the new technologies tipped to dramatically speed up Internet access. In addition to faster connection it will also facilitate the delivery of a range of other services including video on demand, e-commerce, music, interactive advertising, online news, interactive gaming and videoconferencing. Broadband technologies provide 'always on' access, where the connection between a computer and the ISP is permanently connected rather than a dial-up service. The two main competing technologies in broadband access are Asymmetric Digital Subscriber Line (ADSL) and cable modems. Both of these services provide access in the region of 512 Kbps to 2 Mbps. This is approximately 8–32 times the speed of an ISDN line connection.

Fundamentals of broadband and consumer trends

Broadband is widely available in North America but currently has got limited use. Even so, forecasts for broadband adoption is anticipated to be very high. For example Forrester research has predicted 20 million European users by 2003. The fast access and far richer service will be delivered on a flat fee basis enabling unlimited access. For e-commerce to mainstream in Europe customers will demand the time to browse and explore at leisure. The current metered access model is similar to charging people to go window shopping on the high street. Consideration also needs to be given to who controls the Internet communications networks. Currently this is controlled by IAPs (Internet Access Providers) rather than ISPs. IAPs are your cable, telephone and satellite companies while your ISPs are companies such as AOL and Freeserve. Such control puts IAPs potentially in a strong position in being able to promote their own ISP service. This for example is still an unresolved argument in the US.

Research to date on usage patterns of broadband and other systems allowing unlimited use reveal dramatic changes in usage patterns of online services. Consumers on average using such services in the US spend approximately three time as much time online and purchase twice as much as an average dial-up user. For the B2C markets the bandwidth and flat fee is seen as very important in what is expected to be a major shift in purchasing patterns. For the B2B e-commerce sites the automotive industry in North America has been particularly fast to grab the benefits of broadband for speeding up the process of procurement, enabling lower redundant stock levels and lower prices. Broadband. Mr Steele, president of Ford in Europe, has been quoted as stating that the use of broadband speed transmission will create savings of up to $900 per vehicle. Broadband services will also be very useful for off-site maintenance and diagnostic checks. The emergence of broadband services becoming affordable for both business and consumer markets has direct implications for the types of services being developed and consumer requirements across the Internet. The implications to both cost and revenue in the context of e-commerce are illustrated in Figure 11.5.

Current stages of development

- At present neither cable nor telecom companies have adopted a particularly proactive approach towards broadband Internet development.
- Telecom companies in Europe are still at an early stage of deploying DSL. From the companies that have begun the more advanced are France Telecom and British Telecom.
- UPC has been aggressively purchasing cable networks in various countries including the Netherlands, Belgium, France, Austria, Norway, and Sweden. This has enabled them to establish a pan-European broadband strategy.

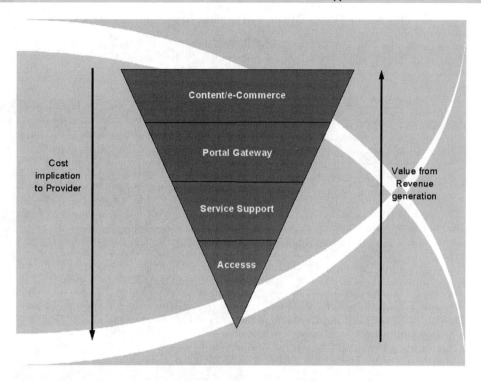

Figure 11.5. Value and cost of Internet content

- Some other companies are also expanding beyond domestic boundaries. For example a European ISP EasyNet has targeted France, UK, Germany, Belgium for Internet access ADSL. Telia is already offering high-speed access to the Internet across both telephone and cable in several Nordic markets.

Third generation (3G) networks

The 3G networks expected to be gradually introduced from late 2000 will make portable computing a real option to a mass market. 3G capabilities will allow sufficient bandwidth to provide remote desktop, Voice over The Internet Protocol (VoIP) services, teleconferencing and eventually shared virtual spaces. For example an office could be replaced by a new form of virtual space through a set of IP numbers, accessed from machines in geographically remote locations. For many 3G technological developments will be the true enabler for the Internet to be a truly mass market product that can offer the visuals and speed consumer users are already familiar with through TV. An organization called On2 (www.on2.com) based in the US provides a good insight into the potential of the next generation of Internet based technology. On2 is recognized as a world leader in the development of broadband content and delivery. On2 is a cutting edge developer of software based video compression/decompression and streaming technologies with

TrueMotion products that have been licensed by companies such as Microsoft and Sega. Recognizing the phenomenal impact of broadband on the Web, On2 is now shifting its expertise to create immersive Internet applications such as music video's and films (Figure 11.6).

Figure 11.6.   On2.com

Conclusion

While it is uncertain in predicting how technological developments will be accepted in the market, some trends are clearly emerging. This chapter has described areas of particular relevance to the marketing profession across global markets and considered the potential implications of such developments. These include:

- A shift to network efficiency through the delivery of Internet access and the acceptance of global networking standards.
- Efficiency in software development through the unprecedented acceptance of open-source solutions.
- Emergence of modern network technologies such as IP into mainstream tele-communications.
- Networking on the move through international mobile technological development standards.

- Web database integration as a tool driving Customer Relationship Management (CRM).
- Development of new higher bandwidth mechanisms and the increasing popularity of more task specific ubiquitous technological devices, such as Personal Digital Assistants (PDAs).

Such advanced technological developments are likely to precipitate a change in the way marketing is structured and fundamentally change many marketing processes. This drives access closer to the customer through the convergence of technologies and at the very least the interchangeable nature of technology is in many ways seen as a vehicle for stimulating innovation and change throughout the marketing processes. As technology continues to bring the customer closer, as a means of enabling improved relationship marketing, interactive marketing will become the norm. Interactive marketing will be truly realized with the emergence of cost effective communications technology that is accessible to mass markets with the use of PC access to the Internet but more importantly when considering business-to-consumer markets handheld devices and other ubiquitous technological devices. The convergence and the ubiquitous nature of emerging technological devices discussed enforce the need to move from competitive to collaborative marketing strategies for sustainable success.

Checklist

1. Open-source solutions are drivers of international collaboration in the creation of innovative solutions. For some markets this will enable new forms of relationship marketing that are more dynamic in nature.
2. Open-source applications are enabling the Internet to become a ubiquitous tool and in many instances offering free solutions.
3. Intelligent agent software applications will be integral to most software of the future and are viewed as essential for marketing management success. Intelligent agents will gradually play a more important role in supporting marketing information systems as the volume and speed of information continues to increase.
4. Intelligent agents currently are primarily designed based on a content and collaborative focus.
5. Mobile push and pull technologies will be central to Internet marketing communications initiatives in the near future. Mobile technologies are now a ubiquitous tool for mass markets and through WAP will be the primary window to the Web in the near future.
6. Web-to-database integration has extended traditional customer relationship management to a phase that is driven by response time and the ability to offer an efficient customized solution.
7. The main obstacle to the Internet has been cost and the richness of applications. Broadband solutions will certainly offer a rich and immersive 'always on' service but it is also intended to be an affordable option to mass markets in the relatively near future.

8. Broadband offers the opportunity for rich multimedia transmission driving interactive marketing to new levels to be able to offer personalized solutions.

References

Balabanovic, M. and Shoham, Y. (1997), Fab: content-based collaborative recommendation. *Communications of the ACM*, 40 (3), pp. 66–70.

Burke, R., Hammond, K. and Kozlovsky, J. (1995), *Knowledge-Based Information Retrieval for Semi Structured Text Working Notes from AAAI Fall Symposium AI Applications in Knowledge Navigation and Retrieval*, AAAI Press, Menlo Park, CA, pp. 19–24.

Kamba, T., Sakagami, H. and Koseki, Y. (1997), Anatagonomy: a personalised newspaper on the WWW, *International Journal of Human Computer Studies*, 46 (6), pp. 789–803.

Kautz, H., Selman, B. and Sah, M. (1997), The hidden web, *AI Magazine*, 18 (2), pp. 27–36.

Krulwich, B. and Burkey, C. (1996), *The contactFinder Agent: Answering Bulletin Board Questions with Referrals*, Proceedings of the 13th National Conference AI (AAAI 96), AAAI Press, Menlo Park, CA, pp. 10–15.

Krulwich, B. (1997), Lifestyle finder, *AI Magazine*, 18 (2), pp. 37–46.

LaMacchia, B.A. (1996), *Internet Fish, A Revised Version of a Thesis Proposal*, MIT, AI Lab and Department of Electrical Engineering and Computer Science, Cambridge, MA.

Leonard, A. (1999), Open season, *Wired Magazine*, May, pp. 140–148.

Lieberman, H. (1995), *Letizia: An Agent that Assists Web Browsing*, Proceedings of the 14th International Joint Conference AI (IJCAI), AAAI Press, Menlo Park, CA, pp. 924–929.

Maes, P. (1994), Agents that reduce work and information overload, *Communications of the ACM*, 37 (7), pp. 30–40.

Mladenic, J.S. (1999), Text-Learning and Related intelligent agents: a survey, *IEEE Intelligent Systems*, July/August, pp. 40–54.

Rucker, J. and Marcos, J.P. (1997), Siteseer: personalised navigation for the Web, *Communications of the ACM*, 40 (3), pp. 73–75.

Shavlik, J. and Eliassi-Rad, T. (1998), *Building Intelligent Agents for Web-Based Tasks: A Theory-Refinement Approach, Working Notes of Learning from Text and the Web, Conference Automated Learning and Discovery (CONALD-98)*, Carnegie Mellon University, Pittsburgh, PA.

Syken, B. (2000), An evangelist for free software, *Time Magazine*, September 18, p. 136.

Vel, O. and Nesbitt, S.A. (1998), *Collaboration Filtering Agent System for Dynamic Virtual Communities on the Web. Working Notes of Learning from Text and the Web, Conference Automated Learning and Discovery (CONALD-98)*, Carnegie Mellon University, Pittsburgh, PA.

Further reading

Autonomy. http://www.autonomy.com.

Brier, S. (2000), Our interconnected future, *Interactive Week*, August 28, p. 39.

Gilbert, D. and Janca, P. (1997), *IBM Intelligent Agents*, http://www.ibm.com.

Korn, A. (2000), *Background Briefing: Broadband Internet Access*, VNU Business Publishing, Ltd. http://vnunet.com.

Krueger, P. (1999), Toure de source, *Wired Magazine*, May, pp. 144–145.

OFTEL (Office of Telecommunications) and OFT (Office of Fair Trade) (2000), Competition in e-commerce: a joint OFTEL and OFT study, http://www.oftel.gov.uk.

Screendigest (2000), The European broadband internet market: full speed ahead, http://www.screendigest.com.

Wireless Application Forum, Ltd. (1999), Wireless Internet Today, October.

CHAPTER 12

Strategic Internet marketing planning

Key topics

- Business and market analysis
- Integrated online marketing communications strategies
- Development paths for strategic Internet marketing planning
- Internet marketing budget and resource allocation
- Vulnerability, risk analysis and contingency planning.

After studying this chapter you will be able to:

- Evaluate the main internal and external data sources.
- Outline development paths for strategic Internet marketing planning.
- Understand budgetary methods and potential implications.
- Identify contingency strategies for volatile markets.
- Build a strategic Internet marketing plan.

Visionary thinking needs to be outlined in a strategic document that describes ends and means required to implement a specific development strategy that is both responsive and flexible. A company's short term success will be dependent on financial performance of the product portfolio, while longer term success in terms of survival and growth will imply the ability to foresee market changes and adapt the product portfolio accordingly (Lambin, 2000). A strategic marketing plan is basically a financial plan but with more emphasis on information that considers the origins and destinations of the financial flows. In a market orientated organization the mission of strategic marketing is to identify prospects for growth and profit. As a consequence the process of strategic planning should result in improved organization integration at a functional level. The principles of strategic marketing planning in the physical marketplace are the same for virtual markets but the conditions and focus are more unique. In particular the Internet typifies more volatile and turbulent markets that are driven by technological development and the ability to adapt rapidly to changing market conditions. Internet marketing planning also has seen a far greater emphasis on what is frequently termed personalized or one-to-one marketing driven by technological advances.

One-to-one marketing and service is not a new concept or approach but is being driven to new levels through the use of the Web for both mass marketing and customized, one-to-one marketing. Both Peppers and Rogers (1997) and McKenna (1999) developed further one to one marketing in the context of technological developments such as the Internet, web and database applications (Figure 12.1).Table 12.1 briefly outlines the principles of how one-to-one marketing differs from target marketing and mass marketing with particular emphasis on the planning process (for more detail refer to Chapter 5).To support such a personalized approach on the Internet an Internet marketing plan needs to provide an highly flexible template that needs to provide you with the foundations for further customization, by yourself in developing your own unique style necessary for specific organizational needs. Many of the areas outlined below will be familiar to a traditional marketing plan but with quite specific changes and additions in supporting

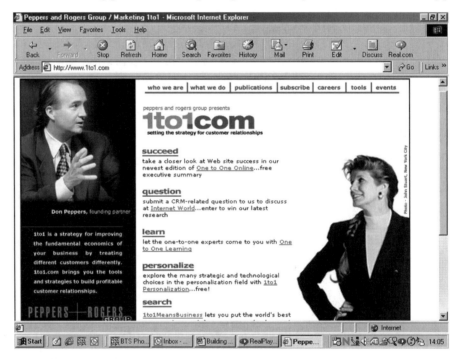

Figure 12.1   1to1.com

Table 12.1   Marketing trends and styles

Mass marketing	One-to-all or one-to-many communications without any form of specialization in the message or medium
Target marketing	One-to-many communications but with specialization of message and/or medium for identifiable market segments
Personalized marketing	One-to-one or one-to-few communications with personalized marketing

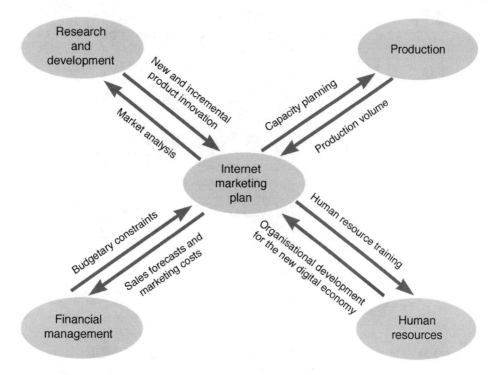

Figure 12.2 Internet marketing plan (adapted from Lambin, 2000)

the transition into the virtual marketspace. Lambin (2000) provides a useful illustration of the cross-functional responsibilities and processes in building a strategic marketing plan that allows both responsiveness and adaptability in ever increasing volatile market conditions (Figure 12.2).

Business and market analysis

This is a description of an organization's background and anticipated future, that will be affected by or will affect a specific Internet marketing plan. The main areas for consideration are as follows: market analysis (customers, industry, patterns and trends), products and services offerings by an organization (product lines, pricing and volume), and future outlook for research and development. In gathering data for manipulation and analysis it is useful to consider the traditional Marketing Information System (MkIS), eloquently described by Kotler (1997). The main shift in emphasis since the mid 1990s has been the move to distributed information with a far greater focus on external data sources (see Figure 12.3). Virtual markets have also 'blurred' the boundaries between what has traditionally been defined as internal and external data sources. The Internet has been the driver of such a change, allowing greater responsiveness to market conditions. Identify any elements of Internet market statistics that support a specific Internet marketing plan. Marketing statistics can be gathered from various sources providing focused industry specific information. The main areas for consideration are general Internet data (worldwide users, business usage, revenue streams) and market specific data (growth in Internet use, geo-demographics, gender, purchasing behaviour).

Both dynamic internal and external data sources have the ability to create a strong customer orientation and this is one of the most important factors in achieving a successful website.

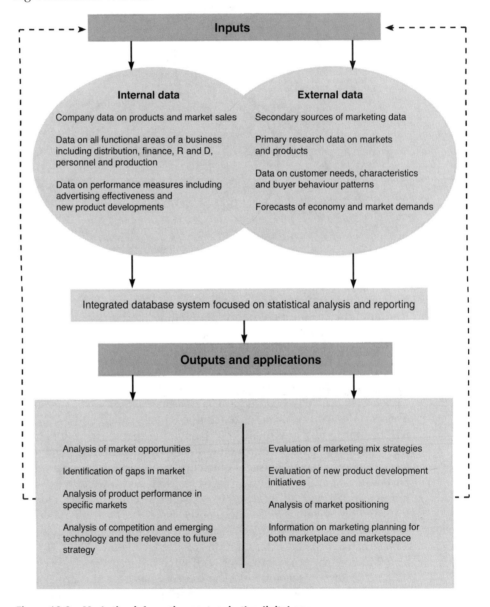

Figure 12.3 Marketing information system in the digital age

Integrated online marketing communications strategies

In formulating online marketing communications strategies for a company you need to consider new forms of marketing communications tools that have specifically evolved for the Internet. Online marketing communications are being driven by the unprecedented growth of e-commerce and the marketing planning process needs to reflect the speed of change and ascertain, where possible, how it will be affected by or will affect your overall marketing plan. Particular emphasis needs to be given to both Internet marketing communications initiatives and also the implications for offline methods. Additional supporting information may be included that demonstrates industry best practice as a means of providing guidance to the implementation process.

The online marketing communications process needs to be considered in the context of: (1) strategies for achieving specific objectives and goals in the age of e-business, (2) perspectives towards migrating a company's brand from marketplace to marketspace, and (3) Internet infrastructure as a platform to support your overall marketing plan.

Integrating strategies for specific objectives

The primary market planning strategies can be organized to achieve the tasks and objectives based on the three categories of Internet hierarchy effects according to Strauss and Frost (1999). We have categorized the major strategies as follows for the planning process:

- Stakeholder communications strategies (cognitive and attitude objectives)
- Selling products and services through the Internet (transaction behaviour objectives)
- Internal efficiency strategies (internal efficiency goals for marketing budgets).

Below are typical tasks and operational objectives for Internet marketing programs grouped by Internet hierarchy effects categories (Strauss and Frost, 1999) plus some additional objectives.

Cognitive and attitude objectives

- Brand awareness and positioning
- Employee incentive programs
- Information dissemination through the Internet, intranets and extranets
- Relationship building evidenced by website tracking
- Build positive attitudes through more effective customer relationship management initiatives

Transaction behaviour objectives

- Build a website that will support sales staff meeting directly with customers
- Increase sales of a product that are distributed directly over the Internet
- Increase the space available on the website for advertising banners
- Develop a global affiliate marketing program as a means of increasing the number of points of sale
- Provide integrated support for trade shows via your company's website.

Internal efficiency goals for marketing budgets

- Decrease offline advertising costs
- Develop a dynamic communications infrastructure with stakeholders through Internet, intranet and extranet applications
- Reduce distribution costs through automated online ordering

Perspectives towards managing the branding process on the Internet

The branding process on the Internet can take various forms depending on the type of organization and in particular if the organization has an existing brand and its relevance to the Internet. As a consequence we need to consider: migrating and existing brand online, creating a variant of an existing brand online, partnering through a strategic alliance with an existing digital brand, or the creation of a new digital brand. In deciding upon your particular branding strategy consideration in the first instance must be given if a company is solely trading on the internet and most probably trading in both the traditional marketplace and market space.

As identified above the brand planning process will be primarily determined by broader marketing strategies driven by the product and service mix. Clarification is needed of how we define a brand in both the physical marketplace and virtual marketspace. In particular emphasis needs to be placed on the development and long term implications for branding.

The American Marketing Association (AMA) defined a brand in relation to its ability to differentiate primarily through being able to provide a core offering along with values relevant to consumers that drives consumers to pay a premium price.

de Chernatony and McDonald (1998) take the early view of the AMA further by describing a brand as 'an identifiable product, service, person or place, augmented in such a way that the buyer or user perceives relevant unique added values which match their needs most closely…'. Many have also suggested the idea of one-to-one branding as being a logical consequence of Internet technology; this has since also been discussed in further detail by Peppers and Rogers (1997).

When considering the development of brands on the Internet we need to accept a greater importance being placed on computer mediated environments. Berry (2000) emphasized the development of Internet branding being more relevant to service branding than physical goods. This is primarily through the dynamics and speed of interaction across the Internet.

In planning brands for the Internet we need to consider the current shift to what is being termed 'experiential marketing'. With the combination of information technology, the supremacy of the brand and the ubiquity of communications we are now moving, in particular on the Internet, into experiential marketing driven by the pleasure seeking consumer which is implemented by experienced providers. Brand experiences are fundamental to success on the Internet, which need to be provided at a rapid speed. The experience for consumers is of far greater importance than an attitude towards a brand on the Internet, which is clearly in significant contrast to the physical world. As a consequence the marketing planning process needs to be designed primarily for 'brand reality' rather than 'brand perception'. The complexity arrives when considering the brand migration process from the marketplace to marketspace. One of the key issues that has been identified as being of primary importance is the notion of a greater reliance on trust. In considering issues of trust on the Internet we also need to consider issues of community building. Hoffman et al. (1998) for example stated the lack of trust on the Internet between buyers and sellers and this is in stark contrast to much of the branding literature primarily focused on the physical marketplace.

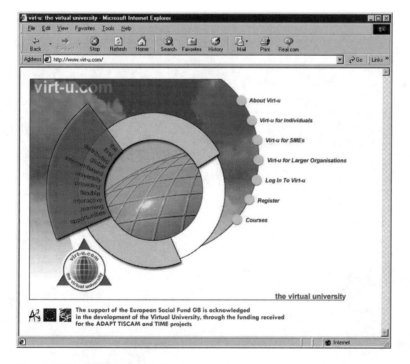

Figure 12.4   Online Education

Developing a traditional brand online

This is the most common route for an organization to take and this can be in the form of a straight migration or through extending the brand further for the virtual community. Clearly this is a fast option but can be quite problematic due to many of the issues just discussed. The primary issue to consider and plan for, if this is a path being adopted, is dealing with the greater emphasis placed on 'brand reality' on the internet in comparison to 'brand perception'. Typically companies that have a well-established brand in the traditional marketplace clearly want to build this further on the Internet. Automobile companies such as Ford and VW are focused on achieving the same brand equity online as they have in the traditional marketplace.

Partner with an existing online brand

With the emergence of web-based 'exchanges', (specialist portals supporting a specific supply chain) primarily used within B2B markets, it can be argued that branding based on the notion of reality and trust can be most easily achieved through a partnership agreement with a dedicated 'exchange'. Consider for example Online Education (www.online.edu) or www.virt-u.com that offers an established online brand that is used as a sign of quality assurance and provides trust in the service experience (Figure 12.4).

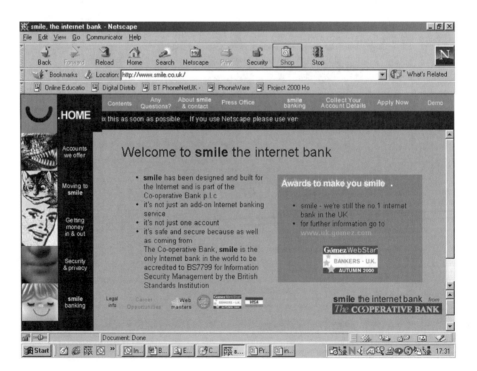

Figure 12.5   New online brand

New online brand

For many organizations a new brand and existence is created for the Web that is in tune with the specific service or product offering and also brand development that harnesses the notion of 'brand reality' through the interactive nature of the Internet. The development of a new online brand has been particularly common within the financial services sector, for example the Egg banking service (www.egg.com) which is part of Prudential or Smile banking (www.smile.co.uk) which is part of the Co-operative bank. Creating a new online brand is a particularly sensible option for businesses operating in an information intensive environment such as software, banking, music and publishing. A new online brand can then permeate throughout the product or service experiences and is viewed as fundamental to success on the Internet (Figure 12.5).

Internet marketing: planning development paths

Now we have considered strategies for meeting specific marketing communications objectives and also approaches towards online branding, we need to consider the various paths that may be adopted in implementing specific Internet development plans. Figure 12.6 below provides a useful framework for considering the three primary paths in planning your Internet marketing presence. As indicated in Figure 12.6 the B and C paths are focused on B2B markets while the A path is typical of a B2C market.

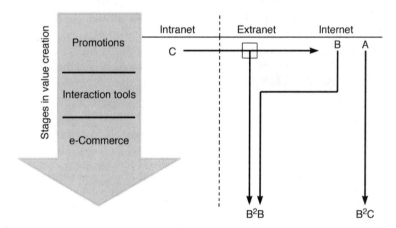

Figure 12.6   'Information to transaction model' for marketing planning

Marketing strategy A focused on B2C markets is a typical evolutionary path and is adapted from Quelch and Klein's (1996) 'information to transaction' model. Information and promotions is typically presented via the Web plus the use of other marketing communications channels such as e-mail. The marketing plan typically illustrates future milestones for further development such as feedback forms and other interactive features, for example, allowing further customization. Many websites currently undertake such developments through the launch of specialist portals offering a gateway to the Web for a defined market segment. The marketing plan would also typically outline the final stage of development in the move towards online ordering. In the development of an online ordering system the marketing plan may incorporate a technical specification with regard to web servers, databases and back end infrastructure or may be referred to a specific complementary technical report.

Strategy B is generally associated with large corporate business. The Web provides an ideal platform for internal communications across geographically remote workspace. Typically a large company may then develop both a greater Internet presence for information dissemination and promotion plus an extranet presence, in particular in B2B markets. In the B2B markets security and speed of communication are of fundamental importance in the planning process. A key feature of this type of strategy is the ability to check stock from suppliers, for example, in the manufacturing sector. The ability to monitor stock securely enables suppliers to be integral to the buyers operations building an highly integrated approach. Finally strategy C is most appropriate for B2B markets such as high technology industries such as aerospace and defence. Typically a company adopting such a strategy would have vast amount of value added information on internal networks that may be made available via the Internet or to selected customers via an extranet. The use of an extranet allows a blurring of organizational boundaries and has the ability to create highly integrated organizational networks across the supply chain. It is also important to note that a strategy adopted by a company could be based on one or a combination of the proposed strategies.

Companies adopting a 'transaction to information' approach are typically organizations trading solely in virtual markets and have formed as an organization through the emergence of the Internet. As a consequence the proposed model is

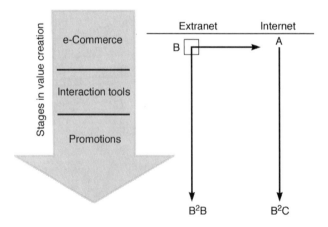

Figure 12.7 'Transaction to information model' for marketing planning

particularly relevant to information intensive sectors including: publishing, software, education and other services. Strategy A focuses clearly on 'goal directed' (Hoffman and Novak, 1996) consumers with a clear need. Strategy B would be typical of an approach for B2B operations that require speed and security such as aerospace industry and various manufacturing sectors with a strong presence of small to medium sized enterprises who are frequently using Internet dial-up accounts and they require factual information and the graphical appearance is not a priority beyond receiving the facts required in an easy to read format. Strategy B typically serves an existing market with information through a new cost effective channel and as a consequence for many sectors Internet developments are replacing traditional EDI based communications (Figure 12.7).

Internet marketing budget and resources allocation

The focus of the budget provided in the marketing plan needs to identify the expected returns from the Internet investment. Cost and revenue information needed to implement the proposed Internet marketing plan need to be outlined. Emphasis needs to be given to the elements of the budget that will be affected by or will affect an Internet marketing plan. The process of identifying the benefits to an organization can be difficult to quantify, similar to IT investment in general due to the intangible nature of many short and long term returns. For example, intangible returns include industry recognition, brand building and possible stakeholder perceptions. The main areas for consideration are typically achieved through adopting a 'bottom up/top down process' (Piercy, 1987) through considering the following:

- Specific cost estimates of Internet marketing – Internet service costs including purchasing and operating a web server and further development costs.
- Internet marketing activity costs such as direct e-mail campaigns and e-promotions.
- Revenue opportunities through Internet advertising and e-commerce activities through product and service offerings.
- Comparison of marketing expenditure against sales opportunities.

Investment costs

Baynes (1997) outlined various methods for estimating specific costs for inclusion in the Internet marketing budget. The Internet marketing budget suggested by Baynes may be based on:

- Previous years Internet marketing budgets
- Percentage of company sales
- Percentage of total marketing budget
- Reallocation of marketing spend
- Industry norm.

The choice of methods will be determined by various factors including existing Internet presence, industry sector, and the specific mix between trading activities in the marketplace and marketspace. More specifically Baynes (1997) suggested the inclusion of four main areas with regard to assessing investment in supporting the path taken in marketing on the Internet. The four main areas of data may include a combination of the following:

- Estimates on Internet services and development costs
- Estimates on an in-house option or partnering with a third party for hosting the Internet applications
- Budget spreadsheet with cost breakouts for each stage of the proposed Internet marketing plan
- Evaluation of the impact of your Internet marketing program on traditional media expenditure.

Development and maintenance cost

The development costs will be dependent on an organizations web presence and secondly the type of development path decided upon. For example, if an organization adopts a 'transaction to information' approach then the initial costs will be far greater than the 'information to transaction' model. Whatever approach is adopted there will be a mix of the following costs:

- Setup cost such as site creation
- Website development costs (promotions, on-going maintenance, relaunch creation)
- Infrastructure costs in terms of using a partner to host the website or hosting internally with dedicated communications channels.

Companies are able to manage the internet marketing costs far more effectively by identifying key milestones and development activities plus having appropriate procedures in place.

Revenue opportunities through the planning process

Investment benefits gained from an Internet operation typically involves either revenue generation or cost reduction (Quelch and Klein, 1996). Firstly consideration needs to be given to whether the Internet is a means of extending a business in the physical marketplace or is solely operating in cyberspace. For a large international organization cost reductions may be through the Internet providing a cheap form of communications or integrating databases through a common platform around the world. In comparison revenue generation as we are all familiar with is directly related to e-commerce applications. The potential cost reductions are frequently overlooked through the desire to developing e-commerce applications but it is important to have an Internet marketing plan that also considers the internal customer in addition to having a external customer centric focus in the planning process (Figure 12.8).

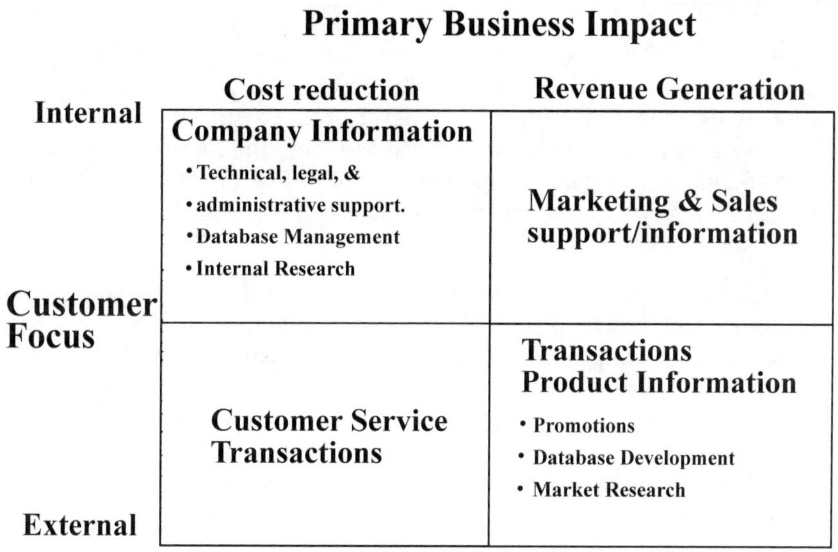

Primary Business Impact

	Cost reduction	Revenue Generation
Internal		
	Company Information • Technical, legal, & • administrative support. • Database Management • Internal Research	**Marketing & Sales support/information**
Customer Focus		
	Customer Service Transactions	**Transactions Product Information** • Promotions • Database Development • Market Research
External		

Figure 12.8   Drivers of Internet business model (adapted from Quelch and Klein, 1996)

Measuring internet marketing performance

Measuring the overall performance is a means of closing the loop and the form of analysis can be in various forms. Before you implement a measurement program you need to review the Internet marketing objectives which may be to increase the Internet customer base, online transactions or brand awareness. Clearly increasing traffic or online sales are very quantifiable and as a consequence will require different measurement tools from evaluating the impact on brand awareness. Similar to more traditional marketing initiatives it is important to have a measurement program that considers both quantity and quality related issues. In addition to monitoring site traffic at different levels throughout a website it is also of prime importance to consider specific product and market data. For example, it is important to monitor and analyze geo-demographics of who is visiting the site, comparative analysis of data over time against target market, longitudinal analysis of the effects of changing the website content style and applications plus many more questions and issues of importance. Such analysis then can feed directly back into the future marketing planning process.

The Internet marketing project team

We now need to consider Internet marketing planning in terms of human resource requirements in undertaking the proposed initiatives which typically include:

- A recommendation on undertaking the project within the organization, outsource or a combination of both.
- After considering organizational structure a further evaluation and proposal will be required on a staffing solution to meet the internet marketing plan.
- Statement on outside partners and potential ad hoc solutions providers for various types of work such as programming, database development specialists, and web designers.

Before considering whether to outsource or undertake the Internet development in-house it is worth exploring if the Internet activities are the core business activities or still a supporting type activity. Clearly for businesses trading solely on the Internet a strong internal team will be required but typically focused on the higher value added activities of the product and service offering and outsourcing non-core activities. If the Internet is still supporting, rather than central, to the product and service offerings then this can be managed internally but is also viable to outsource to a business partner. Achieving the most appropriate mix between in-house and outsourcing will be quite specific to an individual company but before a decision is made ask yourself the following questions:

- Have you got the internal resources to produce a website?
- Are there web design skills available, technical programming skills for both server side requirements and applications end, database specialists and networking people?
- Does the company have a robust IT infrastructure and can or does it support a web server?
- Can the current internal web server support existing and anticipated traffic to the website?
- Is there an integrated multi-functional team in-house to implement the Internet marketing plan?
- Are resources available and allocated within the organization to meet Internet requirements?

Risk analysis and contingency planning

The value of strategic planning is a continuing topic of debate and with the rapid growth of the Internet and the speed of change in virtual markets this questions even more the planning process. The basic structure highlighted earlier for strategic planning continues to be the framework of choice but through the emergence of different market conditions on the Internet we need to change the emphasis placed on various issues. For instance risk analysis and vulnerability related issues are of greater importance due to the volatility of virtual trading conditions.

As a means of testing the robustness of a proposed Internet marketing plan it is useful to consider the issues in Table 12.2 in considering the relevance of strategies.

Table 12.2 Key issues in the development of internet marketing plan vulnerability analysis

Suitability	Consider the potential threats and opportunities in the light of the capabilities of a firm in the context of sustainable advantage
Validity and reliability	Evaluate the relevance of the information, based on reliability and validity of the analysis and data sources
Consistency	The overall vision and how the specific strategies relate to each other
Feasibility	Skills availability in terms of staff resources and commitment
Adaptability	The ability to sustain flexibility in terms of technology, people, systems, processes and organizational structure
Financial Desirability	Value creation in terms of performance forecast balanced against risk assessment
Vulnerability	Risk analysis and contingency routes

In developing an Internet marketing plan consideration needs to be given to a businesses vulnerability in the context of specific markets. The level of vulnerability of a business can be determined through considering the strategic importance of risk and the degree of control a business has over the risk factor (Day, 1986). For businesses trading on the Internet vulnerability analysis is an important area for consideration in the pursuit of a sustainable advantage. A significant amount of information for such an analysis can be obtained through web-based market intelligence tools outlined in Chapter 3.

The vulnerability grid presented in Figure 12.9 is a useful framework to identify and position the risk factors and as a consequence take action on the factors that could cause most damage. Each quadrant represents a specific risk that requires its own particular response in an attempt to minimize the impact on a organization.

- Strategic quadrant. Business activities that have major strategic importance and as a consequence the risk factor has high priority for sustainable advantage. The risk factors have high control through monitoring and managing the business processes. This quadrant may involve distribution channels through product innovation related issues. Typically the strategic quadrant will include companies that have a unique product or service with limited competition within specific markets, e.g. pharmaceutical businesses such as Glaxo-Welcome.
- Vulnerability quadrant. Many businesses operating in the electronics or software industry typically operate in this quadrant. They are reliant on highly innovative products and services through operating in very volatile markets that have significant global competition. Product innovation has very short cycle times

Figure 12.9   Vulnerability grid

and many electronics products for example experience a 3-month cycle time for the release of new products. The degree of control of risk factors positioned in this quadrant is weak but success through minimizing what is viewed as high risk is critical. The risk factors need continuous monitoring and contingency plans should be developed where possible.

■ Experimental quadrant. As both the risk factors and the level of control are weak this will typically involve more experimental projects of which some will be of success and many have limited use for a businesses development. The importance of the risk factors to strategic choice may shift for example into the vulnerability or strategic quadrant through project success. The ability to control the risk factors will be dependent on longer term on both product and market conditions.

■ Incremental quadrant. Here the risk is low while the degree of control is high which indicates that many products have moved into the maturity stage of the product life cycle and operate in relatively stable market conditions.

New roles for the wired marketing planner

Clearly most of the functions of a traditional marketing planner are still valuable and transferable to operating in virtual business communities but new marketing skills are also required. The wired marketing planner needs to be operating at the intersection between marketing applications and new technological developments. We need to drive Internet-based marketing initiatives in parallel with technological developments. For example the rapid growth of viral marketing and affiliate programs is driven purely through technological developments and was unforeseeable in the mid 1990s. Some of the most common functions of a wired marketing planner are as follows:

- Physical and virtual market analysis for top management
- International competitor research
- Sales forecasting and budgeting
- Internal marketing and communicating corporate objectives
- Developing planning systems and techniques
- Evaluating marketing technology applications
- Risk and volatility assessment
- Consulting services.

Formal roles are often viewed as secondary to the role of communicator, facilitator and consultant. Facilitating in a corporate environment has undertaken far greater importance through the commercial acceptance of the Internet in creating truly wired business organizations. Such a focus re-aligns the marketing planner for the 'new economy' and adapts to new internal and external market demands, enabling an Internet marketing plan to be flexible and adaptable to changing market conditions. The marketing planner's focus on the facilitating function allows contingency planning to be integral to the planning process through global Internet communications.

Conclusion

In the pursuit of designing a desired future organization it is important to remember, throughout the planning process, the volatile nature of the Internet. Due to the speed of change on the Internet the marketing plan needs to be viewed as an interactive document that needs to be updated frequently. The time scale for review and changes is constantly being reduced through market demands and technological developments. Even so the Internet marketing plan provides a 'snap shot' of operational issues but also provides a strategic direction in terms of: mission statement, human resource management, innovation, financial requirements and other resource requirements. The Internet marketing plan is based on an external audit which then drives internal operational developments as a means of identifying a sustainable competitive advantage. Finally it is important to remember the Internet marketing plan is very similar to a traditional marketing plan but it is focused on radically different market conditions requiring a new organizational form that can integrate both the marketplace and marketspace into a seamless whole.

1. Business and market analysis

   - Marketing information system in the digital age
   - Integrating strategies for specific objectives
   - Cognitive and attitude objectives
   - Transaction behaviour objectives
   - Internal efficiency goals for marketing budgets

2. Perspectives towards managing the branding process on the Internet

   - Developing a traditional brand online
   - Partner with an existing online brand
   - New online brand

3. Development paths for the Internet marketing communications plan

   - 'Information to transaction' model
   - 'Transaction to information' model

4. Internet marketing budget and resources allocation

   - Investment costs
   - Development and maintenance cost
   - Revenue opportunities through the planning process
   - Measuring internet marketing performance
   - Internet marketing project team

5. Risk analysis and contingency planning

   - Vulnerability analysis

     Strategic quadrant
     Vulnerability quadrant
     Experimental quadrant
     Incremental quadrant

   - New roles for the wired marketing planner.

Checklist

1. A strategic marketing plan is basically a financial plan but with more emphasis on information that considers the origins and destinations of the financial flows.
2. A personalized approach to an Internet marketing plan needs to be developed to

provide an highly flexible template that can provide you with the foundations for further customization.

3. Business and market analysis requires a description of an organization's background and anticipated future that will be affected by or will affect a specific Internet marketing plan.

4. In developing online marketing communications strategies you need to consider new forms of marketing communications tools that have specifically evolved for the Internet.

5. Measuring the overall performance is a means of closing the loop and the form of analysis can be in various forms. It is important to have a measurement program that considers both quantity and quality related issues.

6. Both a responsiveness and adaptable approach in ever increasing volatile market conditions requires dynamic cross-functional responsibilities and processes in building a strategic marketing plan.

7. The emergence of different market conditions on the Internet requires a change in emphasis placed on various issues. For instance risk analysis and vulnerability related issues are of greater importance due to volatile online trading conditions.

References

Baynes, P. (1997), *Internet Marketing Planning*, Wiley, New York.

Berry, L. (2000), Cultivating service brand equity, *Journal of the Academy of Marketing Science*, 28 (1).

de Chernatony, L. and McDonald, M. (1998), *Creating Powerful Brands in Consumer, Service and Industrial Markets*, 2nd ed., Butterworth-Heinmann, Oxford.

Hoffman, D.L. and Novaks, T.P. (1996), Marketingin hypermadiacomputer-mediated environmnets: conceptual foundations, *Journal of Marketing*, July.

Hoffman, D.L., Novak, T.P. and Peralta, M. (1998), Building consumer trust in online environments: the case for information privacy. Unpublished paper, available at http://ecommerce.vanderbilt.edu/papers/pdf/CACM.Privacy98.PDF.

Kotler, P. (1997), *Marketing Management: Analysis, Planning Implementation and Control*, 9th ed., Prentice-Hall, Englewood Cliffs, NJ.

Lambin, J.J. (2000), *Strategic Marketing Management*, McGraw-Hill, France.

McKenna, R. (1991), Marketing is everything, *Harvard Business Review*, Jan–Feb.

Peppers, D. and Rogers, M. (1997), *Enterprise One-to-One: Tools for Building unbreakable Customer Relationships in the Interactive Age*, Piatkus, London.

Piercy, N.F. (1987), The marketing budgeting process: marketing management implications, *Journal of Marketing*, 5 (4).

Quelch, J.A. and Klein, L.R. (1996), The Internet and international marketing, *Sloan Management Review*, Spring.

Strauss, J. and Frost, R. (1999), *Marketing on the Internet: Principles of Online Marketing*, Prentice Hall, Englewood Cliffs, NJ.

Further reading

Bickerton, P., Bickerton, M. and Pardesi, U. (1996), *Cybermarketing*, Chartered Institute of Marketing Series, Butterworth-Heinmann, Oxford.

Peppers, D. and Rogers, M. (1993), *Building Business Relationships One Customer at a Time. The One-to-One Future.* Piatkus, London.

Glossary

Access Provider Company that sells Internet connections. Also called Internet Service Provider (ISP).

ActiveX Microsoft concept that allows a program to run inside a web page.

ADSL A form of broadband communications and information service that offers a dedicated connection to networks such as the Internet. Under the banner of ADSL various levels of service are provided which typically depend on the type of application being used and the speed of connection required.

Anonymous FTP server Remote computer, with a publicly accessible file archive, that accepts 'anonymous' as the log-in name and e-mail address as the password.

AOL America Online. Last surviving online service. Loved by all.

ARPA The advanced research projects agency of the US Department of Defense.

ASCII American Standard Code for Information Interchange.

Attachment File included with e-mail or other form of message.

Backbone Set of paths that carry longhaul Net traffic.

Bandwidth Size of the data pipeline. Increase bandwidth and more data can flow at once.

Baud rate Number of times a modem's signal changes per second when transmitting data. Not to be confused with bps.

Binary file Any file that contains more than plain text, such as a program.

Binhex Method of encoding, used on Macs.

Bookmarks Netscape file used to store web addresses.

Boot up Start a computer

Bounced mail E-mail returned to sender.

Bps Bits per second. The rate at which data is transferred between two modems. A bit is the basic unit of data.

Broadband Telecommunication networks focused on providing relatively cheap multimedia communications infrastructure. Various standards and various services are being introducing including ADSL.

Browser Web viewing program such as Netscape or Internet Explorer.

Buffer Temporary data storage.

Cache Temporary storage space. Browsers can store copies of the most visited web pages in cache. Called temporary Internet files in Internet Explorer.

Ciphertext Encrypted version of transmitted normal text.

Client Program that accesses information across a network, such as a web browser or newsreader.

Crack Break a program's security, integrity, or registration system, or fake a user ID.

Crash When a program or operating system fails to respond or causes other programs to malfunction.

Customer relationship management The primary means of collecting customer data through a set of digital tools which enables you to capture, analyze and respond to customer behaviour in virtual real time.

Cybrary A global digital library.

Cyberspace Coined by science-fiction writer William Gibson, to describe the virtual world that exists within the marriage of computers, telecommunication networks, and digital media.

Default The standard settings.

Digital signing Encrypted data appended to a message to identify the sender.

DNS Domain Name System. The system that locates the numerical IP address corresponding to a host name.

Domain Part of the DNS names that specifies details about the host, such as its location and whether it is part of a commercial (.com), government (.gov), or educational (.edu) entity.

Download Retrieve a file from a host company. Upload means to send one the other way.

Driver Small program that acts like a translator between a device and programs that use that device.

DSL Digital Subscriber Line. Encompasses all forms including ADSL. Sometimes called xDSL.

E-mail Electronic mail carried on the Internet.

E-mail address The unique private Internet address to which your e-mail is sent. Takes the form user host.

FAQ Frequently Asked Questions. Document that answers the most commonly asked questions on a topic.

File Anything stored on a computer, such as a program, image, or document.

Finger A program that can return stored data on UNIX users or other information such as weather updates. Often disabled for security reasons.

Firewall Network security system used to restrict external and internal traffic.

Flame Abusive message posted to Usenet.

Frag Network gaming term meaning to destroy or fragment. Came from DOOM.

FTP File Transfer Protocol. Standard method of moving files across the Internet.

GIF Graphic Image File format. Compressed graphics format commonly used in web pages.

Gopher Defunct menu-based system for retrieving Internet archives, usually organized by subject.

GUI Graphic User Interface. Method of driving software through the use of windows, icons, menus, buttons, and other graphic devices.

Hacker Someone who gets off on breaking through computer security and limitations. A cracker is a criminal hacker.

Header Pre-data part of a packet, containing source and destination addresses, error checking, and other fields. Also the first part of an e-mail or news posting which contains, among other things, the sender's details and time sent.

Homepage Either the first page loaded by your browser at start-up, or the main web document for a particular group, organization, or person.

Host Computer that offers some sort of services to networked users.

HTML HyperText Markup Language. The language used to create web documents.

Hypermedia A non-linear form of distributing information and providing communications. Based on the notion of clicking on media objects that allow the individual interacting to enter new information sources. Hypermedia can be based on text, graphics, audio, animation and video hyper links

HyperText links The 'clickable' links or 'hot-spots' that interconnect pages on the Web.

Image map A web image that contains multiple links. Which link you take depends on where you click.

IMAP Internet Message Access Protocol. Standard e-mail access protocol that is superior to POP3 in that you can selectively retrieve messages or parts thereof as well as manage folders on the server.

Instant Messaging Point to point chat such as ICQ.

Internet A co-operatively run global collection of computer networks with a common addressing scheme.

Internet Explorer Microsoft's weapon in the browser wars.

Internet Favourites Internet Explorer folder that stores filed URLs.

Internet Shortcut Microsoft's terminology for a URL.

IP Internet Protocol. The most important protocol upon which the Internet is based. Defines how packets of data get from source to destination.

IP address Every computer connected to the Internet has an IP address (written in dotted numerical notation) which corresponds to its domain name. Domain name servers convert one to the other.

IRC Internet Relay Chat. Internet system where you can send text, or audio, to others in real time, like an online version of CB radio.

ISDN Integrated Services Digital Network. International standard for digital communications over telephone lines. Allows data transmission at 64 or 128 kbps.

ISP Internet Service Provider. Company that sells access to the Internet.

Java Platform-independent programming language designed by Sun Micro-systems. http://www.sun.com

JPG/JPEG Graphic file format preferred online because its high compression reduces file size, and thus it takes less time to transfer.

Kill file Newsreader file into which you can enter keywords and e-mail addresses to stop unwanted articles.

LAN Local Area Network. Computer network that spans a relatively small area such as an office.

Latency Length of time it takes data to reach its destination.

Leased line Dedicated telecommunications link between two points.

Link In hypertext, as in a web page, a link is a reference to another document. When you click on a link in a browser, that document will be retrieved and displayed, played or downloaded depending on its nature.

Linux A freely distributed implementation of the UNIX operating system.

Log on/Log in Connect to a computer network.

Lycos Web search service at: http://www.lycos.com

MIDI Musical Instrument Digital Interface. Standard adopted by the electronic music industry for controlling devices such as soundcards and synthesizers. MIDI files contain synthesizer instructions rather than recorded music.

MIME Multipurpose Internet Mail Extensions. Standard for the transfer of binary e-mail attachments.

Mirror Replica FTP or website set up to share traffic.

Modem Modulator/Demodulator. Device that allows a computer to communicate with another over a standard telephone line, by converting the digital data into analogue signals and vice versa.

MP3 A compressed music format.

MPEG/MPG A compressed video file format.

Multithreaded Able to process multiple requests at once.

Narrowcasting A web-enabled method of one-to-one advertising.

Name server Host that translates domain names into IP addresses.

Newsgroups These are text-based discussion groups that are primarily driven by e-mail with archives that are frequently viewable via the Web.

The Net The Internet.

Open Source Solutions   Open source relates to software applications that are both free to use but also provide the source programming code also for free. In addition to free usage this also means that programmers around the world can have full access to how applications have been built and as a consequence provide an incentive for developing the product further. This has created numerous successful software applications including Linux and Apache.

Packet Unit of data. In data transfer, information is broken into packets, which then travel independently through the Net. An Internet packet contains the source and destination addresses, an identifier and the data segment.

Packet loss Failure to transfer units of data between network nodes. A high percentage makes transfer slow or impossible.

Patch Temporary or interim add-on to fix or upgrade software.

PDA's (Personal Digital Assistants) A broad term that includes all hand-held devices that provide some form of assistance. This has traditionally been associated with Palm and more recently Visor from Handspring. The boundaries of the traditional PDA's is now broadening significantly to include many other devices.

Phreaker Hacker of telephone systems.

Ping Echo-like trace that tests if a host is available.

Platform Computer operating system, such as Mac OS, Windows, or Linux.

Plug-in Program that fits into another.

POP3 Post Office Protocol. E-mail protocol that allows you to pick up your mail from anywhere on the Net, even if your connected through someone else's account.

POPs Points of Presence. An ISP's range of local dial-in points.

Portal A website that specializes in leading you to others.

Post To send a public message to a Usenet newsgroup.

PPP Point to Point Protocol. Allows your computer to join the Internet via a modem. Each time you log in, you are allocated either a temporary or static IP address.

Protocol Agreed way for two network devices to talk to each other.

Proxies A proxy is a small program that is able to send messages on both sides of a firewall. Requests from outside users for information, files, transactions or communications from the web server are intercepted by the proxy, checked and then forwarded to the server machine.

Proxy server Sits between a client, such as a web browser, and a real server. Most often used to improve performance by delivering stored pages like browser cache and to filter out undesirable material.

RealAudio A standard for streaming compressed audio over the Internet. See: http://www.real.com

Remote login This is where you can connect to a computer at a geographically remote location and which then enables the use of resources, such as library catalogues and databases.

Robot Program that automates Net tasks such as collating search engine databases or automatically responding to IRC. Also called a Bot.

Search engine Database of web page extracts that can be queried to find references to something on the Net.

Server Computer that makes searches available on a network.

Signature file Personal footer that can be attached automatically to e-mail and Usenet postings.

SMTP Simple Mail Transfer Protocol. Internet protocol for transporting mail.

Spam Online equivalent of junk mail. Used as both a noun and a verb.

Streaming Delivered in real time instead of waiting for the whole file to arrive, e.g. RealAudio

Stuffit Common Macintosh file compression format and program.

Supply chain All those activities associated with the flow and transformation of goods from raw materials stage through to the end user, as well as the associated information flows.

Supply chain management Management of the supply chain from raw materials through to finished products and their final delivery to appropriate destinations. The task of companies is to manage information and product flows from suppliers to ultimate users involving the co-ordinating of activities and all entities in the supply chain.

Surf Skip from page to page around the Web by following links.

Synchronous communications This relates to communication that is virtually real time but may be across geographically remote locations. Basically same time and any place.

TCP/IP Transmission Control Protocol/Internet Protocol. The protocols that drive the Internet.

Telco Telephone company.

Telnet Internet protocol that allows you to log on to a remote computer and act as a dumb terminal.

Temporary Internet Files Internet Explorer's cache.

Trojan (horse) A program that hides its true intention.

Troll Prank newsgroup posting intended to invoke an irate response.

UNIX Operating system used by most ISPs and colleges. So long as you stick to graphic interfaces, you will never notice it.

URL Uniform Resource Locator. Formal name for a web address.

Usenet A user's network. A collection of networks and computer systems that exchange messages, organized by subject into newsgroups.

Uuencode Method of encoding binary files into text so that they can be attached to mail or posted to Usenet. They must be Uudecoded to convert them back. Most mail and news programs do it automatically.

Vaporware Rumoured or announced, but non-existent, software or hardware. Often used as a competitive tendering ploy.

WAP (Wireless Application Protocol) The accepted and established protocol allows web pages to be viewed on mobile devices in particular mobile phones. Currently the type of use is quite limited but with the emergence of third generation phones WAP is anticipated to have an important role in enabling access to web-based information and supporting communications.

Warez Software, usually pirated.

The Web The World Wide Web or WWW. Graphic and text documents published on the Internet that are interconnected through clickable 'hypertext'

links. A web page is a single document. A website is a collection of related documents.

Web authoring Designing and publishing web pages using HTML.

World Wide Web See Web, above.

WYSIWYG What you see is what you get. What you type is the way it comes out.

Yahoo The Web's most popular directory at: http://www.yahoo.com

Zip PC file compression format that creates files with the extension .zip using WinZip software. Commonly used to reduce file size for transfer or storage on floppy disks.

Subject index